Key to the New World

For Florida Book Awards

For *[signature]* April 2019

Key to the New World

A History of Early Colonial Cuba

LUIS MARTÍNEZ-FERNÁNDEZ

UNIVERSITY OF FLORIDA PRESS

Gainesville

23 22 21 20 19 18   6 5 4 3 2 1

Library of Congress Cataloging-in-Publication Data
Names: Martínez Fernández, Luis, author.
Title: Key to the New World : a history of early colonial Cuba / Luis
    Martínez Ferández.
Description: Gainesville : University of Florida Press, 2018. | Includes
    bibliographical references and index.
Identifiers: LCCN 2017040578 | ISBN 9781683400325 (cloth : alk. paper)
Subjects: LCSH: Cuba—History—To 1810.
Classification: LCC F1779 .M37 2018 | DDC 972.91/01—dc23
LC record available at https://lccn.loc.gov/2017040578

University of Florida Press
15 Northwest 15th Street
Gainesville, FL 32611-2079
http://upress.ufl.edu

UF PRESS

UNIVERSITY
OF FLORIDA

Para mi mamá, con amor y agradecimiento

Es necesario que debajo de las letras sangre un alma.

JOSÉ MARTÍ

Contents

Figures

Maps

Acknowledgments

Decades ago, I had the good fortune to be professionally trained under two distinguished historians of colonial Latin America, Aída Caro Costas of the University of Puerto Rico and John J. TePaske of Duke University. Working with them opened my eyes to the fascinating world of the colonial era. Under their mentorship, I became familiar with the historiography of the period, the wealth of extant primary documentation, and the methodologies and theories colonialist historians used to decipher and portray Latin America and its people under Spanish rule. I strayed, however, from the colonialist path for two and a half decades as I researched and wrote on the Hispanic Caribbean during the modern period. This colonial-era book is a tribute to their long-lasting impact as great scholars and teachers and as extraordinary human beings.

I wish to acknowledge my gratitude to fellow scholars, too many to mention here, who in one way or another had an impact on the creation of this book. Several friends and colleagues read and critiqued portions of this work and I am grateful for their insights and recommendations. None of them are responsible for any factual errors, misinterpretations, or gaps. Louis A. Pérez Jr. and Jason M. Yaremko thoughtfully reviewed the book's manuscript for the University of Florida Press. Simon Barton, David Head, William F. Keegan, Asela Laguna Díaz, Álvaro Villegas, Jane Landers, and Ezekiel Walker were kind enough to read and criticize earlier versions or sections of different chapters. I am grateful to Antonio Santamarina for his hospitality and guidance during my research residency in 2010 at the Escuela de Estudios Hispano-Americanos in Seville; to Consuelo Naranjo Orovio, Loles González Ripoll, Sherry Johnson, and the other participants of the Islas en la corriente conference in Madrid in 2015; and to a few of my past students, who provided research assistance for this book: Allison P. Sellers, John Settle, David Marina, Pedro Torres, and Onyx de la Osa.

My gratitude also goes to the staff of the Library of the University of Central Florida, especially the librarians of the inter-library loan office, and the staffs of the libraries of Florida International University, the University of Florida in Gainesville, and the Escuela de Estudios Hispano-Americanos.

I also wish to express my gratitude for permissions to reproduce parts of earlier versions of some of the book's chapters, most of which appeared in European and Latin American journals and in essay collections over the last twelve years. I have since substantially revised them; all have been updated and reworked. I am grateful to Blackwell Publishing for permission to reproduce parts of an earlier version of chapter 1 that originally appeared in the online journal *History Compass*; to the editors of *Revista Brasileira do Caribe*, who published a previous incarnation of chapter 3; to Editorial Karolinum for permission to publish sections of the book chapter "The Forging of Creole Cuba" that appear here in chapters 5 and 6; and to the editors of *Revista de Indias* for allowing me to publish an abbreviated and revised version of chapter 7.[1]

Several publishers and specialized libraries allowed me to reproduce images and illustrations from their publications and collections. I want to acknowledge the John Carter Brown Library's splendid collection of digitized books and images and its generous open-access policy;[2] the trustees of the British Museum; Yale University Press; the Society for American Archaeology; Cambridge University Press; Jerome Handler and Michael Tuite, the compilers of *The Atlantic Slave Trade and Slave Life in the Americas: A Visual Record* at www.slaveryimages. org; and Roberto Ramos, who gave me permission to reproduce a painting from his private collection.

I am grateful to Stephanye Hunter, Eleanor Deumens, and their colleagues at the University of Florida Press for accepting this project with open arms and working diligently to make this book much better than it would have otherwise been; and to Kate Babbitt for her kindness and excellent copyediting work.

Finally, I thank my wife, Margie, and my sons, Luis Alberto and Andrés, for their love and support.

A Note on Measurement and Currency

In most of this book, I use English-system units of measurement, often followed by their metric equivalents in parenthesis.

In some instances, I provided units of measurement as they were used in Cuba during the early colonial era. These include *varas*, a measure of length of about 2.8 feet (0.85 meters) and *arrobas*, the equivalent of 25 pounds (11.34 kilograms). Wine was transported in barrels called *pipas*, with capacity for around 155 gallons. Land area was commonly measured in *caballerías*, a unit of measurement that was equivalent to around to 95.5 acres (38.6 hectares). The term *caballería* originally represented the amount of land granted to reward *caballeros* (knights or men on horseback). A *caballería* was between two and five times larger than a *peonía*, the amount of land allotted to foot soldiers. In later centuries, the *caballería* unit shrank to 33 acres.

During the period examined in this book, the official Spanish currency was the silver real, which was equivalent to 34 maravedís, a currency of Arabic origin. Among the period's most common coins were the eight reales (silver pieces of eight), which were equivalent to one silver peso (450 maravedís). The gold ducado was equivalent to 11 reales (375 maravedís). In 1537, the Crown replaced the ducado with the escudo, a unit equivalent to 350 maravedís, but ducados continued to circulate widely in Cuba. In 1566, the value of a ducado was raised to 400 maravedís. The gold eight-escudo coins, known as doubloons, were worth 16 silver pesos. Silver marks, *marcos de plata*, were equivalent to 2,210 maravedís. Most of the coins that circulated in Cuba were minted in Mexico, using the cob method, which produced irregularly shaped coins.

Introduction

Cuba has attracted disproportionate attention from historians and other scholars. This is particularly true for the nineteenth century, when, as a slave society, Cuba was the world's largest exporter of sugar, and for the post-1959 period, when it became the hemisphere's first socialist nation, unpredictably remaining so past the collapse of the communist world in 1989–1991. I myself have dedicated most of my scholarly career to the study of those two periods.

In contrast, few scholars have worked on Cuba's sixteenth and seventeenth centuries. As a result, only a handful of English-language scholarly books that focus on aspects of pre-eighteenth-century Cuba have been published in the last twenty years. The one topical exception is the study of Cuba and the Caribbean's indigenous populations. The dearth of monographs and scholarly articles on early colonial Cuba contrasts sharply with the voluminous historiography of colonial Mexico, Peru, and other regions of Latin America. The same is true in terms of general syntheses of early colonial Cuba. As odd as this may sound, before this book, one had to reach back one full century to find the most recent English-language general history of early colonial Cuba, Irene A. Wright's *The Early History of Cuba* (1916). Moreover, the historiography has focused almost exclusively on Havana, practically ignoring Santiago and much of the rest of the island.[1]

Long aware of and uncomfortable with such serious gaps, I decided to get out of my historiographical comfort zones and write this general history, which covers the pre-Columbian era through the end of the seventeenth century. I have also made a concerted effort to extend coverage beyond Havana and its environs. The idea of this book germinated after I worked on two essays, one on Cuba's geography and its impact on the island's history, and the other on the first explorations of the New World and the early encounters between Europeans and Amerindians. At that point, I recognized the potential for a more ambitious, long-term project: a much-needed comprehensive book on early colonial Cuba. I decided to write several other essays that combined with the first two would provide a wide-ranging scholarly overview of the major developments, themes, and historiographical discussions of Cuba's first centuries. Over the next decade, I wrote several additional chapters as essays meant to both stand alone and serve as building blocks for this book-length project. In the past two years, as I assembled this book, I reworked the individual essays, updated them to reflect the most recent historiography, split and/or consolidated some of them; cut some and expanded others; and wrote four new ones to fill remaining topical and chronological gaps.

This book is the result of the systematic and intentional weaving together of factual information, narrative, interpretation, and discussions of useful concepts. It provides essential information on Cuba's geography, its pre-Columbian inhabitants, and the first two centuries of colonial life and at the same time looks at numerous theoretical frameworks that shed light on the island's complex history.

It traces Cuba's early history at three levels simultaneously: first, the macro level, which allows me to place the island in its broader Atlantic context and discuss the ways that foreign factors and forces, such as piracy, the slave trade, and world market fluctuations, impacted the island. Next is the micro level, which offers more focused attention on specific spaces, such as fortified Havana, the town of Bayamo, and the seventeenth-century sugar plantation Nuestra Señora del Rosario. Lastly, in order to humanize this history, I turn to the individual level, bringing to life numerous historical characters. Some, like Cuba's first governor, Diego Velázquez and the Dutch pirate Piet Heyn, are well known; others are common people whom history simply forgot. In the chapters that follow, readers will learn about a Guayabo Blanco–culture infant who was buried with his mother; the painter Diego Pérez, the first European artist to set foot in the New World; Juan Garrido, one of the first Africans in Cuba, a man who later gained fame and fortune as one of Hernán Cortés's conquistadores; and two Catalinas whose lives could have not been more different—Catalina Hernández, the wealthy widow of conquistador Antón Recio, and Catalina de Fonseca, a six-year-old slave.

This book consists of eight topical chapters that are arranged chronologically and coordinated to minimize repetition and overlap. At the same time, they are tied together by common threads and an evolving narrative.

Three connecting themes stand out. The first theme is the recognition that the sixteenth and seventeenth centuries were times of profound social, economic, intellectual, and political transitions and transformations in Europe. Many interconnected transformations enabled the formation of global empires, which, in turn, spurred and accelerated even deeper transformations worldwide.

The second theme is that Cuban society was forged in a frontier, conquest context where numerous racial, ethnic, and social groups and interests clashed, producing enduring economic, social, political, and cultural characteristics. Some of these had lasting negative consequences, such as a persistent dependence on the sugar monocrop, coercive labor practices, a propensity to mark and accentuate sharp social distinctions, the veneration of strong political and military caudillos, and transgressive practices manifested through violence, vice, and corruption. On the other hand, those same clashes generated a vibrant multiethnic society with a variegated culture in which rich ingredients from various cultural roots came together to produce a new, richly layered culture marked by positive transgressions: cultural experimentation, hypercreativity, gregariousness, a particular type of individualism that is not detached from the collective, and an iconoclasm that permeates the arts, literature, politics, humor, and everyday human interactions.

The third theme is that as early as the 1550s, if not before, Cuban society bifurcated into what I call two Cubas. One is Havana and its hinterland, characterized by a cosmopolitan port city, military fortifications, and institutions of political, military, religious, and mercantile power—an urban space encircled by a virulently fertile agricultural belt composed of staple-food farms, grasslands for various types of cattle, and sugar-producing estates. The other is rural, frontier Cuba, which stretches through the island's central and eastern regions. This Cuba is altogether a different world: sparsely populated, transgressive and rebellious and a producer of hides, tobacco, ginger, and other goods largely meant for contraband trade.

The first chapter, "Geography and the Shaping of Early Colonial Cuba," sets the geographic and ecological stage for the island's history from the arrival of its first inhabitants, between 7,000 and 6,000 years ago, to the year 1700, when the last of Spain's Habsburg monarchs, the feeble Charles II, expired without heirs, marking the transition to rule by the Bourbon dynasty. It provides information about Cuba's geological development and various fundamental aspects of its geography. What makes this chapter different from similar opening geography chapters is that it also traces the ways that humans interacted with their diverse natural and created habitats. It discusses how geographic circumstances opened—perhaps forced—the way to certain historical developments and how Cuba's inhabitants contended with, endured, adapted, or simply benefited from unchangeable realities such as insularity, a specific rainfall calendar, and proximity to important ocean and wind currents. At the same time, human agency had some transformative effects as various groups of inhabitants impacted their environment, whether consciously or unconsciously—constructively by building aqueducts and irrigation systems to quench the thirst of people, animals, and plants or destructively, through deforestation to clear the way for urban living, cattle ranching, and commercial agriculture.

Chapter 2, "Indigenous Inhabitants," studies the socioeconomics, cultures, and interactions of various Caribbean native groups. It discusses different overlapping categorizations such as the Paleolithic, Mesolithic, and Neolithic and the Casimiroid and Ostionoid. It also recurs to V. Gordon Childe's still-useful "Neolithic Revolution" theory.[2] Reflecting recent archaeological discoveries and historiographical developments, the chapter examines the lasting presence of Cuba's original inhabitants, both biological, as evidenced by modern genetic studies, and cultural, as represented by cultural retentions such as smoking tobacco and sleeping in hammocks, the consumption of foods such as boiled *yuca* and guava-based desserts, and the survival of words and concepts that were incorporated into European languages: canoe, barbecue, and savannah, to give but three examples. Reflective of recent scholarship, the chapter goes beyond the traditional population-waves approach; it seeks to paint a more dynamic picture that includes interactions and cultural diffusion among different Amerindian groups.

One of the chapter's topics is the size of the indigenous population of Cuba and the region before contact with the Europeans around 1492. It discusses various estimates and the methods historians and other scholars have used to reach those calculations. The chapter closes by addressing the controversial subject of what is known as Taino revival, a relatively recent phenomenon whereby some Cubans, Dominicans, and Puerto Ricans have embraced Taino identity and practices as their own and have organized themselves into tribes to preserve and celebrate their heritage.

Chapter 3 examines the first encounters between European explorers and the indigenous populations of the Americas. While it provides essential information about the exploration voyages, it goes far beyond that: it discusses those explorations within the broader context of a Europe in transition between the Middle Ages and the Renaissance. The chapter also introduces two stimulating perspectives for the study of Europe's early encounters with the New World: first, Edmundo O'Gorman's thesis of the invention of America, a rejection of the idea of physical discovery in favor of a more complex intellectual process of invention; and second, Alfred W. Crosby's thought-provoking concept of the Columbian exchange, a call to view the so-called discovery as a multifaceted and prolonged multidirectional exchange of people, animals, vegetables, and minerals along with ideas, practices, and material cultures.[3]

The next chapter, "The Manufacturing of Cuba," addresses the conquest and early colonization, including the catastrophic collapse of the indigenous population and the scaffolding of institutions, practices, and laws Spain used to prop up the emerging colonial state and social pyramid. It expands on the thesis that the period surrounding 1492 was a time of profound global transitions, not just intellectually, as discussed in the previous chapter, but in socioeconomic and political terms—in the case of Europe, a transition from feudalism to capitalism and toward an absolutist monarchical model.

The chapter borrows two related arguments: Uruguayan intellectual Ángel Rama's contention that Europeans viewed and treated the New World as a tabula rasa and Trinidadian writer V. S. Naipaul's idea that the Caribbean was indeed a tabula rasa on which Europeans violently "manufactured" colonies to serve metropolitan economic and military needs. In this chapter I argue that during the conquest and early colonization, Cuba was a frontier setting created in the image of another frontier setting—Iberia during the centuries-long *reconquista* war between Christian and Muslim Iberia.[4]

Chapter 5, "The Emergence of Creole Society," looks at the complex racial, ethnic, and social landscape of an emerging colonial society that combined a remnant of indigenous inhabitants, white settlers, enslaved Africans, and free men and women of different hues. It also discusses asymmetrical human interactions among whites, blacks and mulattos, and Amerindians and *mestizos* and pays much attention to conflicting and overlapping hierarchies and to the ways particular groups and individuals challenged those hierarchies. Lastly, in this chapter I expand on the thesis of the two Cubas: one an urban, official, and mercantilist Havana and the other the Cuba of the east, remote, relaxed, and rebellious.

Chapter 6, "The Cuban *Ajiaco*," explores the cultural by-products of multiethnicity, the complex and manifold hybrid cultural manifestations stemming from the human interactions discussed in the previous chapter. The chapter uses Fernando Ortiz's *ajiaco* (Cuban stew) metaphor as representative of syncretic or hybrid cultures forged by transculturation among the cultural contributions of Amerindians, Europeans, and Africans.[5] It brings to life the stories of individuals who are emblematic of transculturation: an unnamed African who lived in an indigenous *encomienda* village; Melchor Sardo de Arana, a cross-dressing, gluttonous Spanish fort commander; Paula de Eguiluz, a slave woman who specialized in potions, amulets, and incantations to lure men and secure their affection; Micaela Ginés, a free black musician, whose acclaimed band toured the island; and two indigenous men and a black boy caught in a boat during a storm inside Nipe Bay.

Chapter 7, "The Cockpit of Europe," discusses various forms of piracy that impacted Cuban ports and Spanish-flagged vessels. Other challenges to Spain's authority included the capture by foreigners of several of its neglected Caribbean colonies during the 1620s, 1630s, and 1640s and the massive military invasion Oliver Cromwell launched in 1654–1655. The chapter's most significant contribution is that it traces developments in Europe and the Caribbean in tandem in order to understand how European wars related to different manifestations of foreign aggression against Cuba and other Spanish possessions. While war in Europe almost always meant war in the Caribbean, the region was located "beyond the line," which meant that European truces and peace treaties were not always honored in the region. This chapter also proposes a periodization and typology of the different waves and types of foreign incursions against Cuba and Spanish vessels. Lastly, it examines how Spaniards and creoles defended the trade routes of Cuba and the empire by militarizing and fortifying the island, convoying trading vessels and warships, launching preemptive attacks, and even arming privateers of their own.

Chapter 8, "Deceivingly Sweet," looks at Cuba's first "sugar revolt"—a term I use to distinguish what happened there from the sugar revolutions that profoundly transformed Barbados, St. Christopher, and most other Caribbean islands beginning in the 1640s. I argue that while the emergence of Cuba's early sugar plantations was transformative, it did not turn the island upside down, as was the case in, say, French Guadeloupe, because in Cuba, sugar production was limited, localized, and did not bring about the demise of other agricultural activities. That said, Cuba's early "sugar revolt" had the same kind of injurious repercussions that sugar revolutions throughout the region had: the expansion of African slavery and manifold destructive, even evil, economic and social ramifications stemming from the demands of a staple crop that has deservedly been called "the sweet malefactor," a "brutal plant," and countless other unflattering names. In his classic book *Cuban Counterpoint*, Fernando Ortiz lyrically chastised sugar as the root of most of the island's economic, social, political, and even moral misfortunes, not least of which was a seemingly eternal dependence on slave or otherwise coerced forms of labor.[6]

The chapter also discusses the nature of the sugar plantation, even in its earliest incarnations, as a distinctive socioeconomic system characterized by the sugar and slavery binomial. It examines the resistance of slaves and free blacks to that system. It looks, for example, at efforts by slaves and free blacks to "reconstitute" (to use Sidney W. Mintz's term) West African peasant practices.[7]

A few words on sources: because this book offers a comprehensive synthesis of the major topics of pre-Columbian and early colonial Cuba, it depends largely on secondary sources, beginning with Irene A. Wright's pioneering works, continuing through the extensive contributions of Cuban historians Ramiro Guerra and Leví Marrero, and including more recent studies by César García del Pino, Alejandro de la Fuente, and others. However, like scholarly monographs, it is also built on the careful examination and interpretation of an extensive array of primary sources. These include documents in the multivolume *Colección de documentos inéditos de ultramar*, sixteenth-century documents from the Archivo General de Indias (Seville) transcribed by Wright or available online through the Portal de Archivos Españoles (PARES),[8] published notarial records, and other primary documents transcribed and published in books and edited volumes of more recent vintage. Plantation inventories, censuses, notarized dowry contracts, slave manumission agreements, minutes of town council meetings, and other revealing primary documents provide valuable windows on key historic, social, and cultural matters and bring to life both major historical figures and common men, women, and children.

1 ❧

Geography and the Shaping of Early Colonial Cuba

En Cuba pueden aclimatarse y prosperar hombres, plantas y animales de todas partes del mundo.

SALVADOR MASSIP

Many human phenomena and characteristics such as behaviors, beliefs, economies, genes, incomes, life expectancies, and other things are influenced both by geographic factors and by non-geographic factors.

JARED DIAMOND

This opening chapter examines the many ways geography and history have intertwined in Cuba. Its primary objectives are first, to provide a dynamic portrait of the island's geological evolution and its most significant geographic traits, including its insularity, shape, location, topography, and climate; and second, to trace the ways Cuba's inhabitants interacted with their environment from the pre-Columbian era until the end of the seventeenth century.

While geographic characteristics are not the deterministic forces many once held them to be, they have some impact on both historical developments and culture. Even today, human beings do not have the capacity to change most aspects of their geographic environment. Over the centuries, Cuba's inhabitants have not been able to change the shape and location of the island, its rainfall calendar, the periodic passage of destructive hurricanes, or the routes of its oceanic and wind currents. Human agency, however, allowed the island's inhabitants to take advantage of favorable geographic circumstances and triumph over some of the natural challenges of their habitats.

Although Spanish settlers could not alter the flow of sea and wind currents, they could locate Havana, the island's eventual capital, in the most propitious location, at the crossroads of important ocean currents. Two earlier capitals,

Baracoa and Santiago, both located in the east, were not as auspiciously situated and thus soon lost importance and population to Havana, which became the de facto capital in the 1550s. While Havana was favored with the passing of ocean and wind currents and a magnificent pouch-type bay, it lacked an adequate supply of fresh water. Its first Spanish settlers used rainwater they collected in cisterns or traveled long distances to fetch water. With the completion of the ambitious Real Zanja aqueduct in 1592, the city received ample amounts of water yearlong from La Chorrera (the Almendares River). To give another example: as soon as French corsairs recognized Havana's strategic importance, it became the object of unrelenting attacks and blockades. Although the city lacked natural protection because of its flat terrain, military and civil authorities made good use of the abundance of local limestone and imported slave labor to erect fortifications that reduced its vulnerability to attacks.

Geological Evolution

In geological terms, the shape, size, and location of Cuba that we are familiar with are relatively recent developments that occurred between the early Maastrichtian Age and the late Eocene Epoch (72.1 to 33.9 Ma [million years ago]), roughly about seventeen minutes ago if we compress the estimated 4.5 billion years of earth's existence into a 24-hour period.[1]

Over billions of years of continental drift, the earth's surface continuously expanded and contracted, moved in different directions, and rearranged itself. This is sustained by the plate tectonics theory, first developed in the early decades of the twentieth century by meteorologist Alfred Wegener, who was seeking to explain the long-term movement of the earth's crust. The theory maintains that the crust is composed of numerous plates that move slowly in different directions, sometimes toward each other, sometimes away from each other. Later scientific discoveries solidified the theory, which has become widely accepted.

At times, various land masses were separated from each other and at times they came together to form supercontinents. The most recent formation of a supercontinent was Pangaea, which came together between 300 and 270 Ma. If we picture the Caribbean/Gulf of Mexico as a closed mouth inside Pangaea, trapped between North and South America and facing west, that mouth began opening around 280 Ma, disconnecting North and South America at the isthmus. During this prolonged rearrangement of tectonic plates, a mass of land that would evolve into Cuba shifted south and west of North America, ending up in the Pacific, where it was reconfigured along a north-south axis. Around

100 Ma, that mass began to move east, until it reached the location of the current American isthmus. It continued to move north and west, until it reached roughly its current position circa 50 Ma, by which time it had reverted to an east-west orientation.[2]

Cuba's geological development was the result of numerous forces operating over millions of years. The primary overarching force was the extended collision between the arc of islands of the proto-Caribbean and the North American plate during the late Cretaceous and Paleogene periods. Other forces shaped specific parts of present-day Cuba. Early on, between the Low Jurassic and Low Cretaceous periods (200–100 Ma), that arc of islands interacted with the Yucatan Peninsula, producing Cuba's westernmost terrain, known as the West Cuban nappe stack. Yet another force, the collision between that arc of islands and the Bahamas Plate, which occurred between the Upper and Lower Jurassic periods (200–145.5 Ma) formed vast portions of central Cuba, primarily through the accumulation of karstic sediment. Because of this clash, Cuba was pushed toward and became part of the North American Plate, its southern coast becoming the tectonic border between that plate and the Caribbean Plate. Thus, while the part of Cuba that is above water is situated in the Caribbean, geologically it is not part of that plate.[3]

More recently, during the Paleogene period (66–23 Ma), the arc of Caribbean islands clashed with the North American Plate, elevating land mass through volcanic and other forces that surfaced above sea level. The coast of southeastern Cuba between Cabo Cruz and Punta de Maisí marks a major stretch of collision between those two plates. As the North American Plate pushed south, the part of the Caribbean Plate known as the Gonâve Microplate was subducted, forming a deep ocean trench known as the Cayman (or Bartlett) Trough. Meanwhile, along the southern border of the North American Plate, steep volcanic mountains rose that became the Sierra Maestra mountain range. Cuba's southeast, one of the most geologically unstable parts of the Caribbean, has a long history of volcanic and seismic activity. Soils of the Nipe type derived from igneous rock testify to the region's volcanic origins.[4]

An extraterrestrial factor further complicated Cuba's geological development. Around 65 Ma, a massive asteroid struck the Yucatan Peninsula. This asteroid is widely believed to have generated the nuclear winter that led to the extinction of dinosaurs and most of the earth's other animal and plant species. The western end of Cuba has some of the largest iridium deposits anywhere in the world. That mineral is extraordinarily rare on earth but is abundant in asteroids.[5]

At times, Cuba was neither an island nor an archipelago. During the Miocene epoch (23–5.3 Ma), most of Cuba was above sea level and thus was connected by surface land to the Bahamas and to what today is the southeastern United States. As recently as 8,000 to 15,000 years ago, when ocean levels were low, the current Cuban archipelago was a single island, connected above water with the Isle of Youth and its surrounding keys. At other times, Cuba was partially below sea level, with only its mountain ranges and volcanic peaks rising above water. During other extended periods—the late Cretaceous period (100–66 Ma), for example—it was completely submerged.

During much of the last glacial period, often referred to as the last ice age (110,000–12,000 years ago), when sea levels were 300–500 feet below their current level, an above-surface land bridge may have connected Cuba and the Yucatan Peninsula. Some scientists theorize that that bridge was destroyed by a southbound megaflood produced by a rapidly melting ice cap that covered most of North America. Its torrent washed away most of Cuba's soluble karstic surface. Earthquakes may also have played a role in the destruction of the land bridge.

In 2000–2001, marine engineer Pauline Zalitski and her husband, Paul Weinsweig, discovered massive rock formations a few miles west of Cuba's westernmost tip, where the theorized land bridge would have been over 10,000 years ago. The structures are geometric; they include large quadrilateral blocks and circular formations. Some are even pyramid-shaped. This led to some speculation that these formations could be the ruins of a sunken Mesoamerican city—an Atlantis of sorts. However, Cuban geologist Manuel Iturralde and the scientific community are not ready to hypothesize, let alone conclude, that this network of rock formations are the ruins of an ancient city built by humans.[6]

Cuba's geology continues to change. As imperceptible as it may be, the island is still in movement, shifting west at the rate of 0.79 inches (2 centimeters) each year. Due to global warming, sea levels around the world have risen at an accelerated rate in the past three decades. Because it has such extensive coastal areas, Cuba is particularly vulnerable to the damaging effects of rising sea levels. A study conducted by Cuban scientists found that sea levels around the island were rising at a rate of around 0.079 inches (2 millimeters) each year.[7]

The Insular Condition

Insularity is Cuba's most salient and historically significant geographic characteristic. Cuba is the largest and most western of an arch of submerged Caribbean islands whose peaks pierce through the blue seas. It is an archipelago that consists of the main island, the Isle of Youth (formerly known as the Isle of Pines), and over 1,600 other islands and keys, some of which struggle to keep their mangrove-capped heads above water.[8]

When Christopher Columbus first encountered Cuba, he believed it was Cipangu (Japan). A few days later, the startled mariner categorically concluded that Cuba was an appendix of the Asian mainland, as indigenous inhabitants seemed to refer to it as Cubanacán, which he took to be an allusion to China's legendary ruler, the Great Khan. In 1508, Sebastián de Ocampo and his crew circumnavigated Cuba, confirming its insularity for Europeans, a fact that its inhabitants had conveyed to Columbus sixteen years before. Perhaps because of the early confusion about whether Cuba was in fact an island, sixteenth- and seventeenth-century maps stressed the fact with the names they assigned it: Cuba Insula and Isola Cuba. Johannes Ruysch's 1507 map captured this ambiguity, portraying it simultaneously as an island and a peninsula.[9]

The island that Columbus refused to recognize as such is by far the largest of all the Caribbean islands. Measuring 42,803 square miles (110,860 square kilometers), the Cuban archipelago is almost the same size as all the other islands

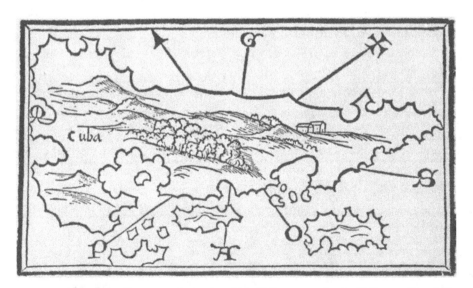

Figure 1.1. This is the first printed map in which Cuba appears by itself. Source: Benedetto Bordone, map of Cuba, in *Libro di Benedetto Bordone nel qual si ragiona de tutte l'isole del mondo* (Venice, 1528).

of the Caribbean combined. The island of Cuba proper measures 40,520 square miles (104,945 square kilometers); it is about the size of Guatemala. Puerto Rico would fit twelve times into Cuba; Barbados would fit 250 times. The archipelago's second largest island, the Isle of Youth, extends over an area of 850 square miles (2,200 square kilometers); it is the sixth largest Caribbean island, behind Cuba, Hispaniola, Jamaica, Puerto Rico, and Trinidad. Once called Treasure Island, the Isle of Youth was close enough to Cuba and well protected enough that it served as a base for generations of foreign pirates and smugglers.

The main island's relatively large size protected it from falling in the hands of French, English, and Dutch maritime plunderers and invading settlers during its early colonial history. While such interlopers attacked and raided Havana, Santiago, and other parts of the island repeatedly, they failed to take over the entire island. The most extensive and prolonged foreign occupation of Cuba, the British capture of Havana (1762–1763), lasted eleven months and included only western Cuba. In contrast, smaller islands such as Martinique or Grenada were more easily dominated in their entirety. Their history was marked by a succession of takeovers by Spaniards, French, and English troops, settlers, and privateers.

Cuba's insularity has strongly influenced the course of its history and culture in ways similar to that of insular nations throughout the world. The condition of insularity generally establishes borders naturally so that the fixed limits of an island (the geography) usually coincide with those of the constituted government (the state) and the population (the nation). Many a war throughout the globe have begun as attempts to make geography, nation, and state coincide. Islanders, furthermore, tend to develop a particular world view in which they distinguish their territory and themselves from continental nations, oftentimes viewing their homeland as uniquely special and even as the center of the world. As far back as the 1500s, Cubans distinguished themselves as *naturales*, in contraposition to Iberian-born settlers. The Cuban sense of identity and nationalism have doubtless been nourished by the condition of insularity. Nineteenth-century Cuban theologian and patriot Félix Varela called for Cuba to be as isolated politically (meaning independent) as it was in nature.[10]

A Caiman-Shaped Island

Often compared to a caiman or crocodile, Cuba has a long and narrow shape that stretches along an east-west axis. The island is twelve times as long (777 miles, 1,250 kilometers) as it is wide (an average of 62 miles, or 100 kilometers). On average, Cuba's most interior locations are only 125 miles (50 kilometers) away from the nearest coastal point. At its widest, Cuba measures 119 miles (191 kilometers) from coast to coast. Its shape makes for a long coastline that is over 3,570 miles (5,746 kilometers) long. That coastline is dented by nearly 200 coves, bays, and inlets, some of which are regarded as being among the world's finest harbors. The bays of Santiago, Havana, and Nuevitas, among others, are of the type known as pouch or bottleneck, consisting of long, narrow entrances leading to protected, lake-like bays.

While Cuba's fine bays have been an asset to international shipping and navigation, beginning in the 1500s, such features became magnets for foreign aggressors and havens for smugglers. Some of Cuba's first settlements, Puerto Príncipe for example, had to be moved inland to protect them from recurrent corsair attacks. Foreign smugglers traded with Cuba's neglected consumers in profitable exchanges of European goods and slaves for local hides, spices, precious woods, and tobacco. Contraband trade was a critical component of the island's economy throughout the first two centuries of colonial history. Early colonial settlements such as Bayamo and Trinidad thrived on smuggling.

The island's elongated shape also makes for long distances between Cuba's east and west. Six hundred miles (967 kilometers) separate Cuba's two major cities, Havana and Santiago. The sun sets over the island's western tip forty-five minutes after it has set on the eastern end. In contrast, only 213 miles (343 kilometers) separate London and Paris, while Boston and Washington, DC, are only 394 miles (634 kilometers) apart. Juan de Ávila, who governed Cuba in the 1540s, claimed to prefer sailing twice to Spain to sailing once between Havana and Santiago against wind and sea currents. During the rainy season, roads that connected the two ends of the island disappeared under water and then turned into mud. When regular mail was established between the two cities in 1755, it took two weeks for correspondence to reach Santiago over land.[11]

During the early colonial era, distance and difficult communications permitted eastern towns such as Bayamo, Santiago, and Holguín to develop beyond the pale of Havana's authority and influence, allowing the east to follow its own historical, economic, demographic, and cultural trajectory. Smuggling activities and racial miscegenation, for example, were more common in the east. Geography divided Havana and Santiago: Havana was an Atlantic society that looked west and north, to Mexico and Florida, while Santiago was a Caribbean society whose closest links were to Santo Domingo, Jamaica, and Cartagena. This bifurcation was politically institutionalized in 1607, when Spanish officials divided the island into two political jurisdictions, one under Havana, the other under Santiago.

Differences between east and west continued to expand, leading to regionalism and even bursts of hostility between Havana and Santiago and, by extension, between west and east.

Latitudes and Longitudes

Cuba's geographic location has influenced its destiny in compelling ways. The island's southernmost point is Punta del Inglés (19°49'36" N); its northernmost point (Punta Hicacos, 23°12'20" N) is less than 31 miles (50 kilometers) south of the Tropic of Cancer, which separates the tropics from northern temperate zones. Cuba is thus located within the tropics, but barely so. Significantly, while Cuba is situated fully within the tropics, its northern neighbor, the United States, is located fully outside the tropics. This combination of proximity and geographic difference has been conducive to trade reciprocity based on complementary agricultural productions, tropical products such as sugar and tobacco heading north and temperate climate products such as grain shipping south.

Cuba's western extreme is Cabo San Antonio (84°57'54" W), and Punta del Quemado (74°7'52" W) is its easternmost point. Although few would visualize it without looking at a map, Havana stands on a longitude that is farther west than Miami; it is actually west of longitudes that run through Cleveland, Quebec, and even the Pacific Coast city of Lima.

Because of their tropical location, Cuba and other Caribbean islands had high incidences of parasitic diseases that were both indigenous and endemic. While the picture of a relatively healthy pre-Columbian world has been widely diffused, scholars from a variety of disciplines have demonstrated that numerous diseases assailed the indigenous populations of the hemisphere, most virulently in its low-lying tropical regions, long before Europeans imported their own catalog of pathogens. Shigellosis was a source of often-fatal gastrointestinal disorders. Tapeworms and hookworms were also endemic infectious diseases, as was leishmaniosis, spread by sand flies, and Chagas disease, transmitted by the so-called kissing bug. When the three big killers—smallpox, measles, and influenza—arrived with Spanish conquistadores, they decimated populations that were already debilitated by disease and that had not developed immunities to the lethal imports. The Caribbean also offered an ideal environment for the spread of two devastating African tropical diseases, malaria and yellow fever. Their vectors, *Anopheles* and *Aedes aegypti* mosquitoes, respectively, were not indigenous to the Caribbean; they came as stowaways in slave trading ships. The lethal cocktail of indigenous parasitic illnesses, European infectious diseases, and African pathogens not only decimated Cuba's indigenous population, it also wreaked havoc among unacclimated European settlers, visitors, and invaders and produced high mortality rates among slaves.[12]

Cuba's location relative to other islands, continental landmasses, and bodies of water has also been of paramount importance in the shaping of its history. Its shores are washed by the Caribbean Sea, the Gulf of Mexico, and the Atlantic Ocean. Havana is strategically located at the crossroads of these major bodies of water and near the three Americas: North, Central, and South. Its location at the intersection of important ocean and wind currents provides its western region with conditions favorable to navigation and ocean trade. The fast-flowing and voluminous South Equatorial Current heads west into the Caribbean. Much of it becomes the Yucatan Current as it squeezes through the narrow Yucatan Channel to enter the Gulf of Mexico, from which it exits through the even narrower strait between Cuba's western tip and Florida's southern keys. Farther north, the current turns into the Gulf Stream and shifts to the northwest toward Europe, gaining unusually fast surface speeds of up to 5.5 miles per hour (9 kilometers per hour) and becoming the navigation conveyor belt that single ships and naval convoys transporting silver from New Spain, sugar from Cuba, and even silk from China used. Havana thus became the main American hub of Spanish colonial navigation, the obligatory stop for all fleets on their way to Iberia.

The island's east was too far from the Gulf Stream and was thus excluded from the transatlantic fleet routes. Local authorities pleaded repeatedly (and unsuccessfully) for the Crown to authorize single vessels to land in Santiago. That city, located next to the Windward Passage that separates it from Hispaniola, is actually closer to three other Caribbean capitals—Port-au-Prince, Kingston, and Santo Domingo—than it is to Havana. Such proximities translated into tighter commercial ties and cultural affinities with Jamaica and Hispaniola. The east did benefit, however, from the currents that flow through the Windward Passage, which facilitated navigation to the northern coast of South America, particularly the port city of Cartagena, with which Santiago developed intimate trade relations. The east also developed close ties with Jamaica and Hispaniola, including smuggling activities with traders and buccaneers from those islands.

While wind currents shift seasonally and even within any given day, they reinforce the routes of prevailing sea currents. Some trade winds, like the South Equatorial Current, follow a westward direction from Africa; the westerlies, meanwhile, roughly follow the Gulf Stream. Because of its proximity to continental North America, western Cuba is often affected by the passage of the continental jet stream, which runs in the opposite direction of the trade winds. At times, this stream brings masses of cold air that lower western Cuba's temperatures significantly.

Gradually becoming aware of prevailing water and wind current patterns, Spanish colonizers who originally established their political, mercantile, and ecclesiastical headquarters in Baracoa and Santiago gravitated west to the island's most auspicious location for navigation to Europe. Originally located on the southern (Caribbean) coast, settlers moved close to Havana's present Atlantic location in 1519. Havana and other port cities were the target of numerous corsair and pirate attacks during the 1500s and 1600s, particularly Havana, because of its role as the last American port of call for fleets returning to Spain. Cuba helped protect the major navigation lanes of the Florida Strait, the Yucatan Channel, and the Windward Passage. The strategic importance that gained Cuba the titles of Key to the New World and Safeguard (*antemural*) of the Indies is evident in the still-standing complex of fortifications erected under Spanish rule, some of which date back to the 1500s. Thus, wind and ocean currents contributed to the bifurcation of the island into two different Cubas: a Caribbean-facing Cuba in the east and an Atlantic-facing Cuba in the west.

Another salient and determinant aspect of Cuba's relative location is its proximity to the North American continent: the proverbial 90 miles. While 4,630 miles (7,450 kilometers) separate Cuba from Spain, its original metropolis, Cuba is much closer to North America. The long distance separating Cuba and Spain impacted the pace and scale of the island's colonization. Travel and communications took a long time and it was difficult to enforce royal authority and deploy troops across the Atlantic. This resulted in an early relative autonomy vis-à-vis Spain and chronic violations of Spanish laws and decrees, including smuggling, tax evasion, extreme labor exploitation, and other corrupt practices.

Cuba's geographical proximity to the United States influenced both countries even before the United States constituted themselves as such in 1776. During the first half of the 1500s, Cuba became the launching pad for expeditions to North America. Notable among these were those of the legendary Álvar Núñez Cabeza de Vaca and Hernando de Soto. The 1565 expedition that Pedro Menéndez de Avilés led, which resulted in the founding of San Agustín, North America's first permanent European settlement, began in Cuba. Two centuries later, proximity between Cuba and the Florida Peninsula shaped history once again. Many of the British troops that captured Havana in 1762 were deployed directly from Britain's North American colonies. The following year, Great Britain agreed to cede Havana to Spain in exchange for the entire Florida Peninsula. In the following decade, Havana's residents exacted revenge on the British by funding the French troops Britain was fighting against during the American War of Independence.

Geographical Features

Other salient traits of Cuba's geography that have influenced the course of its historical, cultural, and economic trajectory relate to the island's topography, hydrography, soils, climate, and natural resources. Unlike most Caribbean islands, its topography is predominantly flat. Two-thirds of its terrain is composed of flatlands, in contrast to, say, Puerto Rico, where only a quarter of the surface is flat. Early in the colonial era, Cuba's predominantly flat terrain facilitated an extensive cattle-ranching economy. A few decades later, sugarcane production, which thrives on flat terrain, developed on the island.

Cuba's mountains are clustered in three main ranges: Guaniguanico (which includes the Sierra de los Órganos) in the west, El Escambray mountain range in the central region, and the Sierra Maestra on the east, which has Cuba's highest mountain, Pico Turquino (6,476 feet; 1,974 meters). Topography is yet another way that eastern Cuba differs from most of the rest of the island; it harbors much of the mountainous terrain that has historically served as a refuge for rebels and transgressors. That is where the Amerindian rebel chief Guamá eluded Spanish forces for over a decade. Generations of Amerindian and African maroons, deserters, and smugglers found shelter in the Sierra Maestra and other mountainous regions. Not coincidentally, the east has historically generated insurgent and even revolutionary movements. Caves, which are abundant, provided shelter for Cuba's first inhabitants and later served as hiding places for generations of runaway slaves. Picturesque *mogotes* are another salient topographical feature, particularly in Pinar del Río Province. Also known as karstic towers, *mogotes* are steep-sided hills formed of residual limestone.

A small number of lakes and lagoons dot the landscape, and very few rivers crisscross the surface. The island's largest lake, La Leche in Ciego de Ávila, measures only 26 square miles (67 square kilometers). Very few rivers are navigable. Most are short and flow along a north-south or south-north course. A notable exception is El Cauto, the island's longest and most voluminous river; it is 230 miles (370 kilometers) long and is one of a few that flows from east (Sierra Maestra) to west, draining into the Caribbean close to Manzanillo. One of Cuba's earliest and most important towns, Bayamo, connects to the Caribbean via a tributary of the same name. At the other end of the island, a few miles west of Havana, the Almendares River (known earlier as La Chorrera) flows into the

Atlantic. It has been the source of the city's drinking water since the 1500s. Some of Cuba's earliest sugar mills were powered by this river's flow.

Cuba's complex geological evolution is reflected in the wide variety of its soils. During the millions of years when Cuba was submerged, accumulated deposits of coral, seashells, and the skeletal matter of other sea creatures produced vast extensions of flat, calcareous rock (limestone) terrain. When these terrains surfaced, they produced highly fertile soils that were optimal for agriculture, particularly sugarcane cultivation, in some regions. Not coincidentally, settlers established Cuba's early sugar plantations on locations with fertile red soils. This created a sugar belt that stretches from the region west of Havana to western Camagüey Province. The limestone-derived sandy soils of La Vuelta Abajo are credited with producing the world's finest tobacco. In general, Cuba's soils are extraordinarily rich and fertile. Today around 90 percent of the surface is made up of soils with agricultural value, either as croplands or as pastures.

The east is richest in metallic minerals, including gold, copper, bauxite, and nickel. Gold, which was first on the agenda of Spanish conquistadores, turned out not to be as plentiful as first believed. By the 1530s, gold deposits were almost depleted. Cuba soon became a backwater of the empire, and the focus of Spanish colonization shifted to the highlands of Mexico and Peru, which were rich in precious metals. Early in the colonial era, however, Cuba was the world's leading exporter of copper. The metal was mined by slaves at El Cobre.

Climate

Cuba's climate is tropical maritime. While the archipelago is tropical, it enjoys a mild climate that is moderated by several factors, including being surrounded by water and having a long shape and extended coastline, the cooling effect of the trade winds and abundant rainfall, and, to a lesser extent, the impact of cooler air masses flowing from North America. Such influences moderate temperatures, making Havana's climate more comfortable, for example, than that of Calcutta or Mecca, which are located at roughly the same latitude. Some of the same moderating influences keep Cuba from experiencing the cold extremes that affect other locations within the same latitude. The yearly mean temperature is 77° Fahrenheit (25° C). The mean for the summer is 81° Fahrenheit (27° C) and the mean for the winter is 70° Fahrenheit (21° C). Thus, differences between the seasons and between day and night are relatively small. During the centuries this book covers, temperatures were somewhat colder and precipitation was scarcer as the result of the Little Ice Age (circa 1350–1850).

This was the optimum period for the forests that once covered over 90 percent of the island's surface.[13]

Cuba's average relative humidity is 81 percent and the average yearly rainfall is close to 55 inches (1,400 millimeters). Certain windward regions, such as the north side of La Sierra Maestra, receive large amounts of rain (more than 78 inches [2,000 millimeters]), while leeward locations such as Guantánamo receive only half that amount and Punta de Maisí, on the eastern extreme, barely gets 20 inches (500 millimeters). The rainy season runs from May to October and the dry season from November through April. This rain calendar matches that of sugarcane cultivation: wet months coincide with the growing season and dry months with the harvest season. Throughout the island, precipitation is usually of the downpour type: large amounts of rain fall in short periods of time (generally in the afternoons).

Natural Disasters

Cuba is periodically stricken by natural disasters, namely hurricanes and earthquakes. It has endured the wrath of numerous destructive hurricanes. Hurricanes are tropical storms with sustained winds surpassing 120 kilometers per hour (75 miles per hour). The hurricane season runs between June 1 and November 30. Interestingly, Tainos depicted hurricanes with a symbol that is uncannily similar to the symbol modern-day meteorologists use. Since the time the island was colonized, over 150 hurricanes have hit Cuba. Historical records note around fifteen devastating hurricanes between 1524 and 1644. According to a contemporary report, a storm named San Rafael devastated Havana on October 24, 1692, leveling all structures with palm-leaf roofs, damaging all wooden buildings, making roads impassable for days, and destroying most crops, including more than half of all sugar-producing units. Hurricanes had a damaging effect on navigation and trade, as they often sank vessels. In 1591, the commander of the Spanish fleet and 500 crew members were killed in a hurricane. On occasion, hurricanes had a silver lining—they destroyed enemy vessels and convoys.[14]

The earliest recorded earthquake to strike Cuba dates to 1578; it generated a plague of snakes that reportedly covered the city of Santiago. Another seven rattled the region around Santiago between then and 1659. Among the most destructive of the colonial period was the great earthquake of 1679, which caused enormous harm in Santiago, including severe damage to the cathedral and the San Pedro fort. Later that year, 800 French buccaneers sought to capitalize on the disaster, but they failed to capture the city and its damaged fortification.[15]

Conclusion

Cuban societies emerged and developed in a strategic geographic location where the oceanic and atmospheric conditions were favorable to transatlantic navigation and trade and under conditions that were ideal for tropical agricultural activities, particularly the cultivation of sugarcane. However, those conditions were also ideal for the spread of tropical diseases and the seasonal onslaught of vicious hurricanes.

Various aspects of geography pushed Cuba's inhabitants into particular economic activities and played a role in shaping their history and culture. Some geographic realities were inescapable and immutable—insularity, currents, and weather patterns, for example. Different populations dating back to Cuba's first inhabitants had the options of moving to more favorable environments, accommodating to the conditions where they lived, or attempting to alter those conditions. Indigenous settlers recognized favorable aspects of their environment and used them to their advantage. When they migrated to the island, they selected locations that offered ideal conditions for fishing and foraging for shellfish. Later groups gravitated to areas that had the fertile soils and adequate irrigation needed for agricultural production. They transformed their ecosystems by using slash-and-burn practices and by altering the terrain with digging sticks and other rudimentary tools. When soils were depleted of nutrients, entire villages moved on to other locations.

Likewise, Europeans recognized favorable aspects of their environment and used them to their benefit. They selected the most advantageous locations to build the first villages, usually near rivers or bays. Baracoa and Santiago proved to be ideal locations during the first decades of colonization, at a time when the Windward Passage was the epicenter of New World trade and navigation. As the Spanish empire expanded west, north, and south, colonists found in Havana an even better location and recognized that its hinterland was optimal for sugarcane cultivation: it was fertile, it had sufficient natural irrigation, and it was close to a major well-protected bay.

Colonial settlers had a detrimental effect on the natural environment. They scarred the terrain with plows, felled forests, and brought pigs and other animal and plant species that further degraded the environment. Sugarcane cultivation and sugar manufacturing, as will be discussed in chapter 8, had a profound ecological impact, including deforestation, soil erosion, and water pollution.

Indigenous people, runaway slaves, deserters, and foreign pirates and smugglers used other geographic circumstances to their advantage. They established their own ecology of resistance and self-imposed marginalization, usually as far away from Havana and sugar plantations as possible. Amerindian and black maroons found shelter in caves, mangrove clusters, forests, and adjacent keys, and smugglers and pirates sought cover in coves and remote locations.

2 ⤸

Indigenous Inhabitants

Oyendo las indias bellas
Y vertiendo puro llanto
De flores de cardosanto
Van adornando sus huellas
Entusiastas como ellas
Los indios de aquella grey
Le llevan a Guanaley
Peces, frutas y yerenes
Y de sus rojos burenes
Las blancas tortas de ajey.

JUAN CRISTÓBAL NÁPOLES FAJARDO

The first revolutionary advance was made when some group
or groups began to cultivate plants and/or breed food animals.
Cultivated plants and domestic animals put the cultivator, herdsman,
and the mixed farmer in control of their own food supply.

V. GORDON CHILDE

Cuba remained uninhabited until around 5000–4500 BCE, when small groups of Amerindians began arriving, most likely from Central America. Other waves of indigenous colonizers followed, each at a higher technological level, culminating with Arawak-speaking agricultural peoples, who continued to filter in until shortly after the first encounters with Spanish conquerors.

This chapter traces the various waves of indigenous migration, categorizes them, describes their material life, and discusses their economic, social, and political organization and their cultural contributions. Reflective of the most recent scholarship on the pre-Columbian Caribbean, the chapter seeks to paint a dynamic picture of interactions among different groups, emphasizing coexistence, trade relations, and cultural diffusion.

A few words on the classification terminology of Amerindian groups are in order. One of the most useful categorizations divides prehistoric human groups along a spectrum of technological and cultural development: Paleolithic nomadic, pre-ceramic hunter-gatherers; Neolithic largely sedentary farmers and ceramic makers; and intermediate Mesolithic peoples. Building on these categories, V. Gordon Childe proposed the theory of the Neolithic Revolution eight decades ago, arguing that the jump from pre-agricultural to agricultural subsistence opened the doors to revolutionary technological, social, and cultural advances.[1]

Archaeologists and other scholars have created classifications of prehistoric human groups that are specific to Cuba and the Caribbean. Irving Rouse's Caribbean-wide typology is still widely used. He recognized six broad categories (series) of indigenous inhabitants: Ortoiroid, Casimiroid, Suazoid, Saladoid, Ostionoid, and Troumassoid. Only two of these have relevance in the case of Cuba: the Casimiroid and Ostionoid. Casimiroids were Paleolithic and have been divided into three subseries, two of which, Casimirian and Redondan, settled the island at different points. Rouse and others have classified Casimirian Casimiroid peoples as Lithic, meaning that they made and used flaked-stone tools. Redondan Casimiroid people groups, on the other hand, are Archaic, meaning that they used tools made of ground stone, bone, and shell. Ostionoids were fully at the Neolithic level. They arrived in Cuba in three different waves (Ostionian, Meillacan, and Chican) and established themselves as two distinct groups, often categorized as Western Tainos and Classic Tainos.[2] Because they shared so many traits, scholars often classify both groups under the umbrella name Tainos.

While this chapter looks at various indigenous groups, it mostly focuses on those broadly categorized as Tainos. According to the different classifications described above, these peoples can be simultaneously categorized as Prehistoric, Neolithic, and Ostionoid. They are also described as Arawak speakers and as sedentary farmers and ceramic people who were organized into socially stratified chiefdoms.

Waves of Migration and Cross-Ethnic Interactions

Archaeologists and other researchers have produced widely accepted theories of the migration processes that led to the original peopling of Cuba and the rest of the Antilles. The Bering Channel–crossing theory contends that the first human migrations to the Americas crossed the Bering Strait around 150,000 years

BCE. It took around 9,000 more years for the first Amerindians to make it to the Caribbean, making the region one of the last to be populated in the hemisphere.

Amerindian groups arrived in Cuba in five distinct waves. The first wave dates to around 5000–4500 BCE, a time when the sea level was between six and ten feet lower than it is today, thus reducing the distance between islands, keys, and landmasses and facilitating navigation of small bands of humans on rafts or canoes.[3] The dominant interpretation is that they came from the Yucatan, but some argue for a possible Floridian origin. These first migrants were Casimiroids of the Casimirian subseries; the best known of them belonged to the Seboruco culture. These lithic-level people subsisted mostly by foraging for mollusks, nuts, and seeds; made rudimentary flaked-stone tools; and dwelled in caves and other natural shelters.[4]

Around 2500–2000 BCE, another wave of Casimiroids, these ones belonging to the Redondan subseries (at the Archaic level), began to move in. It is widely believed that most came from Central America, but some point to a South American origin.[5] The best known Redondan Casimiroid manifestations in Cuba are the Guayabo Blanco. Their sites were located on the western part

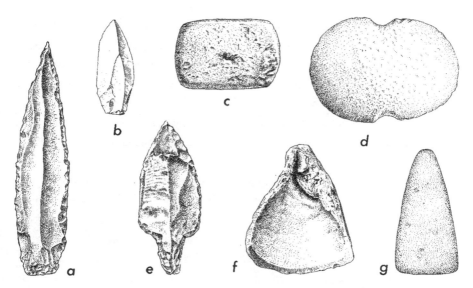

Figure 2.1. Antillean Casimiroid artifacts: *a*) backed knife; *b*) simple flaked tool; *c*) rectangular hammer-grinder; *d*) double-bitted ax; *e*) stemmed spearhead; *f*) shell gouge (from Cayo Redondo); *g*) conical pestle (from Cayo Redondo). After Yale Peabody Museum specimens. Source: Irving Rouse, *The Tainos: Rise and Decline of the People Who Greeted Columbus* (New Haven, CT: Yale University Press, 1992), 56. Reprinted courtesy of Yale University Press.

of the island, including the Guanahacabibes Peninsula, the Zapata Swamp, the southern coast of present-day Matanzas Province, and the Isle of Youth. Often referred to as Guanahatabeyes, they were still present when Europeans first arrived. Cuba's conquistador Diego Velázquez differentiated them from other indigenous groups, describing them as being "like savages . . . [who] do not have houses, nor settlements, nor towns, nor planted fields."[6]

The Guayabo Blanco fished, hunted, and foraged for mollusks and gathered wild seeds, fruits, and vegetables. Their tools were more sophisticated than those the Seboruco used. They manufactured their tools by grinding rather than flaking and they made cutting tools and vessels out of conch shells. They also shaped stones into highly polished daggers and balls. Their fishing equipment included dugout canoes, fishing nets, and hooks.[7]

Archaeological evidence tells us that the Guayabo Blanco buried their dead ritualistically, sometimes with objects such as stone balls.[8] Their bodies were sometimes buried along an east-west axis, but there is no consensus about whether this was done intentionally. The cave cemetery at Bacuranao, Havana Province, sheds light on the funeral practices of the Guayabo Blanco. Archaeologists have found fifty-four inhumed bodies at that site. Two of them were buried together, a woman around eighteen years old and an infant that is estimated to have been between one and a half and two and a half years old. We do not know their names (archaeological records refer to them as burial 4 and burial 27). For the sake of recognizing their humanity, let us call the woman Karaya (Moon) and the child Guey (Sun). We can assume that Karaya and Guey were mother and child; she was buried with the infant on her lap. The fact that Guey's backbone was arched rather than straight suggests that he or she was placed inside a cotton bag or a hammock, as was commonly done in infant burials. Most likely Guey died first and when Karaya died she was buried holding her child's remains.[9]

The most puzzling archaeological findings associated with the Guayabo Blanco include intricate cave paintings in the Isle of Youth that suggest sophisticated cosmological knowledge. Some of these pictographs consist of concentric circles that are interpreted as highly accurate solar calendars marking the solstice, the equinox, and the cardinal points.[10] Since these paintings and some of the polished stone artifacts mentioned above reflect a level of advancement superior to the rest of the Guayabo Blanco material culture, it is possible that they were created by or learned from people who belonged to advanced Central American civilizations.

Another Redondan Casimiroid group, the Cayo Redondo culture, dates to

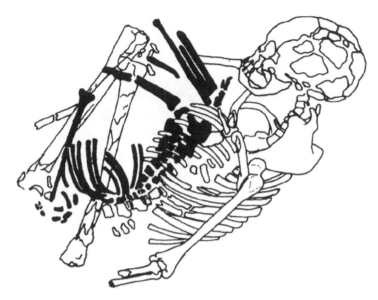

Figure 2.2. Graphic representation of a double cave burial of an adult female (*in white*) and an infant (*in black*) at Bacuranao 1, San José de Lajas, Havana Province. Source: Gabino La Rosa Corzo, "La orientación este de los entierros en cuevas de Cuba: Remate de una fábula," *Latin American Antiquity* 14, no. 2 (2003): 151. Reprinted courtesy of the Society for American Archaeology and Cambridge University Press.

circa 700 CE. There is evidence that they had sites in the west, the center, and the east of the island. The Cayo Redondo culture was more technologically advanced than that of its predecessors, its tribal groups were larger, and its religion and cosmovision were more complex. These people also created ground tools and ceremonial artifacts some of which were highly polished. Recent archaeological excavations have found indications of primitive cultivation practices and pottery production. The Cayo Redondo painted their bodies with ochre for ritual purposes and buried their dead with clay pots and food offerings.

There is plenty of evidence that the Redondan subseries of Cuba's Casimiroid peoples were at the Mesolithic level. What remains unclear is whether they arrived in Cuba as proto-agricultural and proto-ceramic people or they developed those capabilities in situ as a result of interactions with Ostionoid settlers of later arrival. Anthropologist William F. Keegan proposes the provocative thesis that it was the other way around: that the more advanced Ostionoids learned ceramic making from Casimiroid groups.[11]

Although Cuba's Casimiroid peoples had been gradually moving toward agriculture, the Neolithic Revolution did not happen until Ostionoid Amer-indians arrived in three distinct waves. The earliest, Ostionoids of the Ostio-nian subseries, began migrating from Hispaniola around 550–600 CE. By 1500, they had pushed as far west as present-day Matanzas. They were followed by more advanced Meillacan subseries Ostionoids, who also migrated from His-paniola beginning around 800 CE. The last of the Ostionoid waves, the Chican subseries, moved into Cuba beginning circa 1200. By 1492, their geographic extension was limited to a small part of eastern Cuba inside the Punta de Maisí-Baracoa-Guantánamo triangle. First- and second-wave Ostionoids are known as Western Tainos, while those who came during the third wave are categorized as Classic Tainos.[12]

Knowledge of the various waves of migration and the application of strictly defined categories, while useful, present a static view of pre-Columbian Cuba— a snapshot, if you will, taken at one particular moment, say 1492. These move-ments of people and their material culture, practices, and world views were far more dynamic and complex phenomena than this static view would suggest. For one, evidence that groups that originated in Central America kept in contact with and traded with their parent societies suggests that these migrations were multidirectional. Moreover, while there is an inclination to accept the general idea that more advanced groups pushed more primitive groups they came in contact with farther west or absorbed them, recent scholarship has produced evidence of instances when ceramic hunter-gatherer Casimiroids stopped the westward expansion of more advanced Saladoid agriculturalists. Likewise, al-though scholars have long assumed that cultural diffusion always went from more advanced to less developed societies, recent studies provide examples of cultural diffusion in the opposite direction. Keegan, for example, has argued that Cuba's early Ostionoid pottery has its origins in Casimiroid pottery, which influenced ceramic-making in Hispaniola, which in turn was brought to Cuba from that island. Other evidence of bidirectional cultural diffusion and hybrid-ization includes the use of Casimiroid decorative motifs in Neolithic pottery and the use of Casimiroid tools in Ostionoid contexts. If Keegan is right, what happened in Cuba departs from the usual Neolithic Revolution model that pos-its that the development of agriculture and ceramics are interrelated and occur simultaneously.[13]

A systematic focus on migration, geographic overlap, and coexistence among different indigenous groups instead of on cultural boundaries between pre-ceramic and ceramic peoples has sparked novel hypotheses and interpretations. While the roots of island Ostionoids were in northern South America, the material, political, and social culture of this group was far more complex than that of their continental Arawak ancestors. This invites the hypothesis that Ostionoids (Tainos) developed through interaction with and subjugation of lower-level indigenous groups, specifically in the Larger Antilles. It is highly revealing that the most advanced and complex manifestations of Ostionoid culture (Classic Tainos) appear in Puerto Rico, Hispaniola, and the far eastern end of Cuba. Those are precisely the geographical areas with greater and longer coexistence between Casimiroid and Ostionoid inhabitants. Anthropologist Samuel M. Wilson, among others, explains the complexity of Classic Taino societies based on their coexistence with Casimiroid peoples. The Ostionoids' subjugation of Casimiroids made possible the production of larger amounts of food. Subjugated Casimiroids became the bulk of the work force of Ostionoid societies. The Casimiroids produced the bulk of the food, which liberated Ostionoids to engage in tool making, the arts, religion, ritualistic sports, and other non-food-producing activities. This development expanded the size and complexity of Taino communities, which progressed from tribal organizations to chiefdoms.[14]

The Tainos

The Tainos practiced what is commonly referred to as slash-and-burn agriculture: they cleared forests and wild vegetation to prepare soils for cultivation. They called those fields *conucos* and used *coas*, long sticks with burned pointed tips, to push seeds into the ground. To cultivate their main food staples of *yuca* (manioc), *ajes* (sweet potatoes), and other tubers, they prepared mounds measuring nine to twelve feet in diameter. *Yuca* cultivation produced large yields estimated to have approximated 1,160 pounds (525 kilograms) per hectare.[15] Once harvested, *yuca* roots were ground with *guayos* (graters) into a pasty white substance that had to be squeezed inside a cotton cloth sleeve (*sibucán*) to remove its poisonous juice. The *yuca* paste was then shaped into flat cakes and cooked on *burenes* (ceramic griddles) over fire. Taino farmers also cultivated maize, beans, peppers, peanuts, tomatoes, guavas, papayas, and pineapples, among other fruits and vegetables.

The Taino diet also consisted of some animal protein derived from fishing and hunting. Fishing equipment included canoes, some of which could hold as many as 150 passengers, cotton nets, harpoons, and hooks. Tainos mastered the curious practice of using live gluefish (*guaicán*) as lures to trap larger fish. They also caught shellfish, birds, iguanas, *jutías* (hutias), and manatees and domesticated a species of mammal that European explorers referred to as mute dogs.

Figure 2.3. Woodcut of Taino women preparing cassava bread illustrating the different steps of the process: grating *yuca* roots into a paste (*left*), shaping the bread (*center*), and cooking it on a fire-heated *burén* (*right*). Source: Girolamo Benzoni, *La Historia del Mondo Nuovo* (Venice: F. Rampazetto, 1565). Reprinted courtesy of the John Carter Brown Library at Brown University.

These various meats were cooked over hot coals, *barbacoas*, from which the English word barbecue is derived. All told, however, the Taino diet was high in starches and low in proteins.

The archaeological record testifies to a diverse repertoire of manufactured tools and artifacts made from different materials. The most characteristic were earthenware pieces of pottery used to cook and store food and liquids. These maroon-colored artifacts were often ornamented with incised geometric motifs or anthropomorphic and zoomorphic designs. Other artifacts made of stone and other materials included petaloid ax heads, petroglyphs, *macanas* (wooden clubs), *jamacas* (cotton hammocks), *jabas* (cotton or straw handbaskets), and *guanines* (small pendants made from gold). Some artifacts point to increasing levels of hierarchization and specialization and the existence of interisland trade networks: ornamented low wooden seats (*dujos*) for the exclusive use of caciques and shamans, wood carvings created by craft specialists, and imported raw materials such as obsidian and rubber from other islands and beyond.

Taino villages, called *yucayeques*, consisted of dozens of *bohíos* (palm-thatched huts). Village chiefs and caciques lived in larger houses called *caneyes*. The average village had about 100 inhabitants, but the largest chiefdoms could reach populations in the low thousands. The first village Columbus's scouts encountered in 1492, near present-day Bahía de Bariay (in Holguín Province), reportedly had around 50 houses and 1,000 inhabitants.[16] Each village included a *batey*, a central plaza used for religious, social, and recreational purposes. Each village was ruled by a headman. Several villages often fell under the authority of a district chief or sub-cacique, and several districts could belong to a regional chiefdom under one cacique. The names of numerous chiefdoms persist in contemporary place names such as Baracoa, Bayamo, Camagüey, Habana, and Maisí.

Taino communities were hierarchical and complex. According to Alfredo E. Figueredo and other scholars, the lowest category of workers were called *tamemes*; they were most likely Archaic age peoples and their descendants who had been captured by Ostionoids and forced to serve the cacique caste. Then came the *naborias*, who represented the vast majority of the population; they were also likely of Casimiroid ancestry. An intermediary caste consisted of free Amerindians. The ruling elite were the *nitaínos*, a word that meant the good or noble ones. This caste produced the village caciques and regional chiefs.[17] While there were instances of female caciques among Tainos in neighboring islands, Cuban caciques were males who inherited their authority matrilineally, for example by being the son of a cacique's sister. Caciques and other *nitaínos* practiced polygamy and in some cases were buried with their wives. Taino men and unmarried women wore loincloths or nothing at all, but married women wore *naguas* (skirts).

Recent archaeological research in Hispaniola by Kathleen Deagan demonstrates sharp distinctions between upper-caste Tainos and those of lower social standing. She found that the diet of the elite was diverse and included more mammal meat and different—presumably more desirable—types of fish than those non-elite Tainos consumed. Likewise, the former used a larger variety of ceramic vessels.[18]

The religious practices and beliefs of the Tainos are among the best documented aspects of pre-Columbian culture, in part because of the thorough and detailed reports of Fray Ramón Pané, Fray Bartolomé de las Casas, Gonzalo Fernández de Oviedo, and other early chroniclers. Taino religion was animistic in the sense that elements of nature such as the wind and thunder were associated with specific deities. While some spirits were benevolent, others such as the deity Juracán (the root word of the word hurricane) were evil and destructive.

Taino religion provided explanations for many of life's mysteries. The story of Atabey giving birth to Yucahú explained the origin of one of their principal deities, the myth of Yaya and Yayael was their creation story, myths about woodpeckers that castrated men explained physiological differences between men and women, and so on.[19]

Religious rituals were led by shamans called *behiques*, who also played the role of healers. In preparation for healing ceremonies, divinations, and other rituals, *behiques* fasted, practiced ritual vomiting, and smoked potent forms of tobacco or inhaled an herbal hallucinatory powder called *cohoba*. They also used a wide array of medicinal plants. *Behiques*, however, could be blamed, and even killed, for botched curative ceremonies. Religion also played a significant role for Tainos as agricultural people. Their *zemis*, triangle-shaped stone or wooden objects,

Figure 2.4. Woodcut of Taino *behiques* (shamans) healing the sick. Source: Girolamo Benzoni, *La historia del Mondo Nouvo* (Venice: F. Rampazetto, 1565). Reprinted courtesy of the John Carter Brown Library at Brown University.

were fertility idols. Tainos considered their *zemis* to be more than symbolic objects; they viewed them as embodiments of actual spirits.[20]

Taino people engaged in elaborate communal artistic rituals known as *areítos*, which included music, dance, storytelling, and the consumption of intoxicating tobacco and fermented beverages. *Areítos* transmitted a village's oral tradition and celebrated ancestors and past heroes. They included playing maracas, gourd instruments, and drums made out of hollowed-out trunks; chanting; and dancing and could last several hours and even days. Women wore especially elaborate *naguas* during *areítos*, and participants of both sexes stamped their bodies with white and red pigment and wore cotton belts and other accessories. Tainos also played ball games they called *batos* in *bateyes*, or specially designated ceremonial courts. Ten such courts have been discovered in Cuba, nine of them in its extreme eastern region. Participants in ball games wore belts made of polished stone and used balls made from imported rubber. These games may have served as symbolic representations of war. Archaeological digs at El Chorro de Maíta and other sites have documented that Tainos flattened their babies' foreheads for aesthetic purposes and buried their dead in a flexed position.[21]

Pre-Columbian Demography

How large was the indigenous population of the Americas in 1492? How many people inhabited Cuba when European explorers first set foot on the island? Questions such as these have generated much attention and controversy. It is not simply a matter of counting heads, since estimates of the size of indigenous populations that fell precipitously during and after the conquest also have political implications. The larger the pre-Columbian population, the sharper the population collapse and the heavier the guilt of the conquistadores.

Estimates of pre-1492 populations for all the Americas range widely from lows of around 8 million to highs of over 100 million. High estimates were originally produced by chroniclers in an unscientific way. Prominent among them was las Casas, who as chief defender of the Amerindians embraced large precontact estimates that made the conquest and subsequent exploitation look brutally lethal. He guessed that Hispaniola had a population of between 3 and 4 million. Beginning in the 1930s, scholars such as anthropologist Alfred L. Kroeber and Venezuelan linguist Ángel Rosenblat proposed a series of low-end estimates. Their estimates hovered around 13 million for the entire hemisphere and between 200,000 and 300,000 for the islands of the Caribbean.[22]

During the late 1940s through the 1980s, a group of scholars at the University of California at Berkeley that included historian Lesley Byrd Simpson, physiologist Sherburne F. Cook, and historian Woodrow Borah formed what came to be known as the Berkeley school of Latin American demography. They published extensively about Amerindian demography, producing surprisingly high estimates. Using a variety of sources (chroniclers' accounts, censuses, indigenous labor rolls, tribute records) and diverse calculation methods (backward and forward extrapolation and estimates of soil yields), they concluded that the population of Central Mexico at the time of contact was around 11 million. In later studies, they raised that figure to 25 million. They also calculated that the pre-Columbian population for all of the Americas was around 100–113 million people and that Hispaniola alone had 8 million inhabitants.[23]

Most scholars, however, recognize that both low- and high-end estimates are improbable and have embraced middle-ground estimates. William M. Genevan, for example, has proposed estimates of 54 million for the hemisphere, 1 million for Hispaniola, and 2 million for the other Caribbean islands.[24]

There is general agreement that Cuba's population was less dense and smaller than that of Hispaniola and Puerto Rico. Cuban historian Juan Pérez de la Riva calculated the population at the time of conquest to be around 112,000. High-end estimates place it as high as 400,000; las Casas's estimate of 1 million inhabitants is generally dismissed as hyperbolic. Most of these inhabitants, as many as 90 percent, were Tainos who lived on the island's east and center between the present-day provinces of Granma and Matanzas. The other 10 percent, the Casimiroids, inhabited what is now the province of Pinar del Río, on the western end.[25]

Ancestral Legacies Regardless of their numbers, whether 100,000, 400,000, or 1 million, Cuba's native inhabitants came close to extinction within a matter of a few decades of contact with the Europeans. Most succumbed to the violence and pestilence the conquest unleashed. Spanish society absorbed most of the survivors and their indigenous or *mestizo* children. Other survivors were reconcentrated into a handful of Amerindian villages (*reducciones*). Yet others survived on the margins of colonial society in remote and mountainous locations of the interior, where they contributed to an emerging creole culture and mixed-race population along with fugitive slaves, white deserters, smugglers, and other social outcasts.

A 1582 census that included only battle-ready adult males enumerates forty "Indios" in Havana and forty-six in the indigenous village of Guanabacoa, across the bay. Mentions of indigenous inhabitants appear in colonial records as late as the 1800s. As the result of the initiative of Miguel Rodríguez (nicknamed "El

Indio"), in 1700 indigenous people from the Bayamo area founded a new Amerindian village they named Jiguaní. Mid-nineteenth-century accounts point to the fact that indigenous communities remained in existence and that their members performed *areítos* on Sundays. A regiment composed of indigenous people from the town of Yateras fought against Spanish troops during the Cuban War of Independence (1895–1898).[26]

Recent archaeological, genetic, and historical research sheds light on the biological and cultural legacy of Amerindian people. While the vast majority were ultimately absorbed into the dominant society, their phenotypical and genotypical presence is still evident, particularly in parts of the eastern end of the island. In 1964, a Soviet-Cuban team of investigators studied the population of Yateras and Caridad de los Indios. They found widespread physiological evidence of indigenous ancestry, including short stature; light-brown skin pigmentation; straight black hair; dark oblique eyes, many with Mongolian eye folds; and hand whorls and dental patterns specific to indigenous people. More recent genetic and skin pigmentation studies have shown that the current Cuban population exhibits 8 percent indigenous ancestry. In the eastern provinces (Holguín, Las Tunas, and Granma), which were the most densely populated areas before 1492, the average percent of native Cuban ancestry is between 12 and 15.[27]

Some recent studies show that extended family nuclei of Taino descendants exist in the region between Baracoa and Punta de Maisí. Researchers Alejandro Hartmann Matos and José Barreiro contend that as recently as 2011, around 5,000 Tainos lived on the island. In some communities, Caridad de los Indios and Yateras, for example, indigenous biological traits (Type O blood, high cheekbones, copper skin tone, and shovel-shaped teeth) are much more highly concentrated. Recent studies have demonstrated that at least 370 Taino words are still used in eastern Cuba.[28]

Coterminous with an upsurge in scholarship on indigenous cultural retentions is a recent phenomenon called Taino revival. Its proponents have organized into tribal groups in Cuba, Puerto Rico, the Dominican Republic, and the United States. They gather for *areítos* and other ancestral rituals, where they re-create Taino music, dance, and storytelling. One of their primary goals is preserving and representing Taino cultural practices such as using medicinal herbs, planting crops with *coas*, cooking and eating cassava bread, and blowing into conch shells to communicate from a distance.[29]

Yateras resident Julio Fuentes is among the Cubans who have embraced a Taino identity. He told researchers in 2004 that he still used a *coa* to plant his fields and cultivated native food plants according to phases of the moon. He thanked the researchers for "recovering forgotten knowledge." A lot of Tainos, he explained "had knowledge but lived and died without knowing its Indian origin." Upon his first visit to Baracoa's Taino museum, Fuentes exclaimed, "I felt pride because I hadn't seen these things before and because I'm part of this culture."[30]

Whether they embrace a Taino identity or not, Cubans of any race on and off the island who smoke tobacco, take naps in hammocks, eat boiled *yuca* with *mojo* sauce, have guava paste for dessert, play a gourd *güiro*, call a bus a *guagua*, carry groceries from the *bodega* or *supermercado* in a *jaba*, or live in thatch-roofed houses owe that cultural heritage to the Tainos who greeted Columbus five centuries ago.

3 ❧

First Encounters, Inventing America, and the Columbian Exchange

*Al mismo tiempo que Colón y sus compañeros de Europa descubrieron
la América, los hijos de ésta descubrieron a Europa.*

FERNANDO ORTIZ

It is necessary to retrace history, not the history of the discovery
of America but rather of the idea that America was discovered.

EDMUNDO O'GORMAN

What for centuries was called the discovery of America, now more commonly
referred to as first encounters or initial contacts between Amerindians and European explorers, has attracted much attention from historians, other scholars,
and polemicists, some of whom have obvious political agendas. Hundreds if not
thousands of books, articles, editorials, and documentary films hit bookshelves,
newspaper stands, and movie houses in and around 1992 in commemoration of
the 500th anniversary of the events that forever changed the world, connecting
Europe, the Americas, and Africa and initiating a prolonged process of what we
now call globalization.

This chapter explores the foundational encounters between indigenous people
and Europeans and discusses their economic, social, political, and cultural reverberations throughout Cuba, the Caribbean, and the Atlantic basin. It draws
upon interpretative perspectives espoused by Mexican philosopher Edmundo
O'Gorman; American historian and geographer Alfred W. Crosby, who coined
the term "the Columbian Exchange"; and cultural sociologist Eviatar Zerubavel,
author of *Terra Cognita*. The chapter also looks at the competitive exploration voyages of Christopher Columbus and Amerigo Vespucci as a window on a historical

moment of transition between a late medieval religious cosmovision and a Renaissance world view characterized by reason, exploration, and scientific inquiry.[1]

The year 1492 was a most auspicious time for Spain to begin a search for new navigation routes and new lands to conquer. In January of that year, following a prolonged siege, Granada, the last stronghold of Muslim domination, surrendered to Spanish troops. The fall of Granada marked the end of almost eight centuries of the Christian *reconquista* against Muslim occupation. Later that year, the Spanish Crown ordered the expulsion of Muslims and Jews who rejected conversion to Christianity. The publication of the first Spanish-language grammar by Antonio de Nebrija, also in 1492, was symbolic and symptomatic of Spain's national cultural integration. Not coincidentally, that same year, on the outskirts of Granada, after over eight years of incessant lobbying, Columbus finally received the Crown's sanction of and support for his wish to "discover and subdue some Islands and Continent in the ocean."[2]

Spain's political consolidation under a dominant Catholic polity, however, marked the end of what at times had been a relatively harmonious period of coexistence among Christians, Muslims, and Jews. This coexistence, known as *la convivencia*, had proved fertile for cultural hybridization and had made Iberia one of the most dynamic centers of cultural and scientific effervescence. Neil MacGregor, author of *A History of the World in One Hundred Objects*, used a fourteenth-century Spanish-Jewish bronze astrolabe inscribed with Hebrew, Arabic, and Spanish words as a window on the "fruitful friction" between those three cultures. He claimed that these cultural interactions "made medieval Spain the intellectual superpower of Europe." Astrolabes like this one were highly valued as surveying, astronomical, and even astrological tools; Muslims found them useful for finding their way to Mecca. The expulsion of Jews and Muslims who refused conversion in the 1490s ended *la convivencia*.[3]

The Capitulations of Santa Fe, as the original contract between the Catholic monarchs and Columbus came to be known, bestowed upon the Genoese mariner the titles of admiral, viceroy, and governor of all territories to be found and conquered. Such titles were awarded in perpetuity to him and his descendants. The agreement also included generous economic provisions that entitled Columbus to keep 10 percent of the profits derived from all goods found and traded in any territories he discovered and the right to invest in and draw profit from any subsequent enterprise.[4]

Columbus was convinced that he was heading to the Orient by way of the West. Basing his projected voyage on a combination of existing estimates and new calculations, he took China to be much larger than it was and believed that

Figure 3.1. Hebrew astrolabe, circa 1345–1355. This bronze instrument is inscribed with Hebrew, Arabic, and Spanish words. Image © Trustees of the British Museum.

the earth's circumference was about a fourth smaller than it was. Combining these and other miscalculations, he concluded that the Indies, as East Asia was known, were reachable by sailing west from Europe. A self-taught navigator and by no means a recognized scientist or cosmographer, Columbus proposed a voyage that earned him derision from Europe's scientific establishment. Scholars at Salamanca were skeptical about his plans, insisting that his calculations were inaccurate and that the existing naval technology would not permit a voyage from

Europe to the Indies. "Everyone who heard about my enterprise rejected it with laughter and ridicule," he later reminisced.[5] Undaunted, he pursued his plans with the zeal of a crusader, believing that his new route to the Orient would give him and the Spanish monarchs access to the fabled riches and species of Asia and allow Christianity to expand to those parts of the world.

First Encounters

Contrary to the oft-repeated misconception that before 1492 Europeans believed the earth was flat, it had long been established that the earth was round. As far back as the second century, Claudius Ptolemy had calculated the size of the earth, which he estimated to be 28 percent smaller than its actual size. He also produced a fairly accurate map of the known world, which was rediscovered during the Renaissance and became an important source of cosmographic knowledge.

On August 3, 1492, Columbus and around ninety other men boarded the *Santa María*, the *Niña*, and the *Pinta* in the port of Palos in southern Spain. The latter two were caravels, newly developed small, swift, and easy-to-handle vessels that made long journeys feasible and safe. While the crews were mostly composed of poor sailors from the port town of Palos and its neighboring town of Moguer, they included a wide array of individuals, among them relatively wealthy men such as Juan de la Cosa, the owner of the *Santa María*, and the brothers Martín Alonso Pinzón and Vicente Yáñez Pinzón, captains of the two caravels; royal officials, including the *veedor* (royal inspector) Rodrigo Sánchez de Segovia; Luis de Torres, a polyglot Jew recently converted to Christianity who served as interpreter; a painter named Diego Pérez; Bartolomé de Torres, a convicted murderer; three other criminals; a soon-to-be-famous common sailor named Juan Rodríguez Bermejo (aka Rodrigo de Triana); and a cabin boy named Pedro.[6]

Several weeks into the voyage, the ships' crews began showing signs of unrest and desperation. Mutinous conspiracies were spun that Columbus tried to avert by feeding his men false information about the distance they had traveled so far. He kept two daily records, an accurate one for himself and a false one to share with the sailors: "[September 10, 1492] went sixty leagues only reckoned 48." Anxieties and fears were somewhat diffused with the sighting of birds and other evidence of nearby land. According to his grossly inaccurate latitude calculations, his vessels were approaching present-day Nova Scotia. On October 10, Columbus reported that his men "could stand it no longer." But at last, in the early hours of October 12, after seventy days of uncertain navigation, Juan Rodríguez Bermejo shouted "¡Tierra! ¡Tierra!"

Columbus named that first island San Salvador. Later that day, explorers had their first contact with frightened inhabitants, who fled in terror. As the vessels headed south, inhabitants told the explorers of a large and bountiful island located farther south. On his log entry for October 21, Columbus referred to Cuba for the first time: "They call it 'Colba.'" The admiral's preconceptions and the description he heard about the island led him to believe that it was Cipangu (Japan). "Indians tell me," he wrote on October 24, "that it is very large and has much trade, and has in it gold and spices and great ships and merchants." Three days later Cuba came within sight.[7]

On October 28, Columbus and his men landed on the island that above all others delighted his senses and captivated his heart. Crew members spent the next five weeks exploring the eastern end of Cuba's northern coast, intermittently measuring the depth of the inlets of the jagged coastline. They made several landings along the way, planting a cross and saying prayers at every stopping point. Two members of the expedition, Rodrigo de Jerez and the interpreter Luis de Torres, ventured inland for several days, during which they encountered numerous villages and spent time among native inhabitants.

What Columbus and his scouts saw in Cuba failed to approximate the advanced civilization and marvelous riches of Cipangu described in *The Travels of Marco Polo*. Instead of the solid gold–roofed palaces that mathematician and cartographer Paulo Toscanelli had described in one of his letters, what Columbus found were rudimentary palm-thatched *bohíos* and *caneyes*. The admiral now struggled to fit Cuba somewhere else on his nebulous mental map. His indigenous informants also spoke of a nearby Cubanacán, which he believed was the legendary Cathay. Columbus dismissed the local inhabitants' claims that Cuba was an island. "I am certain," he wrote on November 2, "that this is the mainland."[8] They also spoke of a large and rich nearby island called Bohío, which now Columbus took (and mistook) for Cipangu. According to inhabitants, Bohío was rich in gold and was inhabited by fierce cannibals, two things Columbus had read about in *The Travels of Marco Polo*. On December 5, after over a month of sailing along the coast, the expedition headed toward Bohío, which the admiral renamed Hispaniola. The *Santa María* ran aground on a sandbank and sank on Christmas Day 1492. The two surviving vessels, the *Pinta* and the *Niña*, left for Europe on January 16. Around forty crew members and passengers stayed behind, quartered in the small fort of La Navidad that the crew had built from the wreckage of the *Santa María*.

Figure 3.2. The islands Columbus encountered during his first voyage. This 1493 woodcut appeared in early illustrated editions of Columbus's letter about his first voyage. The illustration includes Isla Juana (Cuba), Hispaniola, and four islands in the Bahamas (San Salvador, Santa María de la Concepción, Fernandina, and la Isla Bella). Source: Christopher Columbus, *De insulis inuentis* (Paris, 1858). Reprinted courtesy of the John Carter Brown Library at Brown University.

Although Columbus failed to bring back to Europe convincing evidence that he had reached rich lands of the Orient, the success of his first voyage earned him ample royal support for a second expedition (1493–1496). On September 26, 1493, seventeen vessels and 1,200 people departed from Spain. A few months earlier, the Spanish-born Pope Alexander VI had issued his famously controversial *Inter Caetera* bull, which sanctioned Spain's claims to all lands 100 leagues west of the Azores and granted Portugal equal rights over territories east of that line of demarcation. After making a few short stops in several of the Lesser Antilles, Columbus's convoy sailed toward Hispaniola, where his crew learned that all the Spaniards who had been left behind after the first voyage had been killed, among them interpreter Luis de Torres and painter Diego Pérez.

On April 24, 1494, Columbus set sail toward Cuba on board the *Niña*, convinced that it was the Malay Peninsula protruding from the Asian mainland. He referred to it as the province of Magó, which he believed was located not far from the Great Khan's Cathay. This time, the vessels sailed along the southern shoreline for several weeks, making numerous stops along the way. In his farfetched efforts to sustain the proposition that Cuba was a peninsula, Columbus sailed west until he reached what later became known as Cortés Bay in Pinar del Río Province. Instead of continuing westward, Columbus ordered his caravels to turn back, but not before forcing their crews to take an oath affirming that Cuba was not an island because they "did not see or [hear] of an island which could have 335 leagues on one coast from west to east." Anyone who ever claimed that it was not a peninsula would be punished by having his tongue cut out.[9]

Viewing these events armed with over five centuries of accumulated knowledge and the scientific capabilities of the early twenty-first century obscures the fact those first encounters between the Old and New Worlds were bewildering, filled with uncertainty, fear, and wild speculation. Initial responses ranged from awe and admiration to horror and contempt. These encounters tested the limits of the imaginations of both Europeans and Amerindians. Both scrambled to draw from their respective religions and cosmovisions as they struggled to understand each other, the worlds they represented, and the new world they were beginning to create together.

As Columbus's travel logs and other sources attest, he fell in love with Cuba; it was love at first sight, passionate, and enduring. "I have never seen anything so beautiful," he wrote on October 28, 1492, marveling at its variegated topography, its luscious vegetation, and its splendid bays and rivers, which he claimed were the finest he had ever seen. A month into his first exploration of Cuba, he wrote that it looked "like an enchanted land," and days later he wrote that he did not want to leave the place. The weather seemed to conspire with the natural enchantment, as the convoy was forced to wait several days for favorable winds before it could leave. On his second voyage, Columbus reiterated his predilection for Cuba, calling it "the most beautiful thing that human eyes had ever seen." He remarked on a delightful stop along the south coast on the day of Pentecost in 1494: "We rested there on that grass next to those water springs and the marvelous aroma of flowers that could be felt, and the sweet singing of a multitude of little birds, under the shade of tall and enormously beautiful palm trees."[10]

The Genoese mariner described the inhabitants in laudatory but patronizing terms, highlighting their beauty, their meekness, and their friendly character. He wrote about their olive skin, their high cheekbones, and their lustrous straight jet-black hair. Early explorers were struck by their unabashed nakedness. Columbus erroneously reported that they had no religion and could be easily converted to Christianity and effortlessly subdued: "10 men," he wrote, "cause 10,000 Indians to flee."[11] He and other contemporaries commented on the selflessness of the indigenous people and their willingness to share whatever they had and to trade gold and other valuables for trinkets made of tin or glass. Early European explorers also recounted their first impressions of tobacco smoking, the use of hammocks and canoes, and other curious practices.

The admiral reported to the monarchs that during his first voyage he had not found "any human monsters" but instead had encountered "people of very pleasant appearance." However, he conveyed the fact that indigenous inhabitants repeatedly mentioned the existence of fierce cannibals living in nearby islands: "Men with one eye and others with dogs' snouts who eat men."[12] Columbus and his fellow explorers also heard tales of an island to the southeast inhabited by amazons and of men with tails living somewhere in western Cuba. Later explorers reported visiting villages inhabited by giants; others searched obsessively for the mythical El Dorado and the fabled Fountain of Youth.

The first chroniclers scrambled for words to describe the fauna of Cuba and the Caribbean that were unfamiliar to them. They saw flying fish and manatees they mistook for sirens. The admiral and his contemporaries reported on dogs that did not bark, clouds of polychromatic parrots, dragon-like iguanas, and countless unimaginable species. Later explorations expanded the catalog of seemingly monstrous creatures as Europeans encountered anteaters, vampire bats, armadillos, boa constrictors, toucans, electric eels, piranhas, and hundreds of animals that were unlike anything they had seen or imagined before. Columbus was repulsed by the sight of the iguanas that local inhabitants found so appetizing: "[The] nastiest thing ever seen. . . . They were all the color of dry wood, their skin very wrinkled especially around the neck and above the eyes which looked poisonous and horrific." A few years later, Peter Martyr d'Anghiera described another New World creature: "four-legged in the shape of a turtle, but with scales instead of a shell, with extremely hard skin, to the point that it is not afraid of arrows, covered with a thousand warts, its back flat, its head like an ox's." He was describing a manatee.[13]

These sights tested the limits of the explorers' frame of reference and the vocabularies of European languages, and Columbus and other contemporaries recurred to comparisons with more familiar things. Thus, grass in Cuba was "as tall as it is in Andalusia," "palms [were] different from those in Guinea or Spain," the sea was as "calm as the river at Seville," nuts and rats were "like those of India." *Yuca* roots were like carrots but were white and tasted like chestnuts; tobacco leaves resembled lettuce leaves. Tomatoes were golden apples and potatoes were earth apples; that is where we get the Italian word *pomodoro* and the French term *pomme de terre*. Puzzled Europeans recurred to hyperbole in their efforts to convey the strange world unfolding before them. Columbus spoke of Cuba's mountains that "appear[ed] to reach Heaven," of "flocks of parrots that obscure the sun," of ocean water that was white and as thick as milk. Before departing from Cuba during his first voyage, he wrote in his log that "it does not seem to me that there can be more fertile countries under the sun or any more temperate in heat and cold."[14]

As a symbolic act of possession over Cuba, which he first named Juana in honor of Prince Juan, Columbus christened coastal points, harbors, and rivers as he sailed alongside the island during his first two voyages. He named his first landing point San Salvador (Bahía de Bariay) and subsequently assigned dozens of other place names: Río de Mares or Marte (Bahía de Gibara), Cabo de Palmas (Punta Uvero), Puerto del Príncipe (Bahía de Tánamo), Santa Catalina (Cayo Moa), Puerto Santo (Baracoa), and so on. While sailing along the southern shore in 1494, the admiral continued to hand out names as if he were Adam and Cuba his Eden. Deeming Cuba's westernmost point the extreme eastern end of Asia, he named it Alfa y Omega (Punta de Maisí) and erected two columns and a cross to mark the spot. He later gave the name of Puerto Grande to Guantánamo Bay and named two constellations of keys Jardines de la Reina and Jardinillos. Columbus also named the large island south of Cuba's southwestern coast San Juan Evangelista (Isle of Youth).

Because the extant documentation of the first encounters between Caribbean indigenous people and European explorers was produced exclusively by the latter, it provides much insight into the Europeans' perceptions of Amerindians and their environment. However, it provides very little information about how indigenous peoples perceived the invaders and how they struggled to incorporate them into their Neolithic cosmovision. Had the Tainos been able to record these first encounters, we would have a better understanding of how they grappled with language and cultural limitations to make sense of the shock that was turning their world upside down. It is more than likely that Cuba's indigenous inhabitants first saw Columbus's vessels approaching from a distance. They probably appeared to be large sea monsters, perhaps whales or giant manatees. Perhaps they seemed to be canoes shaped like *bohíos* with large cotton sheets blown by Guabancex, the deity that drives the wind and the waves. The experience of seeing white, bearded, armed men emerge from those vessels was frightening, as evidenced by the numerous accounts of the Tainos fleeing in terror. The Spaniards' metal armor, weaponry, and overall appearance were as disconcerting and awe-inspiring to Cuba's native inhabitants as the Amerindians' nudity, beardlessness, and bodily ornamentation were to the Europeans.

While Europeans viewed indigenous inhabitants as inferior human beings, the latter first deemed the Europeans immortal gods. When Columbus's scouts Luis de Torres and Rodrigo de Jerez visited an indigenous village they were treated as supernatural beings; the villagers believed they had come from heaven. The scouts reported that local residents kissed their hands and feet and touched them to see if they had human skin and bones.[15] The fact that the first explorers had no women with them must have also puzzled Cuba's native inhabitants and perhaps led them to suspect that, like the Caribs, they had come to kidnap their women to make them theirs, as some Spaniards surely did.

Just as Europeans commented on the relatively small value indigenous people placed on gold and how they yearned after beads and hawk bells, the Tainos were surprised and amused by the Spaniards' obsessive lust for gold and seemingly worthless leaves, seeds, and pieces of bark. Bartolomé de las Casas reported that Cuba's inhabitants came to believe that Spaniards worshiped gold as their god. Some European imports to the New World, particularly metal and gunpowder, terrorized the indigenous population. Based on what we know of Taino religion and culture, we can speculate that those bearded, pale-skinned men on horseback appeared like strange human-eating beasts in which horse and rider fused into one, like the centaurs of Greek mythology. European mastiff dogs were fierce and barked menacingly, unlike the quiet, playful pets the Tainos kept. The explorers' muskets and cannon must have seemed possessed by Guatabua, the deity of thunder, who had apparently formed an alliance with the invaders.

Inventing America

So who "discovered" Cuba and America? When were they "discovered"? Every Cuban and American schoolchild knows the answers: Columbus in 1492. But are those answers correct? It depends on what we mean by discovery.

At the time, Spaniards used the verb *descubrir* to mean to unveil and describe something—a mountain, for example—even if there was previous knowledge about its existence. The use of the term discovery in its current meaning is controversial and has in recent years fallen into disuse. Did the first landing at San Salvador on October 12, 1492, or the sighting of Cuba a few days later, constitute discoveries or were these just first steps in a protracted process that involved multiple actors who were engaged in what Edmundo O'Gorman called "the invention of America" and what Eviatar Zerubavel has more recently termed the "mental discovery of America"? In his stimulating book *The Invention of America*, O'Gorman used philosophy to dismiss the idea that Columbus discovered America because the admiral based that conclusion not on facts but rather on a preconceived idea.[16]

The gradual unveiling of the Americas took place in the context of a Europe that was in transition from the Middle Ages to the Renaissance, from feudalism to capitalism, from small regional kingdoms to absolute monarchies, and from a world view dominated by religion and scholasticism to another based on skepticism, humanism, and experimentation. These transitions were gradual and occurred at different times in specific places. Columbus and Vespucci reflected these transitions.

At the risk of engaging in distorting reductionism, Columbus was essentially a medieval explorer. A deeply religious man and a crusader at heart, he looked reverently to the Bible, the fathers of the Church, and cosmological and philosophical authorities, whose knowledge he used deductively as he tried to understand the world he unwittingly unveiled. His search followed the medieval formula historian Yuval Noah Harari has described as Knowledge = Logic x Scriptures.[17] Deeply embedded in his view of the world was the dogma of the Ecumene: that the world consisted of three connected continents (Europe, Asia, and Africa), three oceans (Occidental, Mediterranean, and Indian), three human races (Caucasian, African, Asian and the descendants of Japheth, Shem, and Ham), and three religions (Judaism, Christianity, and Islam). All of these triads reflected the Holy Trinity.[18]

Columbus embraced an unconventional cosmovision based on faulty information that lead to erroneous calculations. He accepted the views of Paolo To-

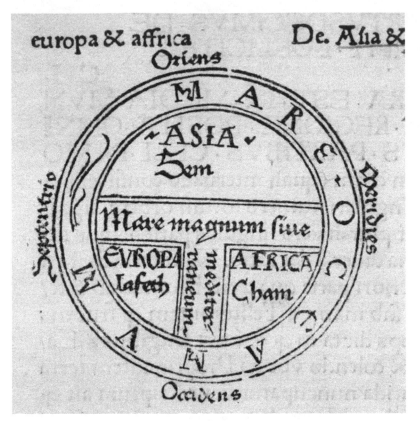

Figure 3.3. The Ecumene. "T-O" map by Isidore, Bishop of Seville (560–636). His rendition of the world divides it into three parts, one for each of Noah's sons: Sem (Shem), Iafeth (Japheth) and Cham (Ham). The fact that Asia appears on top illustrates the primacy of Jerusalem in this world view. Source: *Etimologarvm* (Augsburg: Günther Zainer, 1472). Reprinted courtesy of the Newberry Library, Chicago.

scanelli, a Florentine physician and mathematician whose 1474 map made the world smaller, and Marinus of Tyre's measurement of Eurasia, which was 45 degrees larger than Ptolemy's and 125 degrees longer than it is. The compounding effect of these miscalculations led Columbus to believe that it was feasible to reach Asia by crossing the Atlantic, known then as Occidental Ocean.

Other contemporaries such as Vespucci and d'Anghiera were Renaissance men who challenged the ancient authorities and religious texts with empirical observations and experimentation. They followed a different formula: Knowledge = Empirical Data x Mathematics. In Vespucci's words: "Rationally, let it be said in a whisper, experience is certainly worth more than theory."[19] Vespucci was born and raised in Florence, the epicenter of the Renaissance, where he received a privileged education and later worked as a merchant for the de Medici family. Renaissance minds like his approached questions empirically, seeking and analyzing evidence to decipher the riddle of the islands and landmasses explorers encountered. D'Anghiera, an Italian-born priest and humanist, served on the court of the Spanish monarchs and in 1521 became the Crown's official chronicler of the New World.

Columbus's first and second voyages shook the cosmological, philosophical, and religious foundations of Europe as explorers, cosmographers, theologians, and cartographers worked to understand the puzzling geographic information that gradually made its way to Europe from halfway around the globe. Columbus's burdensome philosophical baggage did not allow him to even consider that Cuba and the other lands he found were something other than the Indies he had set out to reach by way of the west. Meanwhile, Renaissance thinkers such as d'Anghiera were willing to engage in the "mental discovery" of a New World if evidence led them inductively to that conclusion. D'Anghiera was perhaps the first to embrace the notion that the islands that Columbus had found were not Asia but were in fact something previously unknown. In a letter dated November 1, 1493 (only seven and a half months after Columbus's first return to Spain), he referred to Columbus as "he who discovered the New World."[20] He, Vespucci, and other Renaissance cosmographers saw the budding idea of a New World as a hypothesis to be tested with subsequent voyages and explorations.

Columbus and Vespucci were protagonists in the prolonged effort to figure out the location and identity of the islands and continental masses Columbus had found during his first two voyages. Over the next few years, they embarked in parallel explorations to determine the identity of those lands.

During his third voyage (1498–1500), Columbus ventured farther south and encountered the mainland of South America, near the Gulf of Pariah, which separates the island of Trinidad and the coast of Venezuela. Taken aback by this new finding that threatened to destroy the holy concept of the Ecumene, the admiral came up with another conclusion based in religion: he had found the Garden of Eden. His encounter with the mighty Orinoco River flowing off the coast of South America led him to affirm that the earth was not round but rather was shaped like a pear or a woman's breast. Columbus believed that he had reached the earth's nipple-shaped highest point, the lost Garden of Eden from which the world's mightiest rivers flowed. He concluded deductively that because islands could not sustain rivers of such magnitude, the land mass to the south was "a

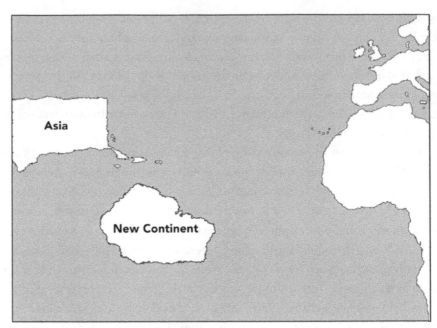

Map 3.1. Map depicting Christopher Columbus's hypothesis (1500). Credit: Luis Martínez-Fernández and Luis Alberto Martínez.

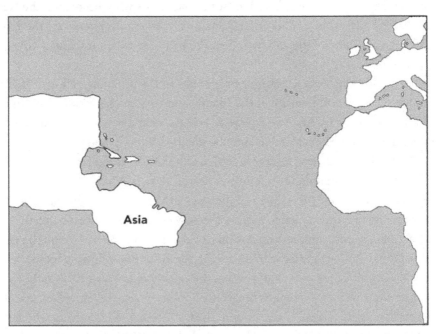

Map 3.2. Map depicting Amerigo Vespucci's hypothesis (1500). Credit: Luis Martínez-Fernández and Luis Alberto Martínez.

mighty continent that was hitherto unknown," which God had concealed from Europeans until that point. This new continent, he believed, was separate from the islands and from the mainland to the north, which he continued to claim were parts of Asia.[21]

A few months later, during his first Atlantic voyage (1499), Vespucci reached the Cape of San Roque near the northwestern tip of present-day Brazil and then sailed west toward Venezuela, where he sailed from the Gulf of Pariah all the way to Maracaibo. Based on observations from this voyage, he came to believe that those coastal areas were part of a large continental mass that belonged to Asia.

These encounters with a massive continent located south of the equator and another large land mass west of the Caribbean sparked two primary hypotheses to be tested in further explorations. Columbus hypothesized that the islands and mainland to the north were Asia, as he had claimed all along, and that the continent to the south was a previously unknown land mass. Vespucci, meanwhile, hypothesized that all the islands and land masses constituted a single continent, Asia.

Both explorers embarked on another round of voyages to test their respective hypotheses. Vespucci set out on his second voyage (1501–1502) to search for more evidence. His strategy was to sail south along the continental coast. His expedition sailed to 34.5 degrees south of the equator, a parallel far beyond the estimated southernmost parts of Asia. This evidence pushed Vespucci to discard the Asia hypothesis and to embrace the idea that what we know to be South America was indeed a new continent; the "fourth part of the earth," as he put it.[22] Reflecting this mental redrawing of the world, Cantino's world map of 1502 showed the Americas as separate from Asia, North and South America as separate from each other, and Cuba as an island.

Columbus, meanwhile, set out on a fourth and final voyage (1502–1503) toward Central America in search of an oceanic passage that separated what he believed was Asia to the north and the new continent to the south. After sailing from present-day Honduras to as far south as Panama without finding any water passage, he discarded the two-continent hypothesis. He embraced religious answers once again: the Ecumene was restored and he concluded that during his journey along the coast of Central America he had found yet another biblical landmark, the prodigiously rich gold mines of Ophir, which had produced the gold used to build Solomon's temple.

On his way back to Europe, still thinking it part of the Asian continent, Columbus saw Cuba for the last time in mid-May 1503. A violent storm pushed his vessels away: "I lost, at one stroke, three anchors; and, at midnight, when the weather was such that the world appeared to be coming to an end, the cables of the other ship broke, and it came down upon my vessel with such force that it was a wonder we were not dashed to pieces."[23] This was a far cry from that refreshing afternoon on the day of Pentecost during his second voyage.

Was the discovery of America and Cuba (if we may use that concept) the result of Columbus's medieval crusading zeal or was it a product of the inductive approach of Renaissance men such as Vespucci and d'Anghiera? Was it a physical encounter or an invention? Arguably it was neither and it was both. The "discovery" and "invention" of America required the mystic zeal of a profoundly stubborn Columbus, whose deeply religious world view allowed him to embark on explorations and embrace theories that his learned contemporaries summarily dismissed. It was also the creation of a Renaissance man such as Vespucci, who proposed hypotheses and sought empirical evidence to make sense of those new lands.

Ironically, the same mindset that pushed Columbus to find Cuba and other islands and mainlands to the west prevented him from recognizing them as new. While Columbus was the first European to encounter the Caribbean, South America, and Central America, it was Vespucci who eventually "invented" America. It was a matter of an unwitting collaboration between a passionate medieval explorer and detached Renaissance cosmographers and navigators. Such convergences of primal passions and intuition, on one hand, and skepticism and experimentation, on the other, have been at the heart of many of the most dramatic transformations and revolutions in human history. The discovery/invention of America ranks high among them.

Sixteenth-century cartography reflects the unfolding debate between the two navigators. In 1500, cartographer Juan de la Cosa, one of the men Columbus had forced to swear that Cuba was not an island, produced the first map in which Cuba appeared as an island. Instead of the mighty continental tongue that Columbus still believed it was, de la Cosa portrayed Cuba as a curled-up shrimp of an island about to be devoured by a gigantic, green continental mass, the mandibles of the Gulf of Mexico's gaping mouth. Neither de la Cosa nor any of his shipmates had their tongues cut out as Columbus had warned they would be if they ever said that Cuba was an island.

Martin Waldeseemüller credited Vespucci with the correct understanding of the New World. His famous map of 1507 portrayed North and South America as connected to each other and stamped the word "America," not "Columbia,"

Figure 3.4. Detail from Martin Waldseemüller's map of the world. This is the earliest map that uses the name "America" to identify South America. Source: Waldseemüller, *Universalis Cosmographia* (1507).

over the southern continent. In later maps, only two of the names that Columbus gave as he sailed past Cuba stuck (Jardín de la Reina and Jardinillos); bays and capes reverted to their Taino names or later settlers imposed names of their choosing. Not even the name Juana stuck, as King Ferdinand ordered it renamed Fernandina soon after Prince Juan died. Fernandina did not stick either; the island came to be known as Cuba, what indigenous inhabitants had first said to Columbus or what he had understood them to say. Havana's founders, perhaps unwittingly, honored Columbus when they named what would eventually become Cuba's capital San Cristóbal de La Habana. Three centuries later Columbus's ashes were moved from Santo Domingo to Havana's cathedral, where they remained until Spain lost possession of Cuba in 1898. In an ironic twist, the Cuban territory where Columbus first landed convinced that he was in the Orient eventually became known as Oriente Province.

The Columbian Exchange

As America was being invented, the Old and New Worlds engaged in what Alfred W. Crosby Jr. has termed the "Columbian Exchange," the idea that the encounter between the New and Old Worlds opened the floodgates to a centuries-long exchange between Europe and the Americas that included peoples, ideas, technology, precious metals, animals, plants, and germs.[24] There is no doubt that these early stages of what is now called globalization dramatically transformed both the Americas and the three continents of the medieval Ecumene.

The early Europeans who explored Cuba and other parts of the New World brought with them their domesticated animals and plants, which they hoped would thrive and flourish in the American context. Among the imported animal species were the horse, for transportation and warfare; the cow, for its milk, meat, and leather; the sheep, for wool and meat; the pig, chicken, and goat as sources of food; and the dog as a pet and hunting companion. Pigs, cattle, goats, and horses were let loose to multiply, reverting to a state of wildness and wreaking havoc on the croplands of the indigenous inhabitants. The Europeans imported plants that provided the food and beverages that satisfied their tastes: wheat, onions, garlic, lettuce, olives, chickpeas, sugarcane, bananas, watermelons, grapevines, coffee, and tea, among others. Some, like sugarcane and bananas, blossomed in the Caribbean to such an extent that parts of the region would eventually be known as "sugar islands" and "banana republics." Other European food plants, such as olives, grapes, and wheat, floundered in the region, although they later flourished in the temperate regions of continental America.

Pre-Columbian inhabitants of the Americas had few domesticated animals; they were largely limited to turkeys, guinea pigs, and llamas. Although a few animals crossed the Atlantic in the other direction, mostly as specimens such as exotic birds, American plants invaded Eurasia and later Africa. One of Columbus's major goals was to acquire exotic spices such as ginger, cinnamon, cloves, and peppers. While Columbus was disappointed that he did not find familiar spices, he and later explorers discovered a vast catalog of food plants, some of which became popular in Europe and beyond. Cuba's main pre-Columbian foodstuffs, *yuca* and sweet potatoes, did not make it to Europe's kitchens but eventually found their way to Africa and Asia, where they became dietary staples. While the practice has been lost in Cuba, in parts of Africa farmers still cultivate *yuca* in mounds, like the Tainos did five centuries ago. Likewise, American corn has reached all parts of the globe. Its high yields help nourish millions of people in China and other countries; it also feeds hogs and other animals. The potato, indigenous to South America, found fertile ground in Europe. Originally suspected of causing leprosy, potatoes later became the staple crop of several European nations, most notably Ireland, and the main ingredient of vodka. Tomatoes also found their way into the European diet, while sweetened chocolate made from Central American cacao captivated taste buds in the Old World. Because chocolate was deemed to have aphrodisiac properties, the Jesuit order at one point prohibited its members from consuming it, lest the treat conspire against their vow of chastity. Perhaps more sinful was an American plant known as tobacco. In his *History of the Indies*, las Casas castigated smoking as a useless vice that was hard to quit. Its addictive qualities turned tobacco into a product that was consumed in great quantities in all parts of the world. Cuba, where Columbus first saw tobacco, produces what is widely regarded as the world's finest cigars.[25]

The Columbian exchange was also a human drama in which entire populations were decimated as others, voluntarily or not, took their place and new populations emerged as various racial groups encountered one another for the first time. In Cuba and much of the Caribbean, Amerindian depopulation rates surpassed 90 percent in just a few decades after the initial contacts. The rate of depopulation reached similar levels for the entire hemisphere. European settlers and their African slaves replaced indigenous inhabitants throughout the Caribbean and elsewhere. Contact between the various racial groups led to miscegenation and the emergence of large *mestizo* and mulatto populations. The coming together of Amerindians, Europeans, and Africans also generated creole cultures that combine elements of those diverse origins.

When humans migrated, they brought their germs and diseases with them. Because the Americas had been isolated from the rest of the world and its pathogens, the Tainos and other Amerindian peoples had neither been exposed to nor developed resistance to diseases that were common in Europe, Africa, and Asia. Smallpox, measles, influenza, and other illnesses that European explorers and settlers imported caused appalling rates of mortality. African parasitic diseases such as malaria and yellow fever wrought havoc not only among Amerindians but also among unacclimated Europeans. In return for such a deadly catalog of new diseases, America gave Europe syphilis. No evidence of syphilis has been found outside the New World before 1492. European colonists, in turn, further syphilized the Americas.

The Columbian exchange also included precious metals. In 1592, largely due to American production, five times more bullion circulated in the world than had been the case a century before. The recorded amount of precious metals exported from the Americas to Europe between 1503 and 1660 was an astounding 407,851 pounds of gold and 35,273,600 pounds of silver. This astonishing outflow of American gold and silver led to what Earl J. Hamilton called the sixteenth-century price revolution (or price inflation), sparked by increased demand for a wide range of old and new products.[26]

Whether we call it "discovery" or "encounter," when Europeans first set foot on the Americas, they initiated a prolonged exchange that forever transformed not just America and Europe but the entire world.

4

The Manufacturing of Cuba

Conquests, Demographic Collapses, and Government Institutions

Comme un vol de gerafauts hors du charnier natal,
Fatigués de porter leurs misères hautaines,
De Palos de Moguer, routiers et capitaines
Partient ivres d'un revè héroïque et brutal.

JOSÉ MARÍA HEREDIA

These Caribbean territories are not like those in Africa or Asia with their own
internal reverences, that have been returned to themselves after a period of colonial
rule. They are manufactured societies, labour camps, creations of empire.

V. S. NAIPAUL

This chapter examines the conquest, early settlement, and formation of a colonial state in Cuba between 1511 and around 1550. It begins by tracing the anteced-
ents of those processes back to the eight-century-long *reconquista* (718–1492),
during which Spanish Christian kingdoms fought to recapture the Iberian Peninsula from Muslim rule, and to the conquest and colonization of Hispaniola,
which began shortly thereafter. It pays special attention to the evolution of contending models of colonization, of government and ecclesiastical institutions,
and of labor legislation and practices.

The chapter engages with the thought-provoking ideas of Uruguayan intellectual Ángel Rama, who argued that European conquerors and colonizers were
handicapped by an "anthropological blindness" that made them perceive and
treat the New World as a tabula rasa. It also draws upon the thinking of Trinidadian author V. S. Naipaul, for whom the Caribbean is composed of manufactured societies that Europeans built from scratch.[1]

Rama recognized the persistence and lasting contributions of indigenous cultures and used the concept of a tabula rasa as a metaphor for a Renaissance ideological construct that freed conquerors and colonists from the material weight of history and allowed adventurers and aspiring mercantilist entrepreneurs to imagine the vast new territories as virgin spaces. In contrast, Naipaul used the term literally. Because a large proportion of the Caribbean's relatively small indigenous population was extinguished and most of the survivors were culturally assimilated within the first four decades of the sixteenth century, Naipaul contends that the region offered Spaniards and other, later European colonizers a virtual blank slate on which they created—manufactured, to use his term—new societies to serve metropolitan imperial needs. Such was not the case, he explained, in subsequent European imperial ventures in Asia, Africa, and the Middle East, where colonized peoples retained "their own internal reverences, that have been returned to themselves after a period of colonial rule."[2]

The Crucible of the *Reconquista*

Spain's earliest attempts to "manufacture" Cuba and other New World societies occurred in the wake of the *reconquista*, during a period of profound transition in Europe as the Middle Ages gradually yielded to the Renaissance, heralding new socioeconomic, political, and intellectual models, some of which were discussed in chapter 3. It was a transition away from feudalism based on the closed manorial system of mutual obligations and serfdom and toward a more socially fluid capitalist system characterized by markets, money, and mechanisms for financing, investment, profit, and capital accumulation. There was a parallel transition from the medieval political model, from robust nobilities and broad municipal autonomy to an emergent model of increasingly centralized national monarchies that eventually gained nearly absolute power over vast territories and large populations. King Ferdinand II of Aragon (1452–1516) is a case in point. He amassed enough power to earn praise from Machiavelli. "He rose from the ranks of the weak," Machiavelli wrote, "to become the first King of Christendom in glory and fame."[3]

The context of the final decades of the *reconquista* also allowed King Ferdinand and his wife Queen Isabella the opportunity to combine political and religious authority by virtue of the Patronato Real, an arrangement with the papacy that gave the Catholic monarchs administrative authority over church matters, including the collection and administration of tithes and the nomination of

·Fernandus·Rex·hyspanie·

Figure 4.1. Woodcut (1493) of King Ferdinand in Granada after the city fell to Christian forces. Ferdinand holds two shields, one of the triumphant kingdom of Castilla León, the other of the vanquished city of Granada. Source: Christopher Columbus, *In laudem serenissimi Ferdinandi Hispania[rum] regis, Bethicæ [et] regni Granatæ, obsidio, victoria, [et] triu[m]phus, et De insulis in Mari Indico nuper inuentus* (Basel: de Olpe Ioham Bergman, 1494). Reprinted courtesy of the John Carter Brown Library at Brown University.

bishops and other prelates. In 1478, as a result of related negotiations with Rome, Pope Sixtus IV, who is famous for commissioning the Sistine Chapel, gave the Spanish monarchs authority to establish the Tribunal of the Holy Office of the Inquisition in Spain. More than a mechanism to combat apostasy and heresy, the Inquisition also facilitated the confiscation of properties that belonged to converted Jews and Muslims.

During the *reconquista*, the Iberian Peninsula was a crucible in which different military, settlement, political, and societal models collided. It was also a frontier setting where Christian, Jewish, and Muslim people, practices, beliefs, and institutions interacted, influenced one another, and generated hybrids. Spanish scholars Ramón Menéndez Pidal and Américo Castro, among others, have argued that the prolonged frontier experience of the *reconquista* and the influences of Jews and Muslims were critical elements of the formation of the Spanish nation and its culture.[4] The Muslim invasion and occupation weakened feudalism, and as Christian monarchs pushed the frontier south, they were able to forge a new feudalism that was highly dependent on a type of royal authority that included features of capitalism. Machiavelli saw a direct link between Ferdinand's war against the Emirate of Granada and the consolidation of the Spanish state.[5]

Visigothic law and the legal code known as Las Siete Partidas that followed in the thirteenth century gave monarchs the prerogative to grant extensive municipal autonomies and privileges known as *fueros*. In the tenth through thirteenth centuries, as a way of promoting Christian repopulation of the Peninsula, monarchs granted municipal *fueros* to localities such as León (1017), Toledo (1108), and Córdoba (1241) that recognized their right to autonomous rule under local laws. This included permission to organize largely independent cabildos that served as the highest municipal authorities. Cabildos had democratic features that included the election of members by the jurisdiction's male property owners. During the latter centuries of the *reconquista*, *fueros* were mostly bestowed upon military orders. Whether municipal or not, *fueros* required military service and unfailing loyalty to the Crown. Soldiers and clergymen enjoyed the protection of *fueros* of their own.

A related institution was the *encomienda*, which Christian monarchs used to lure knights and soldiers to push the frontier with Muslim Iberia farther and farther south. If grantees (known as *encomenderos*) successfully captured enemy territory, they received authority over and the right to receive tribute from those they had defeated, who were now deemed the monarch's vassals. Yet another enticement were the *repartimientos*. When Seville and its hinterland was conquered in 1248, for example, the Castilian Crown assumed direct ownership of the conquered territories and applied the *repartimiento* method, distributing abandoned lands and houses among various constituencies, such as members of the royal family, noble knights, members of religious and military orders, and even foot soldiers. Knights and others with high social status were given special concessions that allowed them to subjugate conquered peoples and collect *parias* (tribute) and taxes from them, usually in the form of gold.

New civil and military offices also emerged. King Alfonso X appointed the first *adelantados*, nobles tasked with conquering new territories. At the municipal level, cabildos were constituted by locally elected *regidores* (aldermen). *Regidores*, in turn, elected local magistrates called *alcaldes* (from the Arabic word for judges). During the last decades of the *reconquista*, however, Spain's Catholic monarchs sought to limit the power of cabildos by appointing *corregidores*, who were specifically tasked with protecting royal interests. The title of *almirante* (admiral) was another by-product of the *reconquista*; it was first granted by Ferdinand III of Castile to Ramón de Bonifaz in 1247, who was charged with arming and organizing naval fleets against Muslim-controlled territories and naval forces. The admiralty, which was based in Seville, offered extensive privileges but at the same time served the interests of the Crown, which laid claim to Seville and its hinterland as exclusively royal property.

These practices, institutions, and offices appeared to have had contradictory results on the Iberian frontier. To meet the demands of war, continue territorial expansion, and persuade nobles and commoners to conquer and repopulate territories, monarchs dispersed incentives that included titles of nobility and lucrative rewards in the form of *parias*, *encomiendas*, and *repartimientos*. Instead of weakening royal power, such enticements created a new nobility that depended on the Crown, expanded royal authority, secured loyalty, and generated wealth for the kingdoms of Castile and Aragon. What emerged from this was a centralized system that retained certain feudal characteristics while developing some features of capitalism whereby royals, nobles, and merchants invested in military and repopulation ventures that generated large profits, much of which they reinvested in subsequent military ventures.

When the last battles of the *reconquista* were being fought, only four Christian kingdoms remained in the Iberian Peninsula. The smallest, Navarre, was in the north. Castile, Aragon, and Portugal all stretched from north to south. The dynastic marriage between Isabella I of Castile and Ferdinand II of Aragon in 1469 was a major step toward unifying Iberia. A decade later, both became monarchs in their own right. When Isabella died in 1504 and the daughter she had with Ferdinand, the feeble-minded Juana la Loca, was declared incompetent in 1506, her husband, Philip V of Burgundy (of the Habsburg family), became King Philip I of Castile. However, he ruled for only a few months. Following Ferdinand's death, Philip and Juana's son, the Habsburg prince Charles, inherited the unified thrones of Castile and Aragon. In 1519, he became head of the Holy Roman Empire, which absorbed the kingdom of Navarre in 1521. In 1526, he married his cousin, Isabella I of Portugal, further extending his power. Until 1556, Emperor Charles V ruled over an empire on which the sun never set.

The *Reconquista's* Transatlantic Sequel

Because of its geographic location, demographic makeup, historical trajectory, and cultural characteristics, Spain was exceptionally equipped to imprint its image on the Caribbean terrain. The *reconquista* afforded Spain, particularly Castile, a culture of military expansionism with civil and political features and institutions such as a unified, powerful, and affluent monarchy; a militaristic nobility that was subordinate to the Crown; and a system of rewards that included *fueros* and other privileges. Spaniards, moreover, had plenty of experience fighting against and coexisting with large "foreign" populations that looked different from themselves and had dissimilar cultures and religions.

The expansion to the New World coincided with and reflected the transition toward monarchical absolutism, producing self-perpetuating and vicious circles of centralized authoritarian rule and imperialism. The consolidation of modern European monarchies such as that of Spain made possible the accumulation of the vast amounts of material and human resources that were needed for the creation of global empires, and bullion and other riches extracted from colonial realms fueled further national consolidation and absolutism.

Not coincidentally, in 1492, in Granada, where the *reconquista* had just been completed, Isabella and Ferdinand gave Columbus their blessing to explore and colonize any islands and continents he discovered in a contract known as the Capitulations of Santa Fe. The terms, which were surprisingly generous, reflected the transitions and contradictions of the *reconquista*. On the one hand, the capitulations were a feudal contract that granted Columbus the titles of admiral and viceroy in return for his service, loyalty, and obedience. On the other hand, the agreement had a clear capitalist orientation that stipulated terms for investments and the distribution of riches and profits: Columbus received the prerogative to invest one-eighth of the costs in any future commercial venture and collect the same proportion of any profits secured. The contract also established that the Crowns of Castile and Aragon would receive 90 percent of all extracted riches and that Columbus would receive 10 percent. The monarchs invested one million maravedís in the first voyage, Columbus borrowed and invested half a million maravedís, and ship owner and navigator Martín Alonso Pinzón procured and invested another half a million maravedís.[6]

As a "tabula rasa"—whether defined in Rama's or Naipaul's terms—the New World became the battlefield not only between conquerors and indigenous inhabitants but also among several contending political forces (the Crown; the Columbus dynasty; the conquistadores, a large percentage of whom hailed from Andalusia and Extremadura; and the Church) and between the socioeconomic and political models outlined above. The unveiling of the Americas gave the Catholic monarchs the opportunity to create a polity and social order essentially from scratch. In Iberia, monarchs had had to negotiate (somewhat reluctantly) with an ancestral and an independent nobility and with new dependent elites who had fought Moors, repopulated reconquered territories, and erected new settlements and fortifications. In contrast, from the very beginning, the conquest and colonization of the Americas were royal capitalistic enterprises and all conquered lands were ultimately the property of the Crown, following the model of reconquered Seville.

To protect their investments and secure authority over New World domains, monarchs created an imperial political scaffolding that combined medieval and feudal institutions and practices with early modern and capitalist ones. Some were based in Spain, others in the colonies. Some were old, some were reshaped, and others were new. Others, such as the cabildo and the "feudal seigniory," as historian Luis Weckmann explains, experienced a rebirth and gained vigor in the Americas.[7]

One of the earliest colonial institutions was the Casa de Contratación (House of Trade), which the Crown inaugurated in 1503 in Seville. It controlled navigation, trade, and migration between Spain and the New World and was in charge of collecting import-export duties and other taxes. It also served the mercantilist and monopolistic agendas of Andalusian merchants. Even more powerful was the Council of the Indies, whose members advised the monarchs about executive, legislative, and judicial matters pertaining to the expanding empire. Founded in 1511 as part of the Council of Castile and established as an independent body in 1524, it took charge of the administration of the Indies, including setting policy, formulating laws, and appointing high-ranking officials.

Spain dispatched a wide array of royal officials and established numerous royal institutions in the New World. The highest-ranking royal officials were the viceroys and governors who had broad executive powers, including the ability to distribute *encomiendas*. Captains-general had military powers as well. Laws designed to ensure that governors remained politically independent from colonial elites failed, for the most part because governors often became connected to local elite families through marriage and through business partnerships. Governors and other royal officials often evoked the principle of *obedezco pero no cumplo* (I obey but do not comply) to justify serving local interests while remaining loyal to a monarch's authority.

Royal treasury officials such as treasurers and *contadores* (comptrollers) were lower in the pecking order. They were charged with overseeing the financial interests of monarchs. Others in this category were the *factores* (business representatives) and *veedores* (inspectors). Royal institutions were set up to provide a check on the powers of civil officials, both royal and nonroyal. Prominent among them were the *audiencias*, three-judge courts of appeal, and *juicios de residencia*, judicial reviews of the performance of outgoing governors and other functionaries by their successors.[8]

Members of the conquest generation, many of whom were veterans of the *reconquista* and the Italian wars, generally opposed absolutist royal authority and demanded feudal arrangements that afforded them titles (military, ecclesiastical, or noble) and special privileges to exploit and collect tribute from indigenous people.

While island governors and captains-general reported directly to the Crown, *fueros* gave local municipal governments considerable local autonomy, including the right of community leaders to elect the *regidores* of their cabildos on the first day of each year. Early American cabildos possessed prerogatives such as the authority to distribute land, issue municipal ordinances, and collect fees for public works. Elected *regidores*, whose numbers depended on the town's size, elected cabildo *alcaldes* (mayors with judicial powers). *Regidores* also elected one or two *procuradores* (lobbyists/delegates), whose task was to represent the interests of nascent colonial oligarchies in regional *audiencias*, the Council of the Indies, and the Spanish court.

In the case of Cuba, local autonomy decreased over time. In 1518, Emperor Charles V began appointing two *regidores* for life in each cabildo, and a few years later all *regidores* became royal appointees. In 1532, the Crown rejected Governor Manuel de Rojas's request that royal officials be excluded from service as *regidores*. Years later, Captain-General Diego de Mazariegos temporarily abolished the election of *regidores*. By 1570, all five Havana *regidores* had lifetime appointments. When *audiencia* judge Alonso de Cáceres traveled from Santo Domingo to Cuba in 1573 to conduct the *residenciamiento* (post-tenure judicial review) of outgoing governor Pedro Menéndez de Avilés, he issued several ordinances that limited the power of the local elite to elect *regidores* and *alcaldes* and attempted to limit the authority of cabildos to make land grants.[9]

In 1559, the cash-strapped monarchy of Philip II institutionalized the sale of public offices, including *regidores*. This practice continued throughout the rule of the Habsburg dynasty. In Cuba, virtually every type of office was available for a price, from a scribe appointment in Havana for 22,000 reales (1678) to the governorship of Santiago for 35,000 reales (1692) to the island's captaincy-general for 140,000 reales (1693). Some offices were bought for lifelong tenure and others could be transferred to relatives or other individuals. Invariably, office purchasers saw the acquisition of saleable appointments as an investment that would generate profit in the form of collectable fees, bribes, and other emoluments.[10]

Tensions between colonial institutions and different sectors of society were interwoven with conflicting ideas about how to manufacture the New World. Columbus was familiar with and promoted the trading post model known as *factoría* (after the Portuguese word for merchant), which Portugal had previously used successfully along the western coast of Africa during the reign of King Henry the Navigator. Columbus had been part of the Portuguese team that negotiated the establishment of the *factoría* of São Jorge da Mina (Elmina) in 1482. The *factoría* model had nothing to do with feudalism and much to do with mercantile capitalism. Portuguese merchants and navigators were seeking the material profit they could gain from trading liquor, weapons, and other manufactured goods for African slaves, gold, and spices.[11]

The Portuguese *factoría* model was well suited for Western Africa because the insalubrious conditions of the hinterland made it extraordinarily difficult for Europeans to survive. This limited the European presence to small contingents congregated in fortified enclaves such as Elmina and Axim and island outposts such as the Cape Verde Islands. The Canary Islands and the Caribbean, in contrast, offered somewhat healthier environments for large waves of conquistadores and settlers who expected and often received rewards similar to those knights and foot soldiers had earned during the *reconquista*.

Although the capitalist *factoría* model promised to be profitable for the Spanish Crown, it limited the geographic extent of royal sovereignty. In contrast, the *reconquista* settlement model offered potentially unlimited fortunes for monarchs but carried the risk of creating a distant, neofeudal aristocracy that would be hard to control. What developed in the Americas was a conflict between those two colonial models. At stake were the interests of the Crown, the Columbus clan, and an ever-expanding number of settlers. Spanish monarchs ultimately decided in favor of the large-scale settlement option.

Hispaniola: Laboratory and Vestibule to a New World

The Spanish conquest and colonization of the Americas began in Hispaniola. Spanish colonial efforts focused on that island, which Columbus had selected in 1492. For fifteen years Hispaniola thus became a colony of many New World firsts: the first Spanish settlement, the first city, the headquarters of the first viceroyalty, the first cathedral, the first *audiencia*, and the first university. Some of the splendid edifices that still stand, such as the Cathedral of Santo Domingo, the Ozama fortress, the palace of Diego Columbus, and the administrative compound known as las Casas Reales, attest to the early primacy of Hispaniola and its capital city of Santo Domingo.

As the Canary Islands had been decades earlier, Hispaniola became the vestibule to the Americas and the testing ground and laboratory for subsequent colonial ventures and institutions. The forces that conquered and settled Puerto Rico, Jamaica, and Cuba all departed from Hispaniola. After decades of sugar production in the Canary Islands, colonists replicated those efforts in Hispaniola, where sugarcane spread like wildfire throughout the region.

Four powerful government institutions with roots in the kingdoms of Castile and Aragon (the viceroyalty, the *audiencia*, the governorship, and the captaincy-general) were transplanted to Hispaniola and thereafter to other New World colonies. The office of viceroy, which had recently been established in the Kingdom of Aragon's Sicilian domains, was first established in Hispaniola to represent the Spanish Crown and dispense its authority. It had jurisdiction over all neighboring islands, including Cuba. Columbus's son Diego served as viceroy in Hispaniola during 1511–1515 and 1520–1524. In 1535, Cuba came under the newly created viceroyalty of New Spain (Mexico). Another powerful institution was the Real Audiencia, which was roughly equivalent to a court of appeals with executive powers.[12] Before the colonization of the New World, two *audiencias* operated in Spain, one with jurisdiction over northern regions, the other for the south. The *audiencia* of Santo Domingo, which Spain established in 1511, was short lived, but in 1526, Emperor Charles V reestablished it. While Cuba was under the authority of the viceroy and governor of Hispaniola, the official title of the island's highest authority was lieutenant governor. From 1535 to 1577, Cuba was ruled by governors, who had broad civilian powers. Beginning in 1577, it was ruled by captains-general, who had both civil and military authority. When Cuba was split into two jurisdictions in 1607, the eastern half came under the authority of a *capitán a guerra*, who was subordinate to the island's captain-general.[13]

The conflict between contending political and socioeconomic models played out in Hispaniola first. The original economic model for the island, while not strictly a *factoría*, had many of the characteristics of one: a small number of settlers, many of whom lived in fortified enclaves, and a markedly capitalist and mercantile economic foundation. In 1497, while Columbus was in Seville organizing his third voyage, colonists in Hispaniola led by Francisco Roldán revolted against Columbus's brother, Bartolomé, who had been left in charge. Increasingly unhappy with the limited opportunities the Columbian enterprise offered, Roldán's men rose up in pursuit of the larger-scale and less constrictive settlement model that included the right to land grants and the privilege of collecting tribute from indigenous inhabitants. When he returned to Hispaniola, Columbus pacified the rebellious colonists. He appeased Roldán with the promise that he would reinstate him as *alcalde* of the village of Isabela and by offering him and other colonists land grants and allotments of Amerindians as personal servants.

When the Crown learned of Roldán's insurrection, it dispatched Francisco de Bobadilla, a veteran knight of the Battle of Granada, to reestablish order, conduct an investigation, and protect the monarchs' interests and investments. Bobadilla was a member of the prestigious religious-military Order of Calatrava. Named after a fortified city recovered from Muslim rule in 1147, the order had acquired numerous *encomiendas* as its warriors gained control over reconquered Iberian territories. As was the case with other feudal institutions, the monarchs gradually stripped the Order of Calatrava of some of its privileges. By 1487, Ferdinand II had gained formal royal control over the order. Bobadilla, who was appointed governor of Hispaniola, arrested Columbus and his two brothers (Bartolomé and Diego) and sent all three of them in chains to face justice in Spain. While the Columbuses were exonerated and their properties restored, they ruled in Hispaniola after that with reduced powers.

The arrival of Nicolás de Ovando in Hispaniola in 1502 with 2,500 settlers further weakened the authority of the Columbus clan. It was also the death knell of the *factoría* model, as it cemented the large-scale settlement model that colonists had demanded for over a decade. Many of the conquerors and early settlers were veterans of the *reconquista* and thus were used to and expected feudal arrangements that afforded them titles and feudal privileges. Ovando, a high-ranking member of the prestigious Order of Alcántara and a protégé of King Ferdinand, bore the title of governor and captain-general. He was handpicked to restore order and expand royal authority. His orders included protecting Amerindians from abuse; establishing the necessary political, civil, and religious institutions; and expanding and diversifying the island's economy. Ovando was also the monarchs' business partner. The monarchs paid for the navigation costs of his expedition and provided about a third of the necessary capital; Ovando and other investors came up with the rest of the capital.[14]

Ovando carried out *repartimientos* and in 1503 distributed the first New World *encomiendas* to his allies and meritorious conquistadores. *Encomiendas* did not include land rights, however, as the monarchs retained sovereignty over the land. *Encomiendas* were originally established in locations with substantial concentrations of indigenous peoples, but as Amerindian villages shrank or disappeared, they were consolidated. As prescribed by law, Amerindian *encomendados* were Crown vassals. They had to be paid salaries, the Spaniards had to ensure that their basic material needs were met, they had to be well treated, and they had to be instructed in the Christian faith.

Also in 1503, the Spanish monarchs allowed Spaniards to enslave indigenous people who resisted the conquest or whose practices were deemed abominable. These included idolatry, sodomy, polygamy, and cannibalism. Enslaved laborers, most of whom had been captured on other islands, in Florida, and in the Yucatan, were often branded with hot irons and distributed among well-connected settlers.

In 1506, two years after returning from his fourth and final voyage, Columbus died in Valladolid, Spain. After a decade of intense litigation, in 1509 the Crown recognized his son Diego as admiral, viceroy, and governor of the Indies with headquarters in Santo Domingo, where he built a palatial fortified house and ruled with diminished authority until 1515. For the Spanish Crown, Diego Columbus served the purpose of curbing the power of an increasingly entrenched Spanish *encomendero* class. However, King Ferdinand also sought to limit the new viceroy's powers by establishing checks and balances through other royal officials and institutions and by pitting the Columbus clan against Ovando loyalists. In 1513, the Crown deprived Diego Columbus of one of his most important sources of power, the right to grant *encomiendas*. Ferdinand further limited Diego's authority by allowing several of his subordinates to communicate directly with the Crown instead of through him.

The Conquest of Cuba and the First Settlements

When Diego Columbus arrived in Hispaniola in 1509, he had orders from the Crown to explore Cuba, specifically to find gold. By that time, the fact that Cuba was an island had been confirmed by expeditions led by Vicente Yáñez Pinzón and Sebastián de Ocampo. Columbus's candidate for the conquest of Cuba was his uncle, Bartolomé, but the Crown preferred a veteran of the Battle of Granada, Diego Velázquez, one of Hispaniola's richest and most respected settlers. It was Velázquez who was appointed *adelantado* and lieutenant governor of Cuba.[15] An untrusting Diego Columbus, however, managed to impose one of his reliable men, Francisco de Morales, as Velázquez's second in command.

The conquest of Cuba began in 1511 (some say late 1510), when Velázquez arrived on the island with four vessels, around 300 men (including some enslaved Amerindians from Hispaniola), and animals, seeds, food, and provisions. He gave the island its third Spanish name, Santiago de Cuba. Among those joining Velázquez were the soon-to-be-famous Juan de Grijalva (his nephew), Hernán Cortés, Bartolomé de las Casas, and Vasco Porcallo de Figueroa. Velázquez loyalist Pánfilo de Narváez arrived from Jamaica with thirty Spanish crossbowmen and a party of indigenous servants.

These conquistadores founded Cuba's first colonial villages. Nuestra Señora de la Asunción de Baracoa (1512), nestled between the Atlantic Ocean and a range of high mountains on the eastern end of Cuba, became the first Spanish settlement, the first capital of the island, and the see of its first bishopric. Soon thereafter, Diego Columbus's trusted man, Francisco de Morales, agitated the colonists to demand that Velázquez distribute indigenous workers to them (just like Roldán had done with Christopher Columbus). Velázquez had Morales arrested and shipped back to Hispaniola.

From their base in Baracoa on the eastern tip of the island, Velázquez and his lieutenants unleashed the violent conquest of Cuba, employing a three-pronged mobilization strategy: one prong, which Velázquez led himself, sailed along the south coast; a second prong sailed along the north coast; and Narváez led a march by land.[16] The conquistadores' arsenal included lethal and terrifying canons and firearms and metal swords, spears, and armor. The native inhabitants' wooden *macanas* and spears were no match for this arsenal. Ferocious mastiff dogs complemented the conquerors' weapons. (Years before, Christopher Columbus had estimated that a fighting dog was worth more than ten men.) Even more terrifying were the Andalusian horses. Narváez equipped his legendarily vigorous mare with bells that magnified the terror the beast and its corpulent redheaded rider instilled.

The first major clashes between Amerindians and Spaniards occurred in and around the Taino village of Bayamo, where Narváez's men massacred hundreds of Amerindians. "A stream of blood ran," las Casas later reminisced, "as if many cows had been slaughtered." On that location, Velázquez founded Cuba's second village, San Salvador de Bayamo, in 1513. Not far from Bayamo, the rebel chieftain Hatuey, who had fled the horrors of Santo Domingo, was captured and sentenced to be burned at the stake. A Franciscan priest offered Hatuey the sacrament of baptism so he could ascend to heaven after death. According to las Casas, Hatuey inquired if there would be Christians in heaven and when the priest replied affirmatively, the chieftain rejected the invitation, saying that he would rather go to hell. Velázquez read the episode differently. He reported to the monarchs that Hatuey's death made it possible to secure much of the island. Farther west, advancing conquerors encountered sporadic resistance in the form of guerrilla attacks.[17]

Shortly after witnessing the massacre at Caonao, las Casas had a change of heart. He gave up his *encomienda* and dedicated the rest of his life to protecting

Figure 4.2. Chieftain Hatuey being burned at the stake after refusing to convert to Christianity. Similar illustrations by de Bry depicting Spanish cruelty appeared in many German, French, and Dutch editions of Bartolomé de las Casas's *Devastation of the Indies*. Source: Engraving by Théodore de Bry, in Bartolomé de Las Casas, *Den Spiegle der Spaensche Tyrannye, Gesscheit In West-Indien* (Amsterdam, 1620). Reprinted courtesy of the John Carter Brown Library at Brown University.

the native inhabitants of the New World. Las Casas tried to persuade Velázquez to stop the atrocities against the Tainos, to no avail. He then traveled to the recently established *audiencia* of Santo Domingo and thereafter extended his lobbying efforts to Spain. The Apostle of the Indians, as las Casas came to be known, became the most unrelenting, vociferous, and prolific voice among the critics of what he once called "the pestilential acts of the Christians." Books he penned like *The Very Brief Account of the Destruction of the Indies* (1552) are filled with graphic depictions of Spanish brutality: infants being grabbed away from their mothers' breasts to be smashed against rocks, mass hangings of indigenous people, the burning to death of 300 nobles, the wanton rape of indigenous women, wholesale mutilations, and countless acts of torture and murder.[18]

Las Casas also condemned one of the conquest's most bizarre practices, the *requerimiento*, a mechanism used to justify the enslavement of Amerindians. Often read at a distance and in Spanish, the text of the *requerimiento* spelled out the lineage of the Spanish monarchs' authority. It offered freedom and peace to those who acquiesced to Spanish authority. Those who resisted, however, were warned: "We shall forcibly enter into your country, and shall make war against you . . . and shall subject you to the to the yoke and obedience of the Church and of their Highnesses; we shall take you and your wives and your children, and shall make slaves of them . . . and we shall take away your goods, and shall do you all the harm and damage that we can." Referring to the *requerimiento*, las Casas once remarked that he did not know whether to laugh or cry.[19]

Unintentionally, las Casas's writings became ammunition in the brewing conflict between northern European nations and Spain, feeding what came to be known as the Black Legend, the systematic denigration of Spain and its people, culture, and religion. Unwittingly, las Casas also became an early promoter of black slavery. He opposed the enslavement of Amerindians on the grounds that they were unjustly enslaved in their own land, but he felt that Africans had been rightfully enslaved by those who had defeated them in war.

After conquistadores founded Baracoa in 1512 and Bayamo in late 1513, colonizers settled five other villages farther west. The immediate founding of towns and cities, which was part of the Latin urban tradition of Spain, also served to secure political privileges for town founders because of strong Iberian beliefs in local autonomy. In 1514, Spanish colonizers founded the villages of Trinidad, Sancti Spíritus, and San Cristóbal de La Habana, the latter of which was originally located on the southern coast. The following year, they founded Santa María del Puerto Príncipe in its original location at Nuevitas Bay on the northern coast. The last of the seven original villages was Santiago de Cuba, which

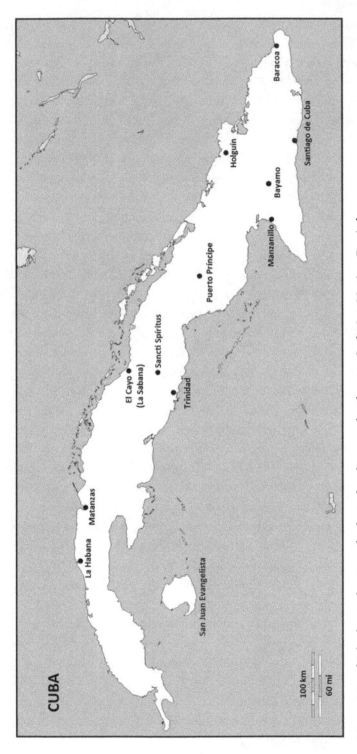

Map 4.1. Map of Cuba showing locations of earliest colonial towns and settlements. Credit: Luis Martínez-Fernández.

was founded in mid-1515. Its original location was on the mouth of the Paradas River. Because of Santiago de Cuba's proximity to Hispaniola and its large natural port, Velázquez moved his residence there from Baracoa, designating it the capital city. Spaniards built a small fort there in 1516. In 1522–1523, the bishopric of Cuba followed the move from Baracoa to Santiago.

The locations of the first Spanish settlements were selected mostly for their proximity to rivers with gold deposits and to sizable Taino villages, where Spaniards could secure indigenous labor. Gold was mostly mined from rivers using forced or enslaved workers. The gold nuggets workers collected were transported to authorized foundries, where a *veedor* secured the monarchs' royal fifth. Gold production peaked in 1517–1519 at 100,000 pesos per year.[20]

To meet pressing labor demands, Velázquez made a temporary allotment of Amerindian labor when he arrived in Cuba. Later, in 1513, the Crown granted him the title of *repartidor de indios*, which officially allowed him to distribute *encomiendas*. An *encomienda* usually consisted of an entire village under the authority of a Spanish *encomendero* (grantee) and often under the direct administration of Taino chieftains, who served as intermediaries. Such was the case in the *encomienda* granted to Royal Accountant Gonzalo de Guzmán (1522), who controlled five caciques and 117 *encomendados*. The *encomienda* system was one of mutual obligations in which the Crown rewarded warriors and other settlers with authority over indigenous vassals, from whom they could extract tribute and labor services in mining or agriculture. According to the 1512 Leyes de Burgos, *encomendado* Amerindians were legally free, were entitled to wages, and

Figure 4.3. Amerindians being forced to pan for gold. Source: Woodcut in Gonzalo Fernández de Oviedo, *Historia natural de las Indias*. Reproduced in Leví Marrero, *Cuba: economía y sociedad* (Madrid: Playor, 1971–1988), 2:4.

had to be taught Christian doctrine. In reality, they were exploited and abused. Colonists routinely ignored the provisions of the law that prescribed good treatment for *encomendados*.[21]

Velázquez used his privilege as *repartidor* to reward his relatives and associates. This produced an island aristocracy that was loyal to him. In 1522, the *encomendero* ranks included his relatives Juan de Grijalva and Manuel de Rojas; his close associates Pánfilo de Narváez, Bachiller de Alonso Parada, and Vasco Porcallo de Figueroa; and fourteen others. Collectively, these men controlled a total of 2,781 *encomendado* Amerindians. A significant portion of the earliest *encomiendas* (eight of eighteen) were located within the jurisdiction of Santiago, and the three largest *encomiendas* were located in that jurisdiction. One was under the charge of Royal Treasurer Pero Núñez de Guzmán (who controlled 307 laborers), one was under the charge of Royal Accountant Pero de Paz (who controlled 269 laborers), and one was jointly held by Pedro Tamayo and Andrés de Duero (who controlled 250 laborers). Farther west, where the pre-Columbian indigenous population had been sparser, there were fewer *encomiendas*, and the farther west one went, the smaller were the *encomiendas*. As the ranks of the *encomendados* dwindled, survivors were rounded up and relocated into *reducciones*. *Encomienda* labor was supplemented by enslaved Amerindians who had been captured and imported from the Bahamas and later from the Yucatan, from Florida, and from other Caribbean islands. While distinctions persisted in law, in practice there was not much difference in the treatment slaves and *encomendados* received.[22]

Some Amerindians fought to protect themselves from the horrors of the *conquista* and from exploitative labor practices. Although the conquest of Cuba had ended by 1525, resistance continued for several years as indigenous people sought to escape the grip of slavery, *encomienda* servitude, and imposed confinement in reservations. Forms of armed resistance included retaliatory attacks on Spanish settlements. Rebels sacked and burned Puerto Príncipe in 1527–1528 and again in the early 1530s, and Baracoa suffered the same fate in 1539 at the hands of Amerindian maroons. Cacique Guamá led a large band of rebels for an entire decade. At one point, he ruled over a settlement of several hundred runaway Amerindians, including several women, among them Margarida, a woman from Jamaica. According to the testimony of members of his settlement, Guamá ruled despotically and killed many of his own people. In 1540, *procuradores* representing the cabildo of Santiago sent an alarming report to the Crown that indigenous people were singing in *areíto* ceremonies that Spaniards would not last long on the island.[23]

As was the case throughout the Americas, the *conquista*, in which courage and military prowess counted as much if not more than lineage and pedigree, blurred social distinctions and was conducive to social and economic mobility. The conquest offered opportunities to gain instant fame and fortune, resulting in prestige and high social standing. In the Americas, where distant monarchs had limited control, social mobility, both upward and downward, was more prevalent and took place on a much larger scale than was the case in the Iberia of the *reconquista*. Salient examples are Hernán Cortés and his distant cousin Francisco Pizarro. Born in poverty in Extremadura, Cortés led the conquest of Mexico, amassed a fabulous fortune, and was appointed marquis of the Valley of Mexico. He had been so poor in Spain that at one point he had had to share a cape with two other men. Even more striking was the case of Francisco Pizarro, an illegitimate, poor, and illiterate pig farmer who was also from Extremadura. With only 180 conquistadores, he conquered the Inca Empire in the early 1530s, was appointed captain-general of New Castile, and became one of the world's richest and most powerful men. His fellow conquistadores, whom historian James Lockhart referred to as the Men of Cajamarca, received prodigious rewards: 4,400 gold pesos and 181 marks of silver for each foot soldier and twice as much for each *caballero*.[24]

In Cuba, the frontier afforded conquistadores and early colonizers opportunities for enrichment and upward social mobility and consolidated an elite group of military and civilian officials in which family names such as Velázquez, Agüero, Cepero, Recio, Rojas, and Soto figured prominently. The Rojas-Soto-Sotolongo clan was the matrix of Cuba's expanding elite. It began around 1540 with the arrival Juan de Rojas and his nephews Alonso de Rojas and Juan Soto in Havana. The nephews married into important families whose members had married into other elite families. The members of these densely interlocked clans amassed political power through membership in Havana's cabildo and favored one another with land grants for cattle ranches and other agricultural activities. Of the 187 land grants the cabildo distributed between 1550 and 1610, 124 went to three clans: 74 to the Rojas-Soto-Sotolongo clan, 29 to the Recio clan, and 21 to the Pérez de Borroto clan. All of these clans were connected by marriage ties.[25]

None of Cuba's conquerors achieved a more seigneurial and autonomous position than the controversial Vasco Porcallo de Figueroa. He was the embodiment of the independent colonial caudillo with vassals under his power. Yet at the same time, he was a capitalist businessman who owned indigenous and African slaves and even his own town. Born in Cáceres, Spain, in 1576 to a noble family, he arrived in Cuba in 1511 with Velázquez. On his westward conquest march, he founded the towns of Trinidad and Sancti Spíritus in 1514 and Puerto Príncipe in 1515. Porcallo de Figueroa later founded his personal fiefdom, La Sabana, also known as El Cayo or San Juan de los Remedios, on the north coast. He was one of the original *encomenderos*; in 1522, he controlled 175 indigenous workers under the direct authority of two caciques in the jurisdiction of Trinidad. One of the island's richest and most powerful men, Porcallo de Figueroa established a sizable multiethnic town with its own church and prison. In 1534, he had 150 *encomendados*, fifty Amerindian slaves, and fifteen black slaves. (At one point, he owned 120 black slaves.) He had a prolonged concubinage with the daughter of the cacique of Camagüey, with whom he had numerous children, some of whom went on to marry into important and powerful Spanish families or gain high political positions. Porcallo de Figueroa earned a reputation for insatiable lustfulness and cruelty. He reportedly sired around 100 *mestizo* children at a time when Cuba's population amounted to a few thousand. He abused and tormented his workers; an investigation concluded that he had killed many indigenous people, in some instances castrating them before execution.[26]

Demographic Collapses

The conquest of Cuba resulted in a demographic catastrophe that reduced the island's population to less than one-tenth of its precontact size in a matter of two or three decades. Historian Juan Pérez de la Riva has estimated the relative weight of the various causes of death. According to his calculations, approximately 12 percent died as a result of the conquest and the brutality the Spaniards unleashed. Another 12 percent perished from starvation due to severe disruptions in traditional agricultural production; the few pigs Velázquez's men let loose when they arrived in 1511 reproduced into hordes of wild roaming beasts that feasted on maize and *yuca* fields. Pérez de la Riva estimated that epidemics caused by diseases the European conquerors and (later) African slaves brought to the island accounted for nearly 20 percent of indigenous fatalities. The first major wave of disease to strike was the smallpox epidemic of 1519; a decade later, smallpox ravaged the island again. In addition, infant mortality increased dramatically. Las Casas put it most graphically: "The milk in the breasts of the women with infants dried up and thus in a short while the infants perished."[27]

In addition to material causes such as war, disease, and starvation, psychological factors contributed to these appalling mortality rates. The conquest shook the social, political, and spiritual foundations of indigenous societies, leading to generalized hopelessness and loss of the desire to live and give birth to children. The practice of inducing abortions by ingesting herbal concoctions became widespread. Suicides, which according to Pérez de la Riva accounted for 35 percent of deaths (perhaps an overestimation), became gruesomely pervasive as masses of Amerindians committed suicide by hanging themselves, jumping off cliffs, eating earth, or drinking poisonous juices extracted from *yuca*. Las Casas wrote about 200 Amerindians who hung themselves, all at the same time. One particularly dramatic case of suicide was that of Cacique Anaya and his wife, who were double-crossed by their *encomendero*, Juan de Vergara. They sought to reunite with their daughter, whom Vergara was keeping illegally in Bayamo. After they rescued her, rather than see her returned to captivity, they hung her, then they hung themselves.[28]

All of these factors reduced a population of over 100,000 to approximately 22,000 in 1519, 10,000 in 1525, and 5,000 in 1555.[29] As numbers fell precipitously, Spaniards congregated survivors in reservation villages (called *reducciones*) such as Guanabacoa, Yara, Mayarí, Yateras, La Güira, and El Caney.

The collapse of the indigenous population prompted another form of demographic collapse. Large numbers of Spanish settlers sought to leave labor-starved and gold-depleted Cuba in search of better fortunes in Mexico and elsewhere. In the process, they drained the island of its inhabitants, horses, vessels, and provisions. In 1517, Francisco Hernández de Córdoba organized a three-vessel expedition to the Yucatan. The following year, Juan de Grijalva took 240 men to the Yucatan and Central America.

The most ambitious and successful expedition of the period was Hernán Cortés's expedition to Mexico in 1519, when Havana was still located on the southern coast. The expedition consisted of ten vessels and around 600 individuals, among them Diego de Mazariegos, a future captain-general, and a few black men, including the African-born Christianized freedman Juan Garrido, who is credited with being the first person to cultivate wheat in New Spain. Eight women accompanied Cortés, one of whom was a famous healer named Isabel Rodríguez. One of the vessels was so overloaded that it ran aground for five days.[30]

Velázquez ordered his lieutenant in Havana, Pedro Barba, to arrest Cortés for insubordination, but Barba was unable to do so. Barba feared that the ambitious adventurer would take the town's entire population with him. When Cortés got to Mexico, he formally broke with Velázquez, an action that prompted the governor to send 1,000 men under Narváez to arrest him. Narváez failed in his mission, losing an eye in battle and getting arrested. Cortés went on to conquer the Aztec Empire. In 1528, Narváez launched another ill-fated expedition from

Figure 4.4. Tainos committing infanticide and suicide through a variety of methods. Suicide was rampant among indigenous people, who lost the desire to live and raise children as a result of the cruel treatment by Spaniards. The image includes a woman aborting her baby, an adult clubbing a child to death, a person jumping off a cliff, suicide by hanging, and a person committing suicide with a sword. Source: Woodcut in Girolamo Benzoni, *La historia del Mondo Nuovo*. (Venice: F. Rampazetto, 1565). Reprinted courtesy of the John Carter Brown Library at Brown University.

Cuba, this time to explore Florida. Only four of 600 men survived; one of them was the legendary Álvar Núñez Cabeza de Vaca.

News of Peru's fabled riches began to reach the Caribbean in 1533. The following year, Governor Manuel de Rojas reported that such news caused "much alteration" and that many settlers were seeking to go to Peru on vessels departing from Santiago or however else they could get there. When the seventeen wealthiest settlers of Trinidad and Sancti Spíritus were polled in 1534, all expressed a desire to leave the island and nine mentioned Peru as their desired destination. Wealthy *encomendero* Porcallo de Figueroa said that he knew Francisco Pizarro and had heard of the riches of Peru. The ensuing exodus not only further depopulated Cuba, it also debilitated its economy as indebted settlers were prone to leave their debts behind. To curb the mounting flight of settlers, anyone who left Cuba temporarily had to post a bond to guarantee his return. There were severe penalties for illegal departures, including mutilation and even death. Even Governor Rojas left eventually, impoverished, indebted, and bitter. He died in Peru.[31]

In 1539, with around 1,500 Spanish settlers remaining, another demographic blow struck when Hernando de Soto, one of the men of Cajamarca, further drained the island's population. He arrived in 1538 with 600 men, but left eleven months later to conquer Florida, taking Porcallo de Figueroa and 900 men.[32] De Soto's wife, Isabel de Bobadilla, remained in Havana, informally acting as interim governor. By 1544, the white population had dropped to around 1,000; by 1550, it had fallen further to between 600 and 700.[33] The village of Trinidad became a ghost town, reportedly without a single white inhabitant. Other settlements teetered on the verge of total depopulation.

Velázquez died in Santiago in 1524. As las Casas, his former protégé, put it, "The devil bore him away."[34] He had come to the island a wealthy man; following two adventurous decades in the Indies, Velázquez had amassed a fortune in silver bullion, three cattle ranches, five farms, 970 heads of cattle, 2,800 pigs, 900 sheep, and 12 farms with 205,000 *yuca* mounds. However, he had lost 40,000 pesos equipping first the renegade Cortés expedition and then the failed Narváez expedition to arrest Cortés. In addition, he had previously invested his own capital in his voyage to Cuba.[35]

The Church

The Roman Catholic Church in Cuba, as elsewhere in the Indies, functioned as yet another colonial institution. Church and Crown often supported each other and had many common goals, such as the desire to keep Jews, Muslims, and new converts from settling in the colonies.[36] They were also intimately tied by the Patronato Real, which the monarchs extended to the Indies. It granted the Crown's lay colonial representatives broad administrative powers over church matters.

In Cuba, the Catholic Church was markedly hierarchical. Bishops were the highest authority of this complex organization. They were followed in the hierarchy by other church officials, priests, monks and nuns, and musicians, all the way down to *perreros de iglesias* (dog catchers). In 1522, Santiago was designated as a diocese.

Cuba's early clergy included members of two religious orders, the Franciscans and the Dominicans. They were later joined by Mercedarians and Jesuits. Dominicans and Franciscans often clashed because the former were far more militant about protecting indigenous people. Regular clergymen, as those belonging to the orders were called, imparted religious instruction to Amerindian slaves and *encomendados* and played leading roles in the administration of hospitals and taking care of orphans and the poor. By 1609, a total of six convents were operating in Cuba, three in Havana (Franciscans, Dominicans, and Augustinians), two in Trinidad (one Mercedarian), and one in Santiago (Franciscan). The first convent for nuns, Santa Clara, was built in the 1640s; it evolved from what had been a cloister for virgin women.[37]

While bishops and other clergymen were bound by the Patronato Real, they clashed with state officials, openly taking sides in political disputes. Government and church officials often pursued conflicting goals, quarreling over matters such as the treatment of indigenous and black slaves, the use of churches as sanctuaries, and the marriage sacrament. During Governor Gonzalo de Guzmán's *juicio de residencia* in 1531–1532, Bishop Miguel Ramírez aggressively supported the outgoing governor and threatened to excommunicate those who dared to testify against him. The *residenciador* counterattacked, accusing the prelate of illegally owning an *encomienda*, using his niece's husband as a front.[38] Later in the century, Captain-General Gabriel de Luján complained to the Crown about the Church's abuse of the power to excommunicate and about the violence church authorities unleashed against their rivals. He added that because Cuba was the last port on the way back to Europe, it had become a magnet for corrupt clerics who had been banished from the rest of the Indies.[39]

Church dictates such as those instructing religious authorities to protect Amerindians from abuse, keep the island free from Jewish and Muslim immigrants, and condemn illicit trade with Protestants clashed with the interests of the local agrarian and mercantile elites, who saw those restrictions as obstacles to profit and economic growth. As a result of secular pressures, church authorities often relaxed their doctrinal stances and adopted an ecclesiastical version of *obedezco pero no cumplo* that some contemporaries derided as the "theology of the Indies."[40]

The most dreaded of all ecclesiastical institutions was the Inquisition. An extension of the Spanish Inquisition, it was led by inquisitor bishops residing in Hispaniola, Puerto Rico, and Cuba until 1571, when it came under the jurisdiction of the newly established Holy Office headquarters in Mexico City. The inquisitors' first victim in Cuba was a Hispanicized Amerindian named Juan Muñoz. He was charged with heresy and burned to death in 1517 or 1518.

A decade later, a Spaniard named Alonso Escalante faced similar charges and suffered the same fate. In 1610, Cuba came under the authority of the new Holy Office of the Inquisition see in Cartagena.[41]

Conclusion

Velázquez and his fellow conquistadores and settlers acted as if Cuba was literally a tabula rasa, with complete disregard for its indigenous population and their culture and for the island's natural environment. They decimated the native population, founded Spanish villages, and introduced the first African slaves. In the process, they brought together the different human and cultural ingredients that converged to form a distinctive colonial creole society.

These foundational decades were characterized by continuous power conflicts among numerous actors and interest groups. These included the violent confrontations of the conquest but also tensions between absolutist, distant monarchs and a brewing colonial proto-aristocracy whose members often ignored royal commands that conflicted with their desire for autonomy and the freedom to exploit local labor and resources. There were also tensions between entitled conquistadores and the royal officials who looked after the Crown's interests and clashes between exploiters of indigenous labor and the few voices that defended their right to be left alone.

5 ❧

The Emergence of Creole Society

Cuba no es india. Cuba no es blanca. No es negra ni amarilla. Cuba es mulata, mestiza, negra blancuzca y color tabaco.

CARLOS FRANQUI

The west flourished as a result of the official presence, in defense of colonial policy; the east flourished as a result of the official absence, in defiance of colonial policy.

LOUIS A. PÉREZ JR.

During the decades following the conquest period, the nascent colonial state and the emerging creole society continued to take shape in a context in which different ethnic and social groups negotiated the tensions between hierarchical castes and estates models and more fluid social structures, between the separation of the races and cultures and miscegenation and cultural syncretism, and between coerced labor and freedom. These were foundational decades, a period when Amerindians, Spaniards, Africans, and white, black, *mestizo*, and mulatto Cubans worked with and against each other to lay the foundations of a distinctive colonial creole society. Many of the resulting fissures and fault lines among estates, classes, races, religious faiths, regions, and generations would continue to mark the island's historical trajectory for centuries. The recurrent political, social, and racial strife that has historically plagued Cuba has roots deep in the sixteenth and seventeenth centuries.

A major topic of this chapter is the bifurcation of Cuba into two parallel but very different societies. Because of its military, commercial, and political roles, Havana became a city that looked out to the sea. It evolved into a distinct society characterized by colonial law and order, commercial agriculture, societal rigidity, and sharp divisions in racial and social status. Meanwhile, Cuba's east lost economic importance. Many factors contributed to the downfall of Santiago and the east. For one thing, in the mid-sixteenth century the capital was moved from Santiago to Havana and as a result of that, island-wide authorities began to neglect the east, reducing its allocations of funds and troops. Neglect of the east worsened after 1607, when that part of the island became officially subordinated to Havana.[1] For another, by the mid-1500s, the *encomienda* system had collapsed. Furthermore, the imposed fleet navigation system bypassed Santiago, further marginalizing the eastern region. Eastern Cuba followed more relaxed rules about the law, commerce, social stratification, and racial mixture. It was an environment that offered greater possibilities for smuggling and other illegal activities and was also more tolerant of social mobility, interracial unions, and religious transgressions.

Economy and Society in the Two Cubas

The gold economic cycle came to an end before the middle decades of the sixteenth century as gold reserves dried up, the native population headed closer to extinction or assimilation, and the Crown dismantled the *encomienda* system in response to humanitarian pleas and in order to secure its goal of keeping colonial oligarchies at bay. Gold production had begun to shrink during the 1520s and 1530s, dropping to 13,000 pesos per year in 1538 and to a negligible 3,000 pesos in 1544.[2] The New Laws of 1542 dealt a severe blow to exploitative labor practices by abolishing the enslavement of Amerindians, limiting *encomiendas* to a maximum of eighty workers, and banning future *encomiendas*. However, those laws generated strong opposition from colonial economic elites. They were not publicized until 1544 and were not enacted until the early 1550s.

These developments translated into the impoverishment of the island and a shift toward less labor-intensive economic activities, namely cattle ranching, horse breeding, and the farming of fruits, vegetables, and tobacco. Post–gold rush Cuba, particularly Havana, became a service entrepôt for the growing Spanish empire, much like Hispaniola had been a few decades earlier: it supplied horses, hides, dried beef, and other provisions for soldiers and settlers heading south, west, and north to conquer new territories. Ranching activities were well suited to labor-hungry Cuba, where hides came to represent close to 90 percent of exports in the period 1560–1620. Toward the end of the 1500s, 50,000 hides were legally exported each year through the port of Havana; illegal

Figure 5.1. *Encomendero* abusing an Amerindian in Mexico. After Spanish colonizers tested the institution of the *encomienda* in the Caribbean, they used it in other conquered territories in Central and South America. This illustration is a drawing made after one that appears in the manuscript Codex Kingsborough, Memorial de los Indios de Tepetlaoztoc, Códice de Tepetlaoztoc, Petition of the Indians of Tepetlaoztoc. It is part of the collection of the British Museum. Source: Leví Marrero, *Cuba: economía y sociedad* (Madrid: Playor, 1971–1988), 1:204.

exports likely surpassed legal ones. Foreign smugglers reportedly paid four to six times more for hides than Havana's merchants.[3]

During the middle decades of the sixteenth century, a bifurcation became increasingly evident between Havana on the west and the eastern and central parts of the island. In the 1540s, because of its location and favorable currents, Havana was designated as an obligatory stopping point for all Europe-bound fleets departing Gulf and circum-Caribbean ports. In 1550, Governor Gonzalo Pérez de Angulo moved Cuba's capital from Santiago to Havana; by that time, the population of Havana had surpassed that of Santiago. Three years later, the *audiencia* of Santo Domingo authorized the formal designation of Havana as capital city.

As the hemisphere's main navigation and commercial hub and as Cuba's main military garrison and capital city, Havana assumed particular roles as a service, bureaucratic, commercial, and military center. The city's primary economic activities were associated with servicing the vessels and their crews, which consisted of up to 1,000 to 2,000 men that converged on Havana whenever fleets arrived. Crews, whose vessels remained in port for weeks and even several months, required water, food, wine and other beverages, entertainment, and other provisions and services. Support services also included ship repair and maintenance, taverns, gambling rings, and houses of prostitution. Havana also developed maritime and defense-related manufacturing activities, including large-scale shipbuilding and even making cannons and muskets.[4]

Although fleet arrivals boosted Havana's economy, delays or failure to arrive had dire economic ramifications. Extant *protocolos notariales* (notarized transaction records) demonstrate that individuals bought a variety of goods and services, including slaves, on credit, with a promise to pay for them when the next fleet arrived. Purchases made in 1587 by Pedro Sánchez, Juan Alonso Saavedra, and Juan Pérez Borroto are illustrative. On January 19, Sánchez purchased a slave couple, Diego and Magdalena, for 212 ducados and promised to pay for them by the end of June "or sooner, if the Fleet of Nueva España or Tierra Firme were to arrive before." Two days later, Saavedra agreed to pay 723 reales to his creditor "eight days after the calling of either of the two fleets." In March of the same year, Havana resident Juan Franco del Río sold a 26-year-old Biafara slave named Catalina to Pérez Borroto on the condition that Pérez Borroto pay him 260 ducados "within eight days after the arrival of the fleet." Likewise, local soldiers who owed money to black women who cooked or washed clothes for them were able to clear their debts only when the next fleet arrived. In 1585, the *mulata* Francisca de Miranda promised that she would complete payment for her self-purchase upon the arrival of expected military funds from Mexico. She anticipated that Havana's soldiers "who I feed and will continue to feed" would soon receive their back pay and be able to pay what they owed her.[5]

The Crown granted Havana the privilege of manufacturing ships as early as 1518. By the end of the century, the city's shipyards employed 116 men. Havana-built vessels replaced many of the ships lost in the defeat of the Spanish Armada in 1588. Havana's craftsmen built some of Spain's largest and finest ships. They were made with Cuban wood except for the masts, which were directly imported from Norway. Nearly sixty ships were built in Havana during the first third of the seventeenth century. These included the formidable 500-ton *Nuestra Señora del Rosario* (1596–1602); the *Nuestra Señora de la Concepción*, which weighed 680 tons (1623); and the Spanish fleet's flagship, *La Magdalena*. In 1620, Havana's shipyards, which were run by Francisco Díaz Pimienta, received authorization to build one-third of the empire's ships.[6]

In support of Havana's roles, a civil and defense infrastructure was erected to service and protect the port city. This included the Real Zanja aqueduct, which channeled water from La Chorrera to the San Francisco square and the Chorro alley, and a network of stone and mortar fortifications. The port city's defensive and service activities translated into prosperity for Havana and its hinterland. It also generated substantial amounts of capital, some of which later flowed into financing and sugar production.

Havana's role as an obligatory port of call and service center made it increasingly dependent on imported food and goods and on outside funds to defray the escalating costs of building, manning, and sustaining forts and garrisons. Cabildo legislation ordered residents in Havana's periphery and Cuba's interior to provide the port city with an adequate supply of beef through a mechanism known as *la pesa*. Another legal instrument, *la sisa*, taxed the sale of wine, beef, soap, and other consumer goods to fund the construction of the Real Zanja.[7] More important, Havana came to depend on periodic monetary allocations, known as *situados*, that came from Mexico to pay for soldiers' salaries and other military expenses.

Historian Louis A. Pérez Jr. has contrasted Havana and the west with the eastern part of the island: "The west," he wrote, "flourished as a result of the official presence, in defense of colonial policy" while "the east flourished as a result of the official absence, in defiance of colonial policy."[8] Cuba beyond Havana developed at its own pace, responding to different economic and demographic realities and generating a distinctive culture. Eastern interior settings such as Bayamo and Manzanillo did not have the regimented and rigidly hierarchical social structure of Havana but rather were characterized by more fluid racial and social distinctions. Such contexts produced a "frontier culture" where whites, blacks, Amerindians, and Cubans of mixed ancestry labored under relative egalitarianism, which in turn was more conducive to creolization and cultural hybridity. Writer Benítez-Rojo has argued that the roots of Cuban nationhood are found precisely there, in the Windward Passage culture of eastern Cuba, where "enterprising people, largely *mestizos* and mulattos . . . lived far from the cities and thus far from the reach of bureaucracy, distant from the military installations and the Church's vigilant eyes."[9]

The economy of the interior was based mostly on hunting the cattle that had turned wild after the conquistadores brought them (the source of hides and beef), tobacco farming, and the cultivation of so-called minor crops: plantains, tubers, ginger, and the like. More than half of the tobacco, hides, and ginger that was produced left the island as contraband in exchange for European manufactured goods such as textiles and tools and for African slaves.

These smuggling activities were more prevalent in the eastern part of Cuba in locations distant from the better-supplied, monopolistic port of Havana, which had the resources to police illicit trade practices. The 1600s were the heyday of smuggling. Contraband trade far surpassed the volume and value of legal commerce. According to contemporary estimates, twice as many hides, the main export product of the period, were exported illegally as were exported legally. The prices foreign smugglers were willing to pay for hides could be six times higher than what Havana's merchants offered. Hides so dominated the illegal trade that they became a widely accepted form of currency: one hide for three *varas* of canvas, three hides for a five-liter jar of wine, twelve hides for one pound of silk, and so on. A notarized sale certificate from 1578 recorded that one slave named Sebastián was sold in exchange for 200 hides. The following year, Francisca, a slave woman from Cape Verde was traded for 260 ducados' worth of hides.[10]

Tobacco was another commonly smuggled product. Demand for it increased as Europeans developed the habit of inhaling snuff. It was such a lure for smugglers that Spanish authorities prohibited its cultivation from 1606 to 1614 and went to the length of forcefully depopulating vast tobacco-producing regions in northwestern Hispaniola. A prohibition against growing tobacco in locations distant from Havana persisted until late in the century. Also in much demand from smugglers were spices such as ginger and sugar (the latter of which was considered a luxury item at the time); precious woods such as mahogany, ebony, and Brazil wood; and medicinal woods such as sarsaparilla and guaiacum, whose extracts were believed to be an effective cure for syphilis, a disease that was rapidly spread by the armies that were crisscrossing war-torn Europe.[11]

These products were bartered for African slaves; a wide range of textiles ranging from the finest Chinese silks to the crudest canvases used to make slave clothing; an assortment of manufactured items such as knives, hammers, needles, and books; and comestibles such as wine from the Canary Islands and

Nicotiana inserta infundibulo ex quo hauriunt fumū Indi & nau cleri.

Figure 5.2. Engraving of a tobacco plant. Source: Pierre Pena, *Stirpium adversaria noua* (London, [1571]). Reprinted courtesy of the John Carter Brown Library at Brown University.

Flemish cheese. Smuggled goods were considerably cheaper than legally imported products, for which Cubans had to pay compounding layers of taxes. Spanish law, which protected the trade monopolies of Seville, Havana, and a handful of other legal ports, made imported products expensive. Laws prescribed that Portuguese-made cauldrons, French textiles, and African slaves, to give only three examples, could not be imported directly but had to be shipped first to Seville, where they were taxed and shipping costs and middlemen profits were added. Then they could be shipped to Havana, where they were taxed one more time and other fees were added. Only then could they be shipped to eastern destinations such as Baracoa or Bayamo. As a result of this, prices of consumer goods shot up: a *pipa* (barrel) of wine that cost 3,740 *maravedis* in Sanlúcar, Spain, sold in Havana for about 24,000 *maravedis*.[12]

Smuggling was widely welcomed by inhabitants in towns such as Manzanillo and Bayamo and even Santiago, and civil and ecclesiastical authorities condoned it by actively participating in it. Illicit trade was carried out so openly that local residents sometimes organized trade fairs when smuggling vessels arrived. One famous fair was one organized with Dutch smugglers in the town of Manzanillo. A contemporary observer claimed in 1604 that this fair's commercial activity rivaled the volume of Havana's legal trade. Also in Manzanillo, sojourning smugglers built facilities that included a variety of shops, doctors' offices, and even bowling allies, all under the protection of a battery of Dutch cannons. Bayamo was the main center of smuggling activity. In 1603, Captain-General Pedro Valdés sent one of his lieutenants with fifty soldiers to investigate the illicit trade activities of the town's residents. He found that virtually all civil and ecclesiastical authorities were complicit. In the words of nineteenth-century historian Jacobo de la Pezuela, "All the well-to-do residents of that part of the island were smugglers: the clergyman, the *alcalde*, the *regidor*, the employee, the soldier, in fact, anyone who had the resources to do it."[13]

Smuggling activities also threatened Spain's Catholic exclusivism, as Protestant traders brought their "Geneva bibles," "Lutheran" religious tracts, and so-called heretical beliefs and practices. So close were the relations between smugglers and local residents that according to one prelate's complaint, residents postponed their children's christenings until the arrival of French smugglers—mostly Huguenots—who willingly served as godparents. Plenty of clergymen, even some prelates, participated in smuggling activities. Numerous accusations were leveled against priests. For example, the parish priest of Baracoa, who was reportedly a frequent visitor to smuggler camps, was described as one of the main partners of "the heretics and enemies." Historian Irene A. Wright deemed priests "the oldest and most unrepentant of smugglers."[14]

Another Cuba existed beyond Havana and the interior towns that was made up of "communities" of diverse races and cultures that precariously coalesced on the margins of society: indigenous rebels, black maroons, military deserters, and castaways. At one point between 1607 and 1609, one roaming band was composed of twenty-seven fugitive slaves (including a few children), two Amerindian men, an Amerindian woman with a *"grifa"* daughter, a free mulatto, and a Spanish man. Groups like that one found refuge in geographic spaces of marginalization such as caves and mangrove-covered wetlands.[15]

A Multiethnic Colony

In the second half of the sixteenth century, the island's population experienced sustained growth. It expanded from less than 6,000 in the 1550s to close to 20,000 by 1607.[16] Its composition also continued to change as the indigenous population fell further to around 1,000 by the end of the century. In contrast, the white population bounced back and the mostly enslaved black population increased with the expansion of the slave trade.

Instead of one neatly defined social hierarchy, Cuba had several contending and overlapping social structures. Some were based on distinctions between estates, others approximated a modern class system, and others were based purely on race. Gender was yet another form of stratification: white women were deemed inferior to white men and endured legal discrimination and subjection to male authority.

Members of different groups embraced stratification models that were favorable to their own aspirations of social and economic mobility. Because Cuba's social pyramid was more complex and more malleable than Spain's estates system, Cubans of all races tested and contested the rigid legally sanctioned hierarchy and used their own criteria to determine social standing and a sense of worth. Some highlighted extraordinary service to the Crown (being a conquistador), some emphasized heritage (descending from a noble), others accentuated wealth (owning trade vessels), others highlighted race (being mulatto as opposed to being black), and yet others stressed legal status (being free as opposed to being enslaved).

Whites were at the top of the racial ladder, and *hidalgos* (*hijos de algo*, literally, sons of something) occupied its very top rung. Estimates are that only 1 percent of Cuba's early settlers belonged the lower nobility, or *hidalgo* estate (Hernán Cortés and Vasco Porcallo de Figueroa were among the few).[17] The way that *encomiendas* and land grants were distributed helped preserve some Old World social distinctions. Early colonial legislation, for example, established that *hidalgos* be granted 100 *encomendado* Amerindians, while commoners received only thirty. By the same token, land usufruct grants to *caballeros* (*caballerías*) measured between one and four to five times as much as the *peonías* that were granted to lower-status whites.[18]

Next in the social hierarchy were *los principales* (the main ones), which included members of wealthy families, high-ranking government officials, military officers, and prelates. Early on, women of the Taino ruling caste married white *principales* and their *mestizo* children were welcomed to that estate. Next were the rest of *los españoles* and some Hispanicized *mestizos*: merchants, farmers, craftsmen, and unskilled workers. Below them were the remaining indigenous inhabitants, with what was left of the cacique caste above all others. One step down were blacks and mulattos, those who were free above those who were enslaved.

Slaves sought to escape their bondage in any way possible, and blacks and mulattos, both slave and free, sought to re-create their own visions of place and social standing. Anthropologist Sidney W. Mintz and others have recognized the generalized inclination of former slaves, and even slaves, to reconstitute peasant communities.[19] Some African-born slaves (*bozales*, literally muzzles) attempted to re-create polygamy and their ancestral pecking orders, distinguishing between kings and nobles and commoners. They also viewed themselves as superior to *criollo* slaves, who in return placed themselves socially above the *bozales*. Mulattos, meanwhile, generally capitalized on their lighter complexion to distinguish themselves from blacks; the general rule was the lighter the better. There was a strong correlation between the racial status of mulattos and the condition of freedom, and free blacks and mulattos adamantly stressed their free status as a way of differentiating themselves from slaves.

In summation, those who were privileged by status, wealth, place of birth, gender, or skin color sought to maintain those distinctions, both in law and in practice. Others challenged the status quo by disputing hierarchical demarcations that impeded upward mobility and improvements in their lives. It is important to highlight, however, that while the various groups were legally separated, they interacted regularly with each other. Masters and domestic slaves lived under the same roofs, and white men fell in love with, lusted after, raped, cohabitated with, and occasionally married women of other races. Men of all races worked together at piers, on plantations, and in shipyards. The farther from Havana one went, the greater was the familiarity between racial and social groups, the more common were interactions among races, the higher the rate of cross-racial unions and the number of mixed-race children.

Los Españoles

The white population evolved during the 1500s in terms of size, composition, demographic makeup, and relations with other racial and ethnic groups. By 1607, the number of whites hovered around 15,000. Originally composed mostly of conquistadores from Andalusia, Extremadura, and Castile-Leon, white society gradually incorporated immigrants from other parts of the Iberian Peninsula such as Portugal, which was tied to Spain through dynastic marriages and was under Spanish rule between 1580 and 1640. Canary Islanders also migrated to Cuba in large numbers, mostly gravitating to agricultural activities in the countryside—mainly cultivating tobacco and supplying cattle fodder. They founded rural settlements and new towns, including Matanzas in 1693.[20] As the sixteenth century unfolded, Cuba also included an increasingly numerous population of creole (Cuban-born) whites and Cuban-born *mestizos*, who were deemed *españoles* by social custom and colonial legislation.

The dominant presence of Andalusians during the early stages of settlement left profound imprints. Thirty-seven percent of those who traveled from Spain to the Antilles between 1509 and 1519 came from Andalusia. Remarkably, 50 percent of all female passengers were from Seville. Statistics gathered and analyzed by historian Alejandro de la Fuente reflect the numerical dominance of Andalusians among Havana's residents during the latter half of the sixteenth century and first decade of the following century; the proportion hovered around 42 percent of all whites.[21] Because the proportion of southern Spaniards in later stages of the conquest and colonization of continental Latin America was lower, Andalusian cultural contributions were more pronounced in the Spanish Caribbean than they were elsewhere in the Americas. Havana and Seville, moreover, were intimate trading partners and those links reinforced other affinities.

Immigration from the Canary Islands increased markedly during the 1600s. That group numerically surpassed all other Spanish origins by the end of the century. Around a quarter of all immigrants who arrived in Havana from 1585 to 1645 were Canary Islanders. They enjoyed the privilege of sailing directly to Cuba from the Canary Islands; other Spaniards had to depart from Seville under much scrutiny. Ship captains who transported Canary families to Cuba received tax exemptions on the merchandise they imported.[22]

Although Cuba's white population originally consisted exclusively of male conquistadores, the island slowly incorporated white women, even though white males continued to dominate numerically and otherwise. Gender imbalances among white settlers were common throughout the Indies. Historian Magnus Mörner calculated that only 10 percent of all licenses to travel to Spain's New World colonies between 1509 and 1539 were granted to women. There is evidence that white slave women were imported to Hispaniola and Cuba during the first years of colonization. A total of only 308 European women arrived in the Indies between 1509 and 1519. The gender imbalance was less pronounced in Santiago than it was in Havana. A 1606 census of Santiago included 217 men and 129 women, a masculinity rate of 1.7. The gender imbalance was also less pronounced among Canary Islanders, whose migration patterns favored family emigration. In fact, during the sixteenth century, there were more women than men among Canary Islanders living in Havana.[23]

The presence of white women was deemed a stabilizing factor that was conducive to the formation of stable families, population growth, and better morality. It also seemed to be preventing colonists from fleeing to other parts of the Americas. To promote the immigration of European women, laws were passed that forced single men to get married, required married men to bring their wives from Spain, and banned bachelors from receiving *encomiendas*. Only two years into Cuba's colonization, the Crown ordered Viceroy Diego Columbus to remove all impediments for transporting to Cuba the wives of soldiers already stationed there. A royal decree of 1526 threatened any married man who left Cuba without a license with death and the confiscation of all properties. A decade later, legislation allowed free passage to Portuguese settlers if they brought their wives.[24] These policies seemed to be effective, at least for some men. When he explained what had kept him from escaping to Peru in 1534, Sancti Spíritus *regidor* Alfonso de Oviedo stated that while he thought about the wealth of Peru, being married held him back. Likewise, fellow *regidor* Francisco Ciborro explained that he would have left if he could have taken his wife and children along.[25]

Because there were so few white women and because they played key roles as social gatekeepers, some appeared to have amassed a considerable degree of influence and even some power. Accusations were leveled against Governor Pérez de Angulo that his wife, Doña Violante, dictated judicial decisions in lawsuits. Similarly, some claimed that Alcaide (fort commander) Melchor Sardo de Arana's wife and mother-in-law coopted soldiers of el Castillo de la Real Fuerza for their personal retinues. Women played important roles when their husbands left to explore and conquer other lands. When Pánfilo de Narváez departed Bayamo on his 1518 expedition, for example, he left his wife María de Valenzuela behind to take care of the family properties.[26] The best-known case was that of Hernando de Soto's wife, Isabel de Bobadilla, who served briefly as interim governor. The legal tradition that protected women's dowries from their husbands also contributed to the relative economic agency of wealthier white women. Upon marriage, however, women lost the right to dispose of their own property and to represent themselves in legal transactions.

The institution of marriage was a tool that members of the island's elite used to consolidate power and separate themselves from lower-status individuals and that newcomers used to integrate themselves into the elite. Members of the elite who had social and economic power also used marriage as a way to gain political power. Governors set the example. Diego Velázquez married María de Cuellar, daughter of Cristóbal de Cuellar, a Spanish noble who served as the king's treasurer. His successor, Governor Manuel de Rojas, married a relative of Velázquez, Magdalena Velázquez. Likewise, two later governors, Diego de Mazariegos and Juan de Ávila, had relationships with local white women of economic means and high social standing. Mazariegos, who had become a widower shortly before he arrived in Havana, began a relationship with Doña Francisca Pérez, the daughter of former governor Gonzalo Pérez de Angulo. She bore him three children and they eventually married. De Ávila, meanwhile, had a scandalous out-of-wedlock relationship with the wealthy, 50-something, twice-widowed Doña Guiomar de Guzmán, whom he favored with allotments of indigenous labor. Governor Gonzalo de Guzmán also used marriage to circumvent legal restrictions against governors owning *encomiendas*; he allotted a 200-worker *encomienda* to Catalina de Agüero and then married her.[27]

A 1604 petition by Jácome Justiniano Velázquez offers a glimpse of the importance newcomers placed on marrying white Spanish or Cuban women and the value Cuban elites placed on pedigree. He supported his petition for a sinecure from the cabildo of Havana by referring to the family tree of his wife, Ysabel de la Gama. The document highlighted the fact that she was the daughter of Captain Bartolomé Cepero and the granddaughter of Francisco Cepero and Ysabel Cepero. Ysabel Cepero was the granddaughter of another conquistador. When Antonio Velázquez Bazán petitioned the Crown for a pension, he stressed that both sides of his family were related by blood to conquistadores: he was the grandchild of one of Diego Velázquez's sisters and the grandson of Captain Francisco Verdugo, one of the conquistadores of New Spain.[28]

While some sought marriage, others avoided it. Concubinage was commonplace, as evidenced by a litany of accusations against governors for condoning such unions and by the clergy's persistent protestations. Governor Manuel de Rojas denounced the problem in a 1534 report: "[Some] persons were cohabiting and in concubinage with indigenous servant women, others with their slaves and others with the daughters of Spaniards or Creoles, serenely and as tranquil as if under blessed unions." Bishop Sarmiento chastised Governor Juan de Ávila for his illicit relation with Doña Guiomar, whom he insulted as a "dissolute witch" and "*puta vieja*" (old slut).[29]

Dowries were common currency in the marriage market. In many cases families were expected to provide a substantial dowry to improve a daughter's chances of a favorable marriage. In other cases, it was the man who had to come up with an attractive equivalent to a dowry, known as *arras* (10 percent of the groom's assets). The value of a dowry varied depending on the bride's family wealth and the desirability of the groom. One of the most expensive dowries, if not the most expensive, was provided by Hernán Manrique de Rojas to seal the marriage between his widowed daughter and a Spaniard from Jerez de la Frontera. It was worth an enormous fortune: 14,450 ducados. In 1609, the parents of Úrsula de Merlo gathered a dowry consisting of 1,500 ducados, 4 slaves, and 200 ducados' worth of clothing and jewels for her marriage with Marcos Solís. That same year, the parents of Inés Posada gave their daughter a 2,400-ducado dowry consisting of a house, slaves, and her wardrobe. Even grooms who earned a living using their hands could expect sizeable dowries, as was the case of Luis Hernández, a mason, whose wife contributed almost 1,000 ducados in cash along with two mattresses, two pillows, two bedsheets, and her own wardrobe. Antón Recio gave his *mestizo* daughters and sons large dowries and *arras* so they could marry advantageously.[30]

The avenues to social mobility that were available during the earlier decades of the sixteenth century became increasingly narrow during the second half of the century. When the conquest and frontier eras ended, the possibilities for mobility decreased. For example, *encomiendas* and royal land grants were no longer distributed. *Limpieza de sangre* (having "uncontaminated" Christian ancestry) became an indispensable requirement for holding even the lowest-ranking public offices. Even some formerly wealthy conquistadores and early settlers fell into the ranks of the poor. Juana, *la princesa gobernadora*, who administered the kingdoms of Castile and Aragon while her brother King Philip II was living in England, intervened on behalf of a few of them. She pitied them for being "poor to the point of having nothing and so old and sick that they cannot earn an income."[31]

Indios and Mestizos

The indigenous population continued to fall during the post-conquest period, dropping from around 5,000 at mid-century to an estimated mere 1,000 by 1600. In 1604–1606, only 77 of Santiago's 625 inhabitants were classified as *indios*, 11 percent of the total.[32] Smallpox and other diseases the Spaniards brought and a host of new diseases imported through the slave trade, including yellow fever and malaria, had fatal consequences for an already debilitated indigenous population. *Mestizaje* and the social assimilation that accompanied it further reduced the indigenous population by producing a large number of *mestizos* who were no longer considered *indios* by Spanish laws and who generally sought to join the social group of their white fathers, into which they were culturally assimilated.

Some Amerindians settled into Spanish villages and settings in the countryside, where they lived in proximity to whites and blacks. In some instances, they received land allocations from the cabildo of Havana. Others, including those freed from slavery, were concentrated in *reducciones* under the supervision of white men. In the early 1580s, only around forty adult male Amerindians and their families lived in urban Havana, among them one named Alonso who identified as "*mexicano*" and had most likely been forcibly brought to Cuba from the Yucatan. Across the bay from Havana, forty-six adult male Amerindians lived with their families in the *reducción* of Guanabacoa under the supervision of a man surnamed Fragoso and his sons. Because of their relative isolation from larger society, *reducciones* like this one were less conducive to *mestizaje* and the communities who lived there were more likely to retain indigenous cultural practices.[33]

Because of the small number of white women during the early colonization phase, many, if not most, male settlers had sexual relations with indigenous women. Such relations ranged from casual sexual encounters (which often were the result of violence) to long-term concubinage to a few instances of true love sanctioned by marriage. Those sorts of cross-racial relations were a central component of the conquest and colonization of the New World. Their by-product, *mestizaje*, was the human foundation of Spanish America. While *mestizaje* continued for centuries in places like Mexico and Peru and *mestizos* eventually outnumbered whites and Amerindians, in Cuba white and Amerindian unions dwindled within a couple of generations and the *mestizos* did not form a separate group outside white society.

For Spaniards of the conquest generation, marrying the daughter of a cacique was a socially advantageous move. In 1534, twelve of the seventeen wealthiest and most powerful residents of Trinidad and Sancti Spíritus were married: five to Spanish women, five to Taino women, and two to *mestizas*. Among those who married or had long-term cohabitation with indigenous women of the cacique elite were Rodrigo de Tamayo and Vasco Porcallo de Figueroa (with Tínima, the daughter of the cacique of Camagüey). Antón Recio had several children with Cacanga, the daughter of the cacique of Guanabacoa.[34] Such relationships became less common as time went on. For one thing, the number of indigenous women decreased, and for another, noble indigenous ancestry lost the value it once had. There is no extant documentation of white women marrying or cohabiting with indigenous men. While some interracial unions were built on mutual love and respect, most unequal liaisons were short lived, exploitative, and even violent. In 1532, Governor Rojas complained that colonists poisoned their Amerindian wives to obtain the freedom to remarry.[35]

The social dislocations of the conquest and colonization had a much larger social impact on indigenous men than on women because the former did not have the political value that daughters of the Taino elite retained for a while. In fact, Amerindian males had enormous difficulty finding mates of any race. As Bishop Diego Sarmiento explained with some hyperbole: "The Spaniards and *mestizos* marry Indian women and the Indian man is lucky to find an eighty-year old wife." Recent genetic studies confirm the bishop's impressions and the sexual dominance of white men, as reflected by the fact that 80 percent of the Y-chromosome (male) ancestry among present-day Cubans is Eurasian and virtually 0 percent is linked to Amerindians. By contrast, Amerindian female ancestry, as measured by mitochondrial DNA, points to a much higher genetic contribution of 33 percent.[36]

The members of the first generation of *mestizos* were welcomed into Spanish society. They tended to identify with and become assimilated to their father's side, both racially and culturally. For the most part, they were *ladinos* (Hispanicized), they were baptized, they had Christian names and Spanish surnames, they spoke Spanish, and they dressed as *españoles*. Governor Velázquez stood as godfather for a son Hernán Cortés had with a Cuban indigenous woman. Another first-generation *mestizo*, Miguel Velázquez, a nephew of Governor Velázquez, was the son of a Castilian man and an indigenous woman. He was sent to be educated at the University of Seville and the University of Alcalá de Henares and later became Cuba's first teacher and first Cuban-born priest. At one point, he served as *regidor* in the cabildo of Santiago.[37]

Early on, *mestizos* born to wealthy and distinguished fathers were able to retain high economic and social standing. Antón Recio's son Juan inherited his father's *mayorazgo*, a Crown-sanctioned indivisible hereditary land grant; it was worth 20,000 ducados. Antón's *mestizo* daughters owned considerable wealth that included slaves and married advantageously with the help of attractive dowries. Porcallo de Figueroa's son Vasco Porcallo served as *alcalde* and *regidor* of Puerto Príncipe, and two of Porcallo de Figueroa's *mestizo* daughters married members of Cuba's white elite.[38] Another *mestizo*, Juan Ferrer de Vargas, whose sister was married to Captain-General Gabriel Montalvo, served for a while as commander of el Castillo de la Real Fuerza. Curiously, Montalvo, himself the father-in-law of a *mestizo*, scorned Juan Recio, for being *mestizo*, an indication that *mestizaje* carried a degree of social stigma even among descendants of powerful white men and women of the vanishing cacique elite.[39]

Being a *mestizo*, however, did not carry the same socio-racial stigma that Spaniards imposed on black slaves and even their free descendants. The labyrinthic racial hierarchy of early colonial Spanish America, the *casta* system, in fact provided opportunities for complete social "whitening" within a couple of generations. According to the brewing racial classification system that was so artistically portrayed in eighteenth-century *casta* paintings, the union of an *español* and an *india* produced *mestizo* offspring. Marriage between that offspring and an *español/a* produced children who were classified as *castizos,* and the children of a *castizo* parent and an *español/a* gave birth to *españoles.*[40] Laws treated *mestizos* as white and assigned them the same privileges and punishments that whites received. In fact, in Cuba the classification of *mestizo* virtually disappeared from official documents in the seventeenth century.

As the sixteenth century unfolded, however, *mestizos* and their descendants lost social ground. By this point, it was only lower-status white males who exhibited a greater inclination to enter cross-racial relationships. Of the sixty-two high-status male adults who appeared in the 1582 census of military reserves in Havana, not one was identified as *mestizo.* Among the seventy described as "residents who live off their labor," only six were categorized as *mestizos* and one as mulatto. However, more than half of the twenty-nine males in the next generation of manual laborers were categorized as *mestizo.*[41] This is evidence that unions among non-elite white males and Amerindian women and *mestizas* were common. Beyond Havana, where larger concentrations of indigenous people had survived, unions between white men and Amerindian and *mestizo* women were even more prevalent.

Black and Mulatto Slaves

The sustained decrease in the indigenous population and the on again, off again restrictions on the use of coerced indigenous labor encouraged—some argued, made necessary—the importation of African slaves, a process that began in the early decades of the sixteenth century. A few of them were Europeanized (*ladinos*) who had arrived from Europe with their masters. Such was the case with African-born Juan Garrido, who joined Ovando's 1502 expedition, participated in the conquest of Puerto Rico, then joined Velázquez's expedition in 1511. By that time, he had become a freedman, and in 1519 he embarked, with Cortés, on the epic conquest of Mexico.[42]

The vast majority of Cuban slaves were brutally uprooted from different regions of West Africa and transplanted to the island directly from Africa, from Cartagena, or from other Caribbean ports. Records dating back to 1515 document the buying and selling of African slaves in Cuba. The accounting unit for slave traffickers was the *pieza*. A *pieza* was the equivalent of a healthy adult male but it could also be the equivalent of a combination of two slaves whose value was considered roughly the equivalent of a healthy adult male. One *pieza* could be composed of, say, an elderly person and a small girl. The *San Pedro*, which landed in Havana in 1628, illustrates this valuation system. Because it transported an unusually large number of enslaved children, its cargo included 230 slaves but was valued at only 142 *piezas*.[43]

Settlers who owned mines and agricultural land incessantly clamored for more lenient restrictions and lower taxes on the importation of African slaves, pleading for opportunities to acquire them on credit and with government subsidies. In 1534, fourteen of the seventeen wealthiest residents of Trinidad and Sancti Spíritus called for government credits they could use to buy African slaves. Porcallo de Figueroa requested a royal loan to buy slaves; he proposed that he pay it off in installments with proceeds from gold mining.[44] Because of the island's relative poverty and the increasing shift of imperial attention toward Central and South America, shipments of slaves tended to head elsewhere; colonists regularly complained about slave cargos being diverted to Cartagena. That was partially the result of a 1556 royal decree that set maximum prices for imported slaves. The limit established for Cuba was among the lowest (100 ducados), while prices in Cartagena and elsewhere were almost twice as high.[45]

By 1582, an estimated 2,000 blacks, most of them slaves, lived in Havana and it is likely that a similar number lived elsewhere on the island. Larger numbers of slaves began flowing into Cuba in 1595; an estimated 1,300–1,500 were brought to the island during the 1590s. The vast majority of imported slaves ended up in Havana and its agricultural hinterland. In 1609, 5,000 slaves were registered in Havana, while Santiago had only 158. In addition to the officially sanctioned slave trade carried out mostly by licensed Portuguese merchants, the smuggling of slaves flourished as a supplement to the legal trade.[46]

Historians Alejandro de la Fuente and David Wheat have periodized the slave trade to Cuba and the Spanish Caribbean. A first stage, which lasted to 1580, consisted of slaves who had mostly originated in the Upper Guinea region. A second stage, in which slaves from the Congo and Angola predominated, ran up to the end of the 1600s. De la Fuente calculated that Upper Guineans constituted at least 60 percent of all slaves brought to Cuba from 1570 to 1594. Representative of that first phase was the human cargo of another vessel named *San Pedro*, which landed in Havana in 1572 with a total of 192 captives, two-thirds of which were male. Its roster listed at least twenty ethnic groups. The most numerous were Bran (51), Biafara (40), and Zape (36), three groups that originated in the Upper Guinea region. Havana's *protocolos notariales* for the period 1579–1588 include sale agreements for 123 slaves whose origins ranged from as far north as Senegal to as far south as Luanda. Among those slaves, two-thirds had ethnic labels from groups that originated in Upper Guinea and the other third were from Angola or the Congo.[47]

The story of the second vessel named *San Pedro* sheds light on the ethnic, gender, and age composition of slave cargoes during the second stage of the slave trade. In 1628 on its way to New Spain from Angola, the *San Pedro* illegally disembarked 230 slaves in Havana. The slaves were quickly bought by at least 149 different individuals from different walks of life, from military officers and a priest to a barber and a midwife. At least two of the purchasers were freed Africans. While it was not uncommon for slave cargos to include children, the case of the *San Pedro* is extraordinary because 72 percent of its slaves were children. An astonishingly high number of the passengers, thirty-six, was nursing babies. Among those children was a boy named Lucas, who was purchased by Francisco de Noriega, himself a former slave.[48]

As a result of slave-trading practices that favored the importation of males, the slave population exhibited a marked masculinity index. The index was 150 among slaves sold in Havana (1578–1588). Among the enslaved population of Santiago and its environs it was 140, and on sugar plantations the masculinity index was a much sharper 530.[49] Seeking to avoid dangerously high masculinity ratios, a royal order of 1527 mandated that half of all slaves imported into the Indies had to be female. This and similar mandates were blatantly ignored, however.[50]

Socially and legally, blacks and mulattos, both slave and free, ranked below the *indios*. Laws were more severe regarding blacks and mulattoes and, significantly, penalties often did not distinguish between slaves and *horros* (freed slaves). After the cabildo banned people from crossing the area between Havana and La Chorrera in 1565—the place name El Vedado (the forbidden place) originated then—whites caught crossing were fined 50 pesos or 100 lashes, but blacks and mulattos, both free and slave, were subjected to *desjarretamiento* (mutilation of the upper calf). In the same vein, indebtedness fines for *horros* were twenty times larger than they were for whites.[51] While blacks were pushed

to the lowest stratum of society by law and discrimination, they had certain social advantages the indigenous population did not have, mostly stemming from
their skills as blacksmiths, coopers, cooks, and even plantation overseers.

The material circumstances of Cuba's first generations of slaves, while generally horrendous, varied widely. How they were treated depended to some extent
on their geographic location and gender and the nature of their work. Urban
slaves had greater chances of earning some income and achieving their freedom.
However, living in cities and their outskirts and under the roof of masters did
not always translate into greater autonomy, better material conditions, or hap-
piness. Domestic slaves usually ate and dressed better, but they did not always
sleep better. This was particularly true for female slaves, who lived under the
constant threat of sexual abuse. Slaves working on sugar plantations endured
some of the worst living conditions and some of the harshest abuse.

Black slaves were forced to work in a variety of tasks. Early on, they replaced
indigenous workers in gold mining. They also labored side by side with Amerindians and whites on farms as cowboys, stevedores, and domestics. Some
worked as town criers and executioners. They also worked in military construction projects and on public works. It is no exaggeration to say that black blood,
sweat, and tears cemented the stones and bricks that fortified Havana. When
needed, slaves were used as soldiers; between 100 and 200 blacks defended Havana against French corsairs during Jacques de Sores's capture of the city in 1555.
In the first decade of the seventeenth century, the permanent work force of the
El Morro fort included 150 to 200 slaves.[52]

Although female slaves were not used in hard labor or to defend the island
from corsair attacks, they were highly visible and active in the economy of Havana. Because they were far more likely to be hired out or to hire themselves
out, they were overrepresented in petty commerce and service lines of work.
Enslaved women worked as laundresses, domestics, cooks, street vendors, and
even as hired mourners for funerals. Some were forced into the world's oldest
profession. Masters rented out slaves of both sexes to work for others or allowed them to work on their own, forcing them to surrender most of their earn-
ings. In 1593, the daily rate for hiring a female slave was 102 maravedís. Slave
laundresses charged a steep 34 maravedís for washing one shirt, the equivalent
of the cost of six pounds of beef. When slaves rented themselves out, masters
forced them to surrender exorbitant amounts; one document states that owners demanded four reales (136 maravedís) per day. This kind of exploitation,
according to the *audiencia* of Santo Domingo, was one of the main reasons
slaves ran away.[53]

Slaves endured extraordinary cruelty at the hands of their masters. *Audiencia* judge Alonso de Cáceres denounced slave masters for the brutal punishments they routinely inflicted, including excessive whippings, *mechar* (inserting explosives into body cavities), *asar* (burning alive), and others too heinous to write about here. Cáceres gave orders to masters not to abuse slaves and mandated that masters provide them with sufficient food and clothing.[54]

Other laws and ordinances were meant to control slave behavior. They prohibited slaves from selling or purchasing wine, carrying weapons, wearing capes, living by themselves instead of with their masters, and being outdoors after curfew. Some restrictions specifically targeted slave women. Women caught selling food in the streets were issued heavy fines, and slave laundresses had to have a special license before they were allowed to provide services to passing fleets (laundry services were often fronts for prostitution).[55]

Rebels, Runaway Slaves, and *Horros*

Slaves resisted their bondage in a variety of ways. At the very least, they tried to carve out some autonomy and better living conditions and ultimately sought to escape slavery altogether. They resisted violently and peacefully, individually and collectively, lawfully and unlawfully. Some instances of violent resistance included the murder of masters and overseers, and some culminated in revolts. Other slaves sought the precarious freedom of the runaway slave. Others took advantage of Spanish and colonial laws that made provisions for self-purchase, either all at once or in installments through the legal mechanism known as *co-artación*. Still others found the ultimate freedom from slavery through suicide, which the slave community deemed an acceptable and dignified way of ending suffering and reuniting with their ancestors.

As Manuel Barcia has demonstrated in his studies of slave resistance in Cuba, West Africans were familiar with and skilled at war and they brought those skills with them and used them.[56] Slave rebellions broke out in the 1530s. In 1533, slaves working at the Jobabo gold mines north of Holguín revolted and reportedly attacked indigenous towns and kidnaped their women. Governor Manuel de Rojas responded swiftly, deploying troops to bring the rebels to submission. The slaves fought to the death. Rojas's men took the bodies of the four leaders to Bayamo, where they dismembered and decapitated them and gruesomely paraded their heads on sticks. Another major slave revolt broke out in 1537 in Santiago, whose residents were reportedly terrified by the prospect of being attacked.[57] Slave rebellions like these, even under the best of circumstances, offered only temporary relief from oppression. Given the zero-tolerance policies of government authorities, slave acts of violence, whether individual or collective, almost always led to certain death.

One of the best documented forms of resistance was *marronage* (slave flight). In 1611, the cabildo of Havana petitioned the Council of the Indies for harsher penalties against maroons who reportedly formed roaming bands of up to 100 individuals who engaged in criminal activities: stealing crops and cattle and luring other slaves away from their masters. The cabildo expressed fears that because there were between 4,000 and 5,000 slaves around Havana, maroons could start a rebellion, attack the city, and kill many people.[58]

Authorities and slave owners responded to slave flight with a heavy hand. They formed parties of heavily armed slave hunters (*rancheadores*) assisted by packs of ferocious dogs. In 1587, Lieutenant Bartolomé Cepero and Juan Pérez Borroto formed a company of *rancheadores*. Its initial resources included a small vessel, four men, three horses, and a few mastiffs. Slave hunters earned reputations for excessive violence and cruelty. In their quest to capture runaway slaves, they illegally entered private farms and *bohíos* owned by free blacks and mulattos, in some instances destroying crops, stealing horses, and ransacking homes. Some *rancheadores* were injured or killed in battle against maroon bands, which were armed with bows and arrows, clubs, and makeshift weapons. When maroons were captured, they were brutally punished with mutilation or 200 to 300 lashes. Their leaders were generally executed by hanging.[59]

Some slaves managed to ameliorate their circumstances or escape slavery by using Spanish laws and practices that considered the condition of slavery "unnatural" and made provisions to protect slaves from extreme abuse, including death at the hand of their masters, and for freedom by way of self-purchase if they so desired. The medieval Spanish legal code known as Las Siete Partidas called slavery "the vilest and most contemptible thing than can exist among men" and allowed slaves to marry other slaves and even free individuals, even if their masters opposed it, and to seek redress from judges if their masters treated them with cruelty.[60]

Although slavery in Cuba was far more racialized and masters got away with much more abuse, Spanish colonial laws stipulated that abused slaves could seek transfer to different masters. The mechanism of *coartación* gave slaves the right to purchase their freedom in installments after coming to an agreement about their value with their masters. These rights, however, were difficult to protect and slaves were often the victims of false promises and fraud. *Coartación* transactions were straightforward: master and slave agreed on the slave's value, the

Figure 5.3. Engraving depicting a runaway slave being chased by slave hunters and ferocious dogs. Source: "Chasing a Fugitive Slave, 1840s," in Edmund Ollier Cassell, *History of the United States* (London, 1874–1877), 3:91, available at *The Atlantic Slave Trade and Slave Life in the Americas: A Visual Record*, compiled by Jerome Handler and Michael Tuite and sponsored by the Virginia Foundation for the Humanities, http://www.slaveryimages.org/detailsKeyword. php?keyword=Cassell&recordCount=10&theRecord=4, accessed September 7, 2017.

slave paid for her or his freedom, and the master issued the freed slave a nota-rized certificate of freedom. In some instances, slaves initiated the process but were unable to come up with the agreed-upon amount of money. Such was the case of a teen-aged *mulata* named María (1579), whose owner, Catalina Hernández, notarized a promise of freedom to be fulfilled if María paid her 200 ducados within the next five months. María was unable to come up with the money. She resurfaced in another *protocolo notarial* when Catalina Hernández sold her for 300 ducados.[61]

Horros were a minority among blacks. In the 1560s, 10 to 15 percent of the free population consisted of black *horros*. Very few *horros* lived in the city center because they were intentionally segregated into particular areas and neighbor-hoods such as Campeche, which was given that name because it also housed in-digenous people from the Yucatan and their descendants. A 1582 military census in Havana included twenty-five free black men, who represented 7.5 percent of all men listed. Among those *horros*, two, Francisco and Villalobos Hernando, are identified as Biafaras and one, Alonso de Aguilar, as a mulatto.[62]

Women were far more likely to earn their freedom through self-purchase and to be manumitted by their owners *por gracia*, without having to pay. That is why most *horros* were female. Statistics for Havana for the period 1601–1610 show that almost 75 percent of those who purchased their freedom were women. For one thing, slave women had many more opportunities to be hired out and to earn and save money for their self-purchase. The Spanish word *ahorrar* (to save money) derives from *horro*. For another, masters tended to manumit women more often than men. Manumission records demonstrate that women outnum-bered men by a 2.5:1 ratio in cases of manumission *por gracia*. The one exception to this was in the mining town of El Cobre, where there were more male than female *horros*. It appears that some masters who had long-term relations with fe-male slaves who produced mulatto offspring were willing to free their children, who by law inherited the status of their mothers.[63]

Law established that slaves could neither own slaves nor represent them-selves in legal transactions. The curious case of a 35-year-old *mulata* from New Spain named Francisca de Miranda demonstrates that at least in her case it was possible to be master and slave at the same time. In or around 1583, Diego de Lara purchased two slaves, Catalina de Fonseca, aged four to six years old, and another Catalina, a woman in her twenties of Bioho ethnicity (one document identifies her as Angolan). Two years later, the truth about that purchase and Francisca de Miranda's status was revealed through a web of interrelated trans-actions registered in Havana's *protocolos notariales*.

One of these documents, dated September 1585, certifies that a man named Diego de Miranda freed his and Francisca's three-year-old mulatto child, Martín, "because he was born in my house and I am very fond of him and love him because Francisca de Miranda, a free black woman, has given me a little black girl named Catalina de Fonseca; she is six years old, more or less." As it turned out, de Lara had stood as the front owner of those two slaves over whom Francisca claimed ownership. In another notarized transaction, we learn that Francisca was actually de Lara's slave until he formally freed her in exchange for a 20- or 22-year-old slave named Catalina valued at 230 ducados and for her promise to pay the balance of her exceedingly high *coartación* valuation of 500 ducados within twelve months. A man named Juan Cabrera guaranteed her promise to pay.[64] This web of documents speaks to the complexity of self-purchase and to Francisca de Miranda's extraordinary quest for freedom, her resourcefulness, her ability to earn money while enslaved, and her keen understanding of the legal system and ways to manipulate it. They also leave many unanswered questions. What or who brought her from Mexico? What type of relation did she have with Diego de Miranda? And how did Catalina de Fonseca end up in her possession?

Another fascinating case of slave ownership by a free black woman was that of Beatriz Nizarda. In 1561, Beatriz requested a land grant from the cabildo with the intention of establishing a farm. Since she requested it by herself, it is almost certain that she was not married at the time. The cabildo denied her petition and encouraged her to apply for a different plot of land "where the other black *horros* live." Almost twenty years later, she and her husband Diego de Rojas surface in official records, this time to notarize their sale of a Congo slave named Damián. The couple owned a farm that included pig pens. Perhaps in need of cash, they sold their 27-year-old Congo slave. These documents shed much light on spatial segregation in Havana and the steps *horros* took to acquire farmland. They also point to commercial interactions that tied together women and men, *horros* and slaves, and blacks, whites, and indigenous people.[65]

While freed women like Francisca de Miranda and Beatriz Nizarda were no longer subjected to the legal and social restrictions of slavery, they still endured the legal and social limitations that women of all races faced, particularly if they were married. Their experiences offer extraordinary glimpses of the convergence of status and gender discrimination. Another free black woman, Margarita de Angola, was married to Simón de Angola, who was enslaved at the time. Although Simón had a lower status than Margarita, she, as a married woman, could not engage in any legal transaction or represent herself in civil or criminal judicial matters. In 1641, in order for Margarita to conduct her own legal affairs, Simón had to authorize her through a notarized statement. Because he was a slave, however, he in turn had had to seek his owner Ana María de Jaén's notarized authorization. The great paradox of Margarita's story is that when she got married she lost some of the rights she had earned when she became a free woman. Ana María de Jaén herself must have been either single or a widow, otherwise she would have had to seek her husband's permission to empower Simón to authorize Margarita to collect debts owed to her and represent herself in judicial matters.[66]

In some cases, former slaves established *cabildos de nación*, social and religious organizations constructed around common ethnicities. The first such cabildo was formed in Santiago in 1535. The first Afro-Cuban cabildo in Havana, Nuestra Señora de los Remedios, was organized by free Zape blacks in 1568.[67]

Spaniards and white Cubans viewed free blacks with suspicion. A 1527 proposal asked that they be deported from Cuba; thirty years later, another proposal sought to ban them altogether from Havana. Multiple laws and ordinances were intended to limit their freedom and range of activities. To reduce their numbers and to discourage slaves from seeking their freedom, free blacks were charged a special head tax. Male *horros* were not allowed to wear capes and hoods or to carry weapons.[68]

Free black and mulatto women were particularly targeted in order to limit their visibility and restrict manifestations of their sexuality. White society perceived them as sensuous seductresses who had loose sexual mores and were endowed with boundless libido. To curb the mobility of free black women, Havana's cabildo issued ordinances that banned them from selling a variety of produce and prepared foods, including fritters, crabs, oranges, and bananas, and prohibited the sale of portable wooden tables known as *tabancos* that were used to sell fruit, seafood, and fritters in the streets. The ban specifically alluded to eradicating street-vending activities by black women "as they do in their homelands." Blacks were prosecuted for selling cassava bread because of the assumption that they were peddling stolen merchandise. If *horras* were caught, they were fined ten gold pesos. Laundresses were often charged and punished for overcharging their clients and for stealing from sailors and other visitors. Havana's cabildo took the extreme measure of voting in 1557 to remove all *horras* from the city "because they are harmful to the republic." Since the Church associated the mobility and visibility of *horras* and slave women with immorality, it too sought to restrict their activities. The 1681 synod reminded civil authorities of a 1678 royal order that banned them from being outdoors after sunset in order "to avoid sins and abominations."[69]

Other restrictions sought to limit the ostentatious dress attributed to free black women by prohibiting them from wearing jewels and luxurious clothing. A 1551 decree barred black and mulatto women, both free and slave, from wearing silk and pearls. There was one exemption, however. A local ordinance from 1571 allowed free black and mulatto women who were married to white men to wear gold and pearl earrings, gold necklaces, and dresses with velvet trimmings.[70]

Because they coexisted with other racial and ethnic groups, black and mulatto women became the sexual partners of white and *mestizo* men. These relationships ranged from exploitative—often violent—casual sexual encounters to long-term cohabitation that was marked by mutual affection but rarely led to marriage or the recognition of the children white fathers sired. Marriage between black women and white men was rare and the reverse combination was out of the question. Havana marriage records for the 1586–1622 period include thirty-five cases of marriage between black or mulatto women and white men, a rate of only one per year. Eight out of the thirty-five brides were registered as *mulatas*. One, named Melchora de los Reyes, from Sanlúcar, Spain, married a man named Alonso Rodríguez from Asturias.[71]

The predominance of Eurasian male ancestors is confirmed by studies of the Y-chromosomes of Cuba's current population, which show an average 80 percent white genetic heritage and 20 percent African. In contrast, mitochondrial DNA studies, which are used to determine female ancestry, show a dominant proportion of African ancestry (45 percent), twice the percentage of ancestry of European background.[72]

Early Cuban society was forged in a crucible of conflict, where people of different races, ethnicities, and national origins interacted and clashed, often violently, producing a multiethnic society. Interracial unions resulting in mulatto and *mestizo* offspring further complicated the structure of creole society. Different social hierarchies coexisted, some codified through legislation, others resulting from ancestral beliefs and practices.

While law and elite white settlers imposed a dominant racial hierarchy (*españoles, mestizos,* Amerindians, mulattos, and blacks), a caste system (*principales,* white and *mestizo* laborers, free blacks and mulattos, *encomendados,* and indigenous, mulatto and black slaves), and the beginnings of a social class structure, individuals in almost every category sought to shake or escape—

even destroy—the official social hierarchy. Common white men and women aspired to upward mobility through marriage and business activities (both licit and illicit), members of the indigenous elite sought to protect what was left of their status by collaborating (sometimes reluctantly) with white *encomenderos*, *mestizos* sought to erase distinctions with whites through marriage to white partners and education, free blacks and mulattos distanced themselves from slaves, and maroon slave leaders assumed the title and roles of African kings.

6 ❧

The Cuban *Ajiaco*

Soy un ajiaco de contradicciones.
I have mixed feelings about everything.
Name your *tema*, I'll hedge;
name your *cerca*, I'll straddle it like a *cubano*.
I have mixed feelings about everything.
Soy un ajiaco de contradicciones.

GUSTAVO PÉREZ-FIRMAT

The real history of Cuba is the history of its intermeshed transculturations. First
came the transculturation of the paleolithic Indian to the neolithic. . . . Then the
transculturation of an unbroken stream of white immigrants. . . . Then at the same
time there was going on the transculturation of a steady stream of African Negroes.

FERNANDO ORTIZ

This chapter explores the emergence and evolution of distinctly Cuban creole
cultures, what anthropologist Fernando Ortiz aptly likened to a slow-cooking
ajiaco (traditional Cuban stew). The *ajiaco* metaphor, which Ortiz introduced
in 1939, is an insightful way to describe Cuba's cultural formation, a process
whereby Amerindian, European, and African ingredients blended to form new
hybrid cultures.[1] Unlike the melting pot metaphor of the United States or the
mosaic metaphor of Canada, the *ajiaco* does not mean melting and amalgamat-
ing into the dominant culture or having distinct cultures coexist side by side.
The Cuban stew simmered slowly. Its meats, tubers, and other ingredients in-
fused each other to create a national dish, which, like Cuban culture, retained a
variety of discernible individual flavors, aromas, colors, and textures.

That *ajiaco*, I argue, also serves as an allegory for Cuba's conquest and early
colonization. This was the recipe: indigenous *yuca* paste and cornmeal were

violently stirred and heated to the point of virtual evaporation. Only a reduction (pun intended) remained, along with other autochthonous tubers and pun-
gent *ají* peppers. Conquistadores and colonizers tossed in pork, beef, garlic,
and onions, among other ingredients. With reluctance, they ate *yuca* bread as
substitute for wheat bread and acquired a taste for guava and pineapple juice,
fresh or fermented. Soon thereafter, African slaves were forcibly transplanted
by the tens of thousands, a bitter experience that paradoxically sweetened the
slow-boiling stew with the ripe plantains and yams they added to the stew.

Ortiz's most impactful intellectual contribution is the concept of transculturation, which he defined as the cultural phenomena that result from "extremely
complex transmutations of culture" that occur when different ethnic groups come
into contact with each other. While transculturation was not exclusive to Cuba, the
island's multiethnic population and other historical circumstances, Ortiz and others posit, were particularly propitious for such complex cultural developments.[2]

The scholarship on early cultural encounters in the Caribbean has demonstrated that peoples of the three primary cultural roots were themselves products of centuries-long processes of cultural hybridization. Cuba's Amerindian
cultures were the result of multiple processes of transculturation that included
the importation and use of gold ornamentation crafted in South America and
obsidian blades of Maya origin, keeping monkeys and other exotic pets, and
copying styles of pottery and ornamentation from other indigenous groups.
Moreover, conquistadores and settlers fought against, enslaved, and interacted
with Amerindians from Florida, the Yucatan, and neighboring islands, whose
cultures differed from that of the Tainos.

Spanish conquistadores and settlers came from a nation "fashioned by many
hands," as writer Carlos Fuentes described it: "Iberians and Celts, Greeks and
Phoenicians, Carthaginians, Romans, and Goths, Arabs and Jews."[3] Most hailed
from Andalusia, the theater of the latter phases of the *reconquista* and the most
culturally syncretic region of Spain. And African cultural contributions came
from many ethnicities and a broad range of regions. While there were significant
cultural variations among West African ethnic groups, linguists such as Joseph
H. Greenberg have recognized that most West African languages were closely
related; they belonged to a broad family of languages known as Niger-Congo.
The same is true for religion. West Africans shared a religious system in which
different ethnic groups recognized equivalent deities and spirits, albeit with
different names and some variations. Moreover, as David Wheat has recently
highlighted, parts of West Africa such as Luanda and islands such as the Cape
Verde Islands were places where cultural hybridization (as well as racial mix-

ture) took place because of the coexistence and interactions among Portuguese settlers and West Africans. This produced what Wheat calls "Luso-Africans."[4] Further transculturation occurred inside the putrid hulls of slave ships and the process continued in plantation settings, on the wharfs of Havana, and even in *encomienda* villages.

Despite ethnic and regional variations, first-generation African-born slaves and their descendants shared common aspects of West African culture and they strove to retain some of them, such as monarchical tribal systems, polyrhythmic music, peasant socioeconomic structures, and the belief that spirits inhabited some inanimate objects and manifested themselves in natural phenomena. In some cases, freed blacks of the same ethnic background maintained a degree of ethnic identity and solidarity, as manifested through the formation of lay religious and ethnic-specific social organizations known as *cabildos de nación*. This preference to remain connected with Africans of the same or related ethnicities was even evident among runaways, who escaped and regrouped along ethnic lines. Marriage patterns among slaves and *horros* also evidenced high rates of endogamy; over 60 percent of individuals from these two groups married someone from the same African region. Ethnic identity remained important even at the time of death. Such was the case with a Terra Nova *horro* from the Bight of Benin named Francisco de Rojas. When he had his will drafted and notarized as he faced death in the summer of 1579, his sense of ethnic identity or perhaps his ancestral belief in being interred next to kin drove him to specify that he wanted to be buried in Havana's main church "in the tomb of blacks from Terranoba."[5]

This chapter discusses several specific instances of transculturation during the sixteenth and seventeenth centuries. It explores transculturation in diet, music, dress, and popular religiosity. It also brings to life actual men, women, and children who contributed to various forms of transculturation: an unnamed black man buried at an *encomienda* village cemetery; a commander of el Castillo de la Real Fuerza who habitually ate fried foods sold by black street vendors; Paula de Eguiluz, a slave woman who owned an enviable wardrobe; and the legendary Juan Moreno and the Hoyos brothers, to whom la Virgen de la Caridad del Cobre first appeared.

Transculturation and *Mestizaje* at an *Encomienda* Village

In the second half of the 1980s, Cuban scholars led by Guarch Delmonte found one of the island's richest and most revealing archaeological sites, a multiethnic cemetery at El Chorro de Maíta in Holguín Province. A total of 133 bodies have since been identified. It dates across a span of over two centuries, including the last century of the pre-Columbian era and the first fifty years of European presence. Originally, El Chorro de Maíta was a Taino village of several hundred inhabitants, but Spanish settlers subjugated them and forced them to work under the *encomienda* system. The site offers multiple insights onto the interactions of indigenous inhabitants with other racial and ethnic groups and supports the contention that Taino culture contributed to many areas of Cuban culture, including diet, art, and social structure.[6]

The transformation of villages into labor camps brought about many demographic and cultural changes. These have been meticulously studied by archaeologist Roberto Valcárcel Rojas and his colleagues. Archaeological evidence points to a massive and rapid collapse of the indigenous population and an increasingly complex ethnic composition. To supplement the shrinking labor pool, Spaniards forcibly imported Yucatecan workers, as evidenced by a small number of bodies that show traces of ritual cranial deformation and dental modification, as practiced in regions of Mesoamerica.

The presence of Europeans was also evident. Biologically, it was reflected in the remains of two people with partial European ancestry, one a *mestizo*, the other a mulatto. The material goods Europeans brought to the village are evidenced in fragments of ceramic olive oil jars and small brass objects such as lace tags. European coins minted between 1505 and 1558 were also found at the site.[7]

The El Chorro de Maíta site is rich in evidence of cultural diffusion and transculturation. This is reflected, for example, in changes in burial practices. The bodies buried in the earlier Taino tradition were in a flexed position. Later burials (about 10 percent of the cases) show signs of Christian influence, manifested in bodies in a stretched position with the arms crossed over the chest. Two of the bodies found at El Chorro de Maíta provide extraordinary glimpses of the cultural interactions that took place there during the first half of the sixteenth century. One is the remains of a Taino woman, who was buried dressed in European-style clothing with European-manufactured brass ornaments. She also wore ornaments of gold and gold-and-copper alloy, artifacts that had been imported from South America or fashioned after South American jewels. The latter suggest that she was of high social status. Her clothing and the fact that she was buried in a Christian fashion strongly suggest that she was the wife (or concubine) of a Spaniard, perhaps the village *encomendero*. The other body belonged to a man of African origin, a slave or perhaps a servant to the *encomendero* or some other Spaniard. Like the Taino woman of high social standing, he appears to have been at least superficially Christianized. His body was buried lying fully

Figure 6.1. Cemetery at El Chorro de Maíta. On the left are the skeletal remains of an African man buried in an extended position with arms crossed above his chest. Photograph by Roberto Valcárcel Rojas. Source: Roberto Valcárcel Rojas, *Archaeology of Early Colonial Interaction at El Chorro de Maíta, Cuba* (Gainesville: University Press of Florida, 2016), 247. Reprinted courtesy of the University Press of Florida.

stretched out with his arms crossed over his chest and he was clad in European-style garb, of which only the European-manufactured brass ornamentation has survived. Transculturation is also evident in other burial goods found at the site, such as indigenous-made ceramic objects (vases and jars) in a European style.[8]

El Chorro de Maíta thus was a microcosm of the biological and cultural interactions of Europeans, Africans, and Amerindians from the Caribbean and from Mesoamerica. They lived and worked together, each according to their social rank. They had sexual relations with and perhaps even married individuals from other racial groups, with whom they had children of different hues. Their roles and places in El Chorro de Maíta's hybrid social structure followed them to the grave, as attested by the significant differences in body position, clothing and ornamentation, and food and other provisions for the afterlife.

"*A falta de pan, casabe*"

Changing culinary practices and diets provide valuable information about how the contributions of Spanish settlers, indigenous peoples, and African slaves transformed each other. The Amerindian diet consisted of *yuca*, maize, beans, other vegetables and fruits, and fish, turtles, and iguanas. Spaniards brought dietary tastes and ingredients of their own, mainly an Andalusian menu that was largely influenced by Mediterranean and Moorish cuisine. Import records include a wide variety of Mediterranean products that were brought to Cuba. High on the list of imports were wine and wheat flour, neither of which could be viably produced in the tropical setting. Other imported foodstuffs included codfish, cheese, raisins, nuts and berries of various kinds, olives and olive oil, figs, capers, and spices such as cinnamon, cloves, cumin, and oregano. Some of those imports came in as contraband. In 1610, a single smuggling vessel brought in 30,000 cheeses, most likely from the Netherlands. This was more than enough to provide one unit to every person on the island.[9] Those imports satisfied those who preferred Spanish culinary traditions, but they were too expensive for the general population

Figure 6.2. Indigenous ceramic jar modeled after a European form, excavated from El Porvenir Site, Yaguajay, Sancti Spíritus Province. Photograph by Roberto Valcárcel Rojas. Source: Roberto Valcárcel Rojas, *Archaeology of Early Colonial Interactions at El Chorro de Maíta, Cuba* (Gainesville: University Press of Florida, 2016), 71. Reprinted courtesy of University Press of Florida.

Explorers, conquerors, and settlers brought a wide array of domesticated animals that expanded food options and made the diet richer in animal protein with an assortment of new meats, including beef, pork, poultry, and goat meat. As evidenced by research conducted in Hispaniola by Kathleen Deagan, consumption of small pre-Columbian mammals by Amerindians dropped significantly, in large measure due to the displacement of indigenous men away from hunting activities to conscripted labor in mining and agriculture. Cow meat, which was more abundant, cost 25 to 50 percent less than pork. Cows were so plentiful that hunters routinely left the animals to rot after removing their valuable hides. The meat of bulls was deemed unhealthy, though.[10]

Wine was a vital consumer good and was a necessity for the Catholic Eucharist. While some was imported, much of it had to be produced locally by fermenting a variety of vegetables and fruits—maize and pineapples, for example. Wine was sold in different ways; it could be bought from free black peddlers or in taverns. Itinerant sellers from the Canary Islands hawked wine and molasses-derived *aguardiente* in rural areas. Havana alone had fifty taverns in 1570 and around eighty during the 1670s and 1680s. Cabildo ordinances limited the sale of wine to whites; black and mulatto tavern keepers could not sell to other blacks, regardless of their status, or to Amerindians.[11]

The punishing climate and exuberant exotic flora of the tropical context forced Spaniards to accept some aspects of indigenous material culture. Early settlers lived in palm-thatched *bohíos* and many slept in hammocks. Not a few became habituated to tobacco in its various forms. Ecclesiastical authorities also raised complaints of settlers keeping the bones of their dead relatives in their houses, a Taino practice.[12] Spaniards had no option but to embrace foods that were alien to their palate. Cassava bread made from *yuca* became an unwelcome substitute for wheat bread, which cost twice as much. This is the origin of the saying still used by Cubans to express resignation: "*a falta de pan, casabe*" (If there is no bread, cassava cakes shall suffice). Gradually, as the black population expanded, plantains displaced cassava bread. While cassava bread never made it to Spain, *yuca* became a staple of the African diet. The Taino way of planting *yuca* in soil mounds was also transplanted to Africa.

Cuba's Deep Africanity

Fernando Ortiz, Antonio Benítez-Rojo, Pedro Pérez-Sarduy, Nancy Morejón, and other Cuban intellectuals have highlighted the centrality of African cultural traits in Cuba, where they permeate virtually every facet of the island's culture. These go far beyond music and dance and include religion, diet, orality, the quintessentially Cuban type of humor known as *choteo*, speech patterns, gregariousness, and rebelliousness. Ortiz argued that elements of the culture that are deemed to be most authentically and essentially Cuban stem from the contributions of Afro-Cubans.[13] More recently, Benítez-Rojo asserted that African cultural influences in Cuba—which racially is one of the least African nations of the Caribbean—are stronger than almost everywhere else in the region: "Cuban religious beliefs, music, dance, painting, literature, and folklore show an African influence unequaled in any other Antillean nation except Haiti." He underscored the fact that culture is independent from race, adding that "even those who can trace back their four grandparents to European provinces know that their cultural mother, their great mother, originates in Africa." The poet Nancy Morejón also emphasizes the depth of African cultural contributions. "The cadenced specificity of the Spanish of Cuba," she wrote, "has much of the syncopation of our rhythms of African origin; of our biting sense of humor, the *choteo*; and of our ingenious ability to create unexpected metaphors, such as referring to a beer carton as a 'lizards' cage.'"[14]

Historian David Wheat has looked at another aspect of African contributions, arguing that Africans and their descendants throughout the early modern circum-Caribbean were not only the majority of the population but also did the bulk of agricultural work and thus were the region's true colonizers. The major problem with that thesis is that as subordinates of white colonials, Africans and their descendants had very limited power, in large measure because local authorities exerted control over the types of work they could do, where they could live, and even how they should dress.[15]

African cultures also contributed to the simmering *ajiaco* through cuisine, religious practices and beliefs, and sexual mores in port cities and interior towns, in quarries and on wharfs, on plantations and *palenques*, in churches, in taverns, on merchant ships, and in *encomienda* villages. Although black Cubans made Spanish their lingua franca, they retained West African vocabularies, cadences, intonations, and sentence structures. And although slaves were sprinkled with holy water when they arrived, they managed to maintain their animistic and polytheistic beliefs and continued to practice divination and the cult to their ancestors. They also concocted potions and cast spells. Afro-Cubans appeared to venerate clay and wooden images of the Virgin Mary and Catholic saints such as Santa Bárbara, the martyred red-clad patron saint of artillerymen, but in many instances, were actually communicating with, worshiping, and offering sacrifices to syncretic Afro-Cuban gods like Ochún and Changó.

The Fort Commander and the Street Vendor

In 1580, Captain Melchor Sardo de Arana arrived in Havana to take charge as *alcaide* of el Castillo de la Real Fuerza. The fort, which had just been finished, housed a 50-man garrison. Sardo de Arana moved into the fort with his wife and mother-in-law, a domestic arrangement that irritated Captain-General Gabriel de Luján. The captain-general also complained about Sardo de Arana's behavior, accusing him of neglecting his responsibilities and engaging, against the law, in lucrative commercial ventures. *Protocolo* records document his sales of imported goods (most likely contraband) to local merchants. According to witnesses who testified against him, on one occasion, at the house of a fellow officer, he dressed up in a petticoat and a turban and performed a sketch in which he mimicked a street prostitute. His behavior in public also earned him censure; reportedly, he was seen wearing a "negligee" while buying meat at the market.[16]

During his *juicio de residencia*, Sardo de Arana was accused of behaving like a "low person" who had compromised the dignity of his office by, among other things, buying a fried plantain (the staple of the Afro-Cuban diet) from a woman street vendor (an African-derived practice). He ate it right then and there, continued the *residenciador*, and he burned his tongue.[17] The implicit accusation was that he had ceased to be a Spaniard and had become something else; he had become *aplatanado* (banana-like), as generations of creolized Spaniards would continue to be for centuries.

From Silk Gowns to a Penitential Garb

Paula, the daughter of a Biafara woman, was born in Santo Domingo in 1590 or 1591. At the age of thirteen, her owner gave her to another man, named Yñigo Otaco, to cancel a debt. Otaco took her to Puerto Rico to serve him as a domestic slave and a sexual companion. His wife became jealous of the young black woman and forced him to get rid of her. Paula ended up in Cuba, where she became the property of one of Cuba's wealthiest and most powerful men, Juan de Eguiluz, the administrator of the copper mines of El Cobre. He took her in as his concubine, had three children with her, and showered her with gifts that included jewelry and fine dresses and accessories. She was suspected of securing de Eguiluz's lust and love by means of *brujería* (witchcraft), using a love potion or a spell.[18]

Paula de Eguiluz dressed like a European aristocrat, something that caused consternation and envy because as a black slave she was not supposed to dress that way; it was actually against the law. She came to own what must have been one of the most luxurious collections of fine clothing on the island. Her wardrobe included eight skirts in five different colors, one of which was made of Mediter-ranean blue damask with eleven trimmings of green and white silk; three full dresses, among them a yellow and white dress with silver cords; four petticoats; seven blouses, two of them made of fine Dutch linen; four corsets; a polychro-matic assortment of scarfs and veils; and a belt with a silver-plated buckle that was described as a *Cinto de San Agustín* (an Augustinian belt). This last item is intriguing and makes one wonder how she acquired it and what she knew about it. *Cintos de San Agustín* were distinctive belts granted exclusively to members of the Spanish religious Cofradía del Cinto de San Agustín; bearers of such belts were given two extraordinary plenary indulgences that absolved them from any sin, one committed during life, the other in purgatory.[19] Given Paula's savviness and interest in and knowledge of religions, it is likely that she acquired the belt knowingly and probably believed that it would protect her in some way.

Paula's entire world, including her status and lifestyle and her relative free-dom, came tumbling down when on May 13, 1624, Inquisition commissars ar-rested her, accusing her of practicing *brujería*, engaging in incest, having sex with demons, and a host of other sacrilegious actions. They placed her on a vessel bound for Cartagena, the see of the Inquisition that had jurisdiction over Cuba. She was thrown into a secret dungeon and subjected to horrific interroga-tions. Her forced confessions of 1624 and 1633 offer a fascinating window onto her life, her beliefs, and how she blended religious, healing, and match-making powers from three different traditions, a veritable *ajiaco*: indigenous Cuban, European by way of the Canary Islands, and West African ingredients.[20]

According to Paula's confession, an indigenous man known as el Indio Do-mingo taught her how to prepare herbal liquid concoctions that she splashed on her body to attract whichever man she wanted to capture romantically. In her testimony, she referred to two herbs from Cuba's Amerindian pharmacopeia, *hierba del tostón* (*Boerhavia erected L.*) and *hierba de curia* (*Justicia pectoralis*), both of which are still used on the island for medicinal purposes. Nearly four centuries after Paula de Eguiluz learned about its powers, *hierba de curia* is still used by some Cubans as an aphrodisiac.[21]

During her travels to Havana, Paula spent time with Afro-Cuban women who taught her to make amulets for the purpose of attracting and charming men. She testified that she had learned from a slave woman named María how to make an amulet to bind the love of a man. To make it, she put pieces of *hierba de curia* root and hair from the desired man into a small bag. She confessed to having used one such amulet to romantically tie a young white man named Pedro. María's recipe combined the indigenous herbal tradition of Cuba with West African practices of using hair, nails, and even human remains to make amulets that had the power to activate sexual attraction. The Inquisition also accused a black man of Havana named Antón, who was of the Carabalí nation, of prescribing herbs "so that men want and love women in a dishonest way."[22]

Paula's love charms included the practices of yet another cultural tradition: European witchcraft, as compiled in manuscript texts known as *Clavicula Salomonis* (Key of Solomon), which was inaccurately attributed to the author of the Book of Proverbs. Daniel Bellingrad and Bernd-Christian Otto point to these texts as emblematic of "the transcultural nature of 'Western Learned Magic.'" Among many other incantations, the *Clavicula Salomonis* offered spells to bind a woman's husband and to guarantee his fidelity. According to one witness, Paula cast such spells. In one case, she requested a piece of the man's underwear; four days later, she brought it back tied into knots and pierced through by seven pins. Apparently it did not work; the witness described the whole affair as a fraud.[23]

When Paula was first convicted in 1624, she was sentenced to 200 lashes, the same number inflicted upon second-offender runaway slaves in Cuba. She also was forced to wear a humiliating penitential garb made of coarse cloth, not too dissimilar from those that were distributed to slaves in the wintertime. Her wardrobe, once the envy of Havana, had been reduced to one paltry piece.[24]

The Ginés Sisters Band

Music, which brought together singers and instrument players from different backgrounds, was fertile ground for transculturation. Cuba's most acclaimed musical group of the 1580s and 1590s was an *ajiaco* of sound and movement in which European melodies tamed African rhythms as Spanish and Taino instruments dueled with each other. According to a 1598 description, the band included Pedro Almanza, a violinist from Málaga; Jácome de Viceira, a Portuguese *zampoña* (a type of flute) player; Pascual de Ochoa, a *sevillano* who played the violoncello; and vocalist and band leader Micaela Ginés, a master of the *vihuela*, a Renaissance-era string instrument. They were accompanied by Andalusian women who clacked castanets as *mestizo* musicians stroked *güiros* that wept monotonously, as if channeling the sadness of the vanishing Tainos.[25]

Micaela and her sister Teodora were free black women who had been born in Hispaniola. Some scholars say that the sisters composed what some believe was the first song in the Cuban genre known as *son*. First transcribed in the nineteenth century, the song was entitled "Son de Ma' Teodora."

¿Dónde está la Ma' Teodora? (Where is Mom Teodora?)
Rajando la leña está (She's out splitting wood)
¿Con su palo y su bandola? (With her stick and her mandolin?)
Rajando la leña está (She's out splitting wood)
¿Dónde está que no la veo? (Where is she, that I don't see her?)
Rajando la leña está (She's out splitting wood)
Rajando la leña está (She's out splitting wood)
Rajando la leña está (She's out splitting wood)[26]

. . . .

Renowned writer and scholar Alejo Carpentier studied Micaela's band and this particular song in an effort to trace its multicultural roots. There was a clear dominance of European instruments in the band, namely strings and a rustic flute. While African instruments, such as drums, are not mentioned, Carpentier argued that through the action of *rasguear* (strumming), stringed instruments were transformed into voices of percussion. Moreoever, Ma' Teodora's son mentions the *palo* (a long wooden stick stumped on the ground to mark rhythm, a practice tied to West African fertility rites). Also mentioned are *güiros* (rasping gourds of Taino origin) and castanets; along with rhythmic hand-clapping and shoe-tapping, similar to what later came to be known as flamenco, the sounds produced would have complex polyrhythms characteristic of West African music.[27]

Carpentier saw "Son de Ma' Teodora" as a derivation of a type of Spanish song known as *romance extremeño* but noted that it incorporated the ubiquitous West African antiphonal model of call and response, followed by multiple repetitions of the chorus: "*Rajando la leña está*" (She is out splitting wood), slang for singing and dancing.[28]

According to contemporary sources, Micaela's band was formed in Santiago, where it played at the main church. Later it moved to Havana, but Teodora apparently stayed behind. Their music was in very high demand, and when the group resettled in Havana, the cabildo paid them to perform in churches and in special processions such as those that celebrated Corpus Christi Day and St. Christopher's Day. They were so heavily booked that anyone who wanted to hire them had to entice them with bonuses that included transportation, food and wine, and even some food to take home.[29]

Cultural diffusion and transculturation were Atlantic-wide, bidirectional phenomena. Zoila Lapique Becali has studied the movement of Cuban syncretic music and dance to Europe. Using references from Miguel de Cervantes's works, she traced the trajectory of two Caribbean genres to Spain and beyond. One of the songs Cervantes referred to begins:

> *Esta Indiana amulatada,* (This mulatto-hued American woman,)
> *de quien la fama pregona* (who is credited with)
> *que ha hecho más sacrilegios* (partaking in more sacrileges)
> *e insultos que hizo Aroba* (and insulting more people than Aroba ever did)[30]

The song's lyrics mention the musical genre *zambapalo* ("the haughty *zamba-palo*"), which the Royal Academy of the Spanish Language defines as a "grotesque dance brought to Spain from the Indias Occidentales, used in Spain during the XVI and XVII centuries." Philip II banned that genre, which *flota* crewmen had brought to Spain. A related American genre, the *zarabanda*, was tamer and slower paced. There is documentation that Spanish performers danced it, accompanied by guitars and castanets, to entertain the French court.[31]

Micaela Ginés, Emilio Bacardí claimed, lived a long life, probably up to the mid-1600s. In her old age, she was hunched and walked with a cane but always remained close to the *vihuela* that made her Cuba's first celebrity musician.[32]

Juan Moreno, the Hoyos Brothers, and the Mulatto Virgin

A culturally *mestizo* and mulatto people created the need for a mixed-race patron saint. Three different deities—one Taino, one brought from Illescas, Spain, and one from West Africa—blended through transculturation to produce new and different divine manifestations that eventually became central components of Cuban Catholicism and African-derived Santería.

One of those three root divinities/deities is la Virgen de la Caridad, patroness of the town of Illescas, located twenty miles north of Toledo. According to Catholic tradition, the first image of la Virgen de la Caridad was commissioned by the Apostle Luke and was brought to Spain in the first century. Extant images represent a dark-hued Virgin Mary in the Romanesque tradition of black virgin images. She is dressed in golden garb and is holding a much-lighter-skinned baby Jesus. From Illescas, the veneration of la Virgen de la Caridad spread to other parts of Spain, notably to the Atlantic port city of Sanlúcar.

Meanwhile, over 4,000 miles away, the Tainos of the Greater Antilles worshiped the female goddess Atabey, one of their two primary deities (the other was Yaya, the god of creation). She was an animistic representation of fertility,

Figure 6.3. *Nuestra Señora de la Caridad del Cobre*, oil painting by an unknown artist, circa 1750. Unlike later renditions, this representation of la Virgen de la Caridad del Cobre is true to the original story, which includes a ten-year-old black child, Juan Moreno, and two Amerindian brothers, Rodrigo and Juan de Hoyos. The virgin has dark skin and is holding a white baby Jesus. Reprinted courtesy of Roberto Ramos.

love, and bodies of water, including rivers and the ocean. According to Antonio Benítez-Rojo, Atabey was the product of cultural syncretism that originated in the Orinoco Basin. Taino representations of Atabey portray a nude female body with prominent genitalia. There are some parallels between Atabey and the Virgin Mary. Both were credited with conceiving and giving birth to major deities without sexual intercourse. Atabey gave birth to twins; one was Yucahú, the highly venerated spirit of fertility for *yuca*, the Tainos' bread of life. Yucahú's virgin mother was also the deity of the sacrifice of virgin males.[33]

Other deities originated from different African religious traditions. One was Kianda, the goddess of the sea, an Angolan deity that had power over the ocean and its creatures and protected fishermen. It was similar to Mama Chola or Chola Wengue, whom Congo-Bantu slaves venerated as the spirit of rivers, sexuality, and beauty. Another was Oshun of the Yoruba tradition, brought by slaves from present-day Nigeria, who arrived in large numbers beginning in the 1700s and became predominant in western Cuba. Oshun was the most important among a handful of female deities in the Yoruba pantheon. Like Atabey, she was the spirit of rivers and of fresh and ocean water. But in contrast to the Virgin Mary, she was neither virginal nor chaste. She was credited with an insatiable sexual appetite and with having numerous affairs with both gods and demigods, among them the polygamous Shango, the red-clad god of thunder and lightning. In West Africa, Oshun was venerated as the goddess of fertility, love, passion, pleasure, sexuality, and luxury. She shared many of these attributes with Mama Chola.[34]

The veneration of la Virgen de la Caridad de Illescas began in Cuba in 1597, when Captain Francisco Sánchez de Moya imported an image of the patroness of his hometown. Philip II had commissioned the artillery captain to protect Cuba's copper mines from pirate attacks and erect a church in their vicinity.[35] What began as a purely Spanish Catholic representation of the Virgin Mary was transformed when Tainos and Africans projected their religious beliefs and practices onto the Virgin. When Tainos were exposed to Catholic doctrine, they naturally connected the Virgin Mary to their own virgin goddess, Atabey. Tainos actually viewed Catholic images the way they saw their own *zemis* (idols), as physical embodiments of actual spirits, and they often buried them in the ground just as they did their own idols. Two Taino chiefs, Cueiba and Macaca, got hold of images of the Virgin Mary and embraced them as dual Taino-Christian talismans. Because the majority of slaves who arrived from Africa in the sixteenth century were from Angola, the earliest transculturations of the Virgin are likely to have been with Kianda. The Virgin was also likely associated with Mama Chola. All three shared the trait of dark skin and yellow or gold clothes.[36]

A more formal syncretic union occurred later with the Yoruba goddess Oshun, who, like Atabey, was the spirit of rivers, bodies of water, and fertility. This transculturation, which blended Atabey, la Virgen de Illescas, and Oshun, began to crystalize in the second decade of the seventeenth century as the result of a miracle three boatmen witnessed. According to the testimony of one of them, Juan Moreno, the Virgin Mary appeared to them while they were rowing off the coast of Nipe Bay, on the island's northeast. They were caught at sea in a canoe during a storm and were saved by the Virgin, whose wooden statue appeared to them floating on the water.[37]

Both the geographical setting and the race of the three boatmen are relevant. This epiphany happened in Cuba's northeastern end, where the Taino presence had been and remained the strongest and where indigenous religious beliefs survived longer. Two of the boatmen, the Hoyos brothers, were indigenous, while the youngest of the three, ten-year-old Juan Moreno, was black—*moreno* means precisely that. Juan Moreno described the Virgin as a dark-skinned *mestiza* who was holding a light-skinned Infant Jesus. Like Atabey, the Angolan deity Kianda, and Oshun of the Yoruba tradition, the Virgin had mastery over bodies of water, which she demonstrated by calming the sea on that stormy day. This manifestation of la Virgen de la Caridad (later renamed Virgen de la Caridad del Cobre) was no longer just a Spanish Catholic saint. She had assumed a different identity and new miraculous powers, evidenced by the fact that the statue's clothes were dry when the boatmen pulled it out of the water. The story of this new transculturated Virgin did not remain static, as evidenced by its subsequent iconography. Images produced in the nineteenth century show a different racial makeup among the boatmen; one of the original Amerindians, Rodrigo, was replaced with a white man named Juan, so that each of the boatmen represented each of the nation's foundational races. To further underscore the nineteenth-century aspiration of creole unity and independence, the boatmen were now referred to as the three Juanes. Curiously, in nineteenth-century Spain, images of la Virgen de Illescas gradually developed noticeably lighter skin, as if to emphasize the growing distance between multiracial Cuba and white Spain.

While the syncretic Virgen de la Caridad del Cobre became Catholic Cuba's primary devotion and patron saint, Ochún, a parallel transculturated deity, assumed a central role in the pantheon of the syncretic religion of Santería. As slaves and their descendants purported to be worshipping la Virgen de la Caridad del Cobre, they were actually venerating Ochún. Like her African counterpart Oshun, Ochún had a special and intense sexual relation with the male deity Changó, whose Yoruba counterpart was Shango, the deity of thunder, drumming, fire, war, and virile leadership. Africans and their descendants transposed Shango (and Changó) onto Santa Bárbara, the patron saint of artillerymen. Although Changó was male and Santa Bárbara was female, they were connected because both wore red clothes and by the fact that the thunder of Changó and canons fired by artillerymen made similar sounds.

Another dark-skinned virgin, la Virgen de Regla, according to Catholic tradition had its origins in Christian northern Africa during St. Augustine of Hippo's lifetime. Its image also survived a storm on its way to southern Spain, earning la Virgen de Regla the role of patron of seamen. A statue of that Virgin was brought to Cuba in the late 1600s and placed inside a shrine in a town across the bay from Havana. The town, which had a substantial Afro-Cuban population, was eventually renamed Regla. Like la Virgen de Illescas, she was eventually syncretized with another Yoruba deity, Yemaja, patron of mariners and goddess of the oceans, resulting in the Santería deity Yemayá. All three wore dresses of blue and white, blue for the ocean and white for the waves. Like Oshun (Ochún), Yemaja (Yemayá) was married to the polygamous Shango (Changó).[38]

Sevillian Castanets and *Mudéjar* Architecture

Andalusians, who predominated among Spanish immigrants during the 1500s, contributed to Cuba's hybrid cultures in numerous ways. *Andaluces* from Seville, Sanlúcar, and elsewhere in southern Spain brought a rich cultural package when they came to Cuba. Some elements of their culture survived because so many *andaluces* came to Cuba and because of continuing commercial ties between Cuba and Seville. Southern Spain already had deeply syncretic cultures that Christians, Jews, and Muslims, as well as substantial African and African-descended populations in Seville and Cádiz, had contributed to. Andalusia's contributions to the Cuban *ajiaco* included musical instruments such as tambourines and castanets, culinary preferences such as frying food in olive oil, and popular expressions of religiosity such as wearing *nazarenos* (pointed-hood robes), which are still worn in processions in Seville. Southern Spaniards also contributed their sense of humor and penchant for hyperbole, verbosity, overstated notions of honor, a propensity for hierarchic distinctions, and a passion for thoroughbred horses. Cuban friendliness, flamboyance, and zealousness can also be partially traced to the first Andalusians who settled the island.

Linguists and students of architectural history have underscored the influence of the language and *mudéjar* (Moorish-inspired) architecture of southern Spain on the Hispanic Caribbean. Cuban Spanish borrowed characteristics of the Spanish spoken in Andalusia, such as the weak pronunciation of consonants, particularly the aspiration of consonants at the end of syllables and the aspiration of the letter *s*; *seseo* (the merged pronunciation of *c*'s and *z*'s); the use of "*ustedes*" rather than "*vosotros*" for the pronoun "you"; and ending words with "*ao*" instead of "*ado*" (*pescao* instead of *pescado*, for example).[39]

Andalusian immigrants brought the aesthetics and architectural expertise of southern Spain, which was imprinted on Havana's early colonial architecture and urban design, including narrow streets that offered protection from the sun, *mudéjar* arches and exterior balconies, *zaguanes* (roofed spaces between exterior walls and entrances to houses), and intricately laced wood ceilings known as *alfarjes*, which feature characteristic Muslim Spanish motifs such as the eight-pointed star. Convents and other buildings were adorned with blue glazed tiles that had been made in Triana, Seville, and other parts of Andalusia.[40]

The recipe for the Cuban *ajiaco* was complex. Its ingredients were both local and exotic. They included practices such as the cultivation of maize, which was indigenous to Central America, and *yuca*, which was transplanted from the Orinoco Basin; African animistic religious beliefs; and *mudéjar* architecture, itself a syncretic combination of Moorish and Iberian styles.

7 ❧

The Cockpit of Europe

Tiene el tercer Filipo, Rey de España,
la ínsula de Cuba, o Fernandina,
en estas Indias que el oceano baña,
rica de perlas y de plata fina:
aqui del Anglia, Flandes y Bretaña
á tomar vienen puerto en su marina
muchos navios á trocar por cueros
sedas y paños, y á llevar dineros.

SILVESTRE DE BALBOA

Caribbean history, conceived in international rivalry,
was reared and nurtured in an environment of power politics.

ERIC WILLIAMS

This chapter explores the roles Cuba, particularly its fortified capital, played during the sixteenth and seventeenth centuries in the defense of the expanding Spanish colonial empire. Because of its privileged geographic location, Havana was the natural hub of Spain's complex transatlantic trade and navigation system. The mainstay of that system was the transfer of massive amounts of bullion from New Spain and other gold- and silver-mining centers to Iberia. Foreign intruders who sought to wrest some of that wealth from the empire routinely committed acts of piracy against Havana and other Spanish ports. Spain responded by militarizing and fortifying its port cities, establishing a fleet system, and having coast guards and small armed fleets patrol the region to curb smuggling. While Havana was not a major production center like bullion-rich New Spain or Peru, the port city became one of the most important, and therefore most coveted, cities in the New World. Its primary roles were to service and defend trade routes and the fleets.

Although Spain insisted on maintaining a monopoly on colonization and trade in the Caribbean and beyond, other European nations challenged its claim of a *mare clausum* and sought to benefit from the riches and commercial opportunities the Americas offered. These challenges varied over time and manifested in different ways, including various forms of piracy and smuggling and eventually the formation of colonies and buccaneer enclaves in Spanish-claimed domains.

This chapter traces the complex and oftentimes chaotic interplay between war and peace in Europe and conflicts in Cuba and the Caribbean, a region historian Eric Williams aptly named "the cockpit of Europe."[1] It was a cockpit that was governed by its own set of rules: cocks fighting whoever, wherever, and whenever they wanted. It also discusses the dynamics of piracy against Cuba and how Spanish authorities and Cuban creoles protected themselves and retaliated against all forms of foreign incursion. The chapter closes with a brief discussion of the cultural ramifications of Havana's roles as a privileged commercial port and military bastion.

Throughout most of the period between the 1510s and the year 1700, Spain remained in an on again, off again state of war with France, England, the Netherlands, and other European nations, which also intermittently clashed with each other. The endless cacophony of war echoed loudly throughout the Caribbean, oftentimes more stridently than in Europe, as pirates, privateers, buccaneers, and, later, regular naval and land forces attacked Spanish vessels and Spain's colonial possessions. While war in Europe translated into bellicose actions against Cuba and other Spanish possessions, peace in Europe did not necessarily mean peace in the Caribbean. In fact, a 1559 peace treaty between France and Spain guaranteed a truce north of the Tropic of Cancer and east of the 46° W longitude but allowed the continuation of hostilities south and west of those lines. This gave rise to the concept and phrase "no peace beyond the line." Historian Richard S. Dunn expanded this idea to include a generalized disregard for European rules. "To live 'beyond the line,'" Dunn wrote, "meant more than a flouting of European treaty obligations. It meant a general flouting of European social conventions."[2]

A few definitions are in order. While they are often used interchangeably, the words pirate, privateer, corsair, and buccaneer mean different things. The term pirate is broadly applied to those who plundered vessels on the high seas and raided ports and harbors. That is the way contemporary Spaniards used the term. In its most specific definition, however, the word applies only to violent booty seekers who operated without license or sanction from a particular nation. Pirates were lawless and stateless predators.

Privateers carried out acts of piracy with special charters from European monarchs and were generally less brutal than their unlicensed counterparts. When privateers worked for stock companies such as the Dutch West India Company, investors received dividends from successful raids. Privateers operated with different degrees of loyalty and obedience to the states that granted them privateering charters. In some instances, they were treated in a way that was similar to how regular soldiers were treated and were even allowed to use royal naval vessels. But sometimes they ignored their monarchs' commands, fought in times of peace, and attacked neutral nations. Corsair means roughly the same thing as privateer but is usually applied to those the French Crown had licensed.

Buccaneers also engaged in piratical activities. They had their origins among hunters of wild cattle who settled in unpopulated, Spanish-claimed locations and made a living by selling dried and smoked meat to passing vessels. When they recognized how profitable piracy was, they converted "from butchers of cattle into butchers of men," as Philip Gosse put it.[3] They mutated into seagoing pirates and began to target port towns in Cuba and Hispaniola and Spanish ships. Buccaneers, while not fully stateless, had loose ties with their respective monarchs and generally operated with a large degree of autonomy.

European incursions against Cuba and the other Spanish islands unfolded in distinct but overlapping stages that roughly mirrored the course of Spain's conflicts with other European powers: first a French corsair phase (1521–1559), followed by a period of aggressive smuggling by English merchants (1558–1567), then by a phase of English piracy (1568–1584) and a phase of English privateering (1585–1603). Then came two periods of intense Dutch privateering (1594–1609, 1620–1648). The second half of the century was the heyday of buccaneering that targeted Spanish vessels, port cities, and even inland towns. This chapter is organized according to this periodization.

Beginning in the 1620s and 1630s, non-Spanish privateers and merchants, supported by their respective states, began to settle permanent colonies and trading posts on islands Spain had neglected. These colonization efforts spread throughout the region, from the Bahamas in the northwest to Tobago in the southeast. Likewise, but less officially, French and English buccaneers settled in places such as the island of Tortuga, the northern and western coasts of Hispaniola, and, later, Jamaica. Whether they were formal colonies such as English Antigua and French Dominique or buccaneer enclaves such as Jamaica's Port Royal, these foreign bases became launching pads for smugglers and for attacks against Cuban ports and vessels that were calling in or passing through waters surrounding the island.

Unlike previous phases of Caribbean piracy, in which Spanish ships and ports were the exclusive targets, during the second half of the seventeenth century, Dutch, French, and English pirates and privateers began to attack each other and raid each other's ports. Oftentimes these clashes reflected ongoing European conflicts; for example, clashes between English and Dutch privateers during the Anglo-Dutch Wars (1652–1674).

Show Me Adam's Will (1521–1558)

The first corsairs were privateers who engaged in piratical activities with the sanction of the French Crown. Corsair attacks against Spanish vessels began in the Atlantic in the early 1520s, soon after France declared war on Spain in 1521. At the time, enormous treasures from New Spain had begun to cross the Atlantic en route to Spain. Not to be left without access to this enormous flow of wealth, French monarch Francis I challenged Spain's exclusivist claims to the New World and its riches, demanding to see "the clause in Adam's will which excluded me from my share when the world was being divided."[4]

The first recorded French incursion in the Caribbean happened in 1528, when a lone corsair vessel appeared off the coast of Santo Domingo and its crew sacked the village of San Germán near the western coast of Puerto Rico. In the mid-1530s, corsairs, most of whom were Huguenots (French Calvinists), routinely attacked Spanish vessels and raided Caribbean ports and coastal towns. The most coveted were Havana, Santiago, Santo Domingo, and San Germán. Corsair raids in Cuba and elsewhere in the region usually followed the ransom model, in which the perpetrators seized villages and cities and kidnapped residents and demanded payment for their release. If there were no hostages to take, corsairs demanded ransom in exchange for sparing towns from obliteration. Whether ransom was paid or not, corsairs looted, committed unspeakable violence against their victims, and desecrated churches and holy images, leaving smoldering reminders of their attacks.

In 1536, France and Spain went to war again and French corsairs launched a series of assaults on Spanish Caribbean settlements and vessels. The waters off Cuba's northwest became particularly alluring to French corsairs because commercial vessels returning to Spain had to squeeze through the 90-mile-wide strait between Key West and Havana. In 1537, a corsair vessel appeared menacingly off Havana, its commander demanding a ransom of 700 ducados. Spanish men-of-war soon arrived and scared off the intruding vessel, but it returned soon thereafter to demand yet another ransom. Santiago was also

Figure 7.1. French corsairs raiding a village at La Chorrera, west of Havana, 1530s. Engraving by Théodore de Bry. Source: Bartolomé de las Casas, *La destruction des Indes* (Frankfurt: Jodocus Winghe, 1598).

victim of an attack that year, and both Santiago and Havana endured raids again in 1538. During one of the attacks on Havana, Huguenot corsairs looted church bells and desecrated an image of St. Peter, which they pelted with oranges for the fun of it. In 1537–1538, French corsairs captured and sacked nine Spanish vessels.[5]

Even though France and Spain were at peace between 1538 and 1542, beyond-the-line corsair activity persisted. When war erupted between them again, it echoed even louder in the Caribbean. A particularly vicious attack on Havana in 1543 killed 200 settlers. In all, between 1535 and 1563, French corsairs carried out around sixty raids against Spanish settlements; they captured over seventeen Spanish vessels from 1536 to 1547.[6]

Spain developed a mostly defensive military strategy. It responded to such aggressions by fortifying and militarizing Havana and other ports. Captain-General Hernando de Soto was charged with the task of leading military construction projects. The city's first fortress, later known as Castillo de la Fuerza Vieja, was erected in 1539 and 1540. The city of Santiago reportedly built a very small fort in 1516.[7]

Another defensive strategy was the practice of having merchant vessels cross the Atlantic in *flotas* (fleets), convoys escorted by naval ships to reduce the chances of capture by corsairs. This practice began in the mid-1520s and was formally organized in the 1560s. While the fleet system varied over time, it generally included one convoy that left Spain in April and another one that left in August, both laden with European products. The final destination of the first one, known as the Fleet of New Spain, was Veracruz; it returned with American and Asian products such as silver, natural dyes, precious woods, bone china, and silk. The second one, called the Galleons of Tierra Firme, departed from the port of Callao, Peru, and made its final call in the Pacific port city of Panama. Because Havana was favored by the Gulf Stream and westerly winds, it served as a gathering port for all ship convoys en route to Europe. The system had both advantages and disadvantages. Vessels that sailed all at once with the protection of Spanish men-of-war were better prepared to avoid and confront attacks by corsairs and pirates. However, the system was cumbersome, rigid, and slow, and a single storm or a successful pirate attack meant greater losses of ships, crews, and cargoes.

The number of vessels in transatlantic convoys rose sharply during the peak decades of Mexican silver production, the 1580s to the 1630s. Fleets would anchor in the bay of Havana for weeks or months at a time. Five hundred forty-one registered fleet vessels passed through Havana between 1585 and 1600, but the actual number of vessels was much higher.[8]

Following a brief truce in Franco-Spanish hostilities, both countries clashed once again in 1552. The following year, the notorious Huguenot corsairs François le Clerc (Peg-Leg) and Jacques de Sores raided Havana, which that year had been designated the island's principal city. Later, they attacked and sacked the de jure capital of Santiago, causing such severe damage that the city did not recover from it for a long time. These attacks marked the beginning of a new era of more militarized, violent, and vicious attacks by better-trained corsairs who attacked with larger numbers of vessels and artillery pieces.

The most devastating and best-documented attack of the period took place in 1555, when 200 men commanded by Sores took Havana's woefully vulnerable la Fuerza Vieja by siege. They took as hostages its commander, Juan de Lobera, and some civilians who had found refuge at la Fuerza Vieja. Sores demanded 30,000 pesos and a substantial amount of cassava bread to feed his ships' crews. Governor Gonzalo Pérez de Angulo had retreated to the nearby Amerindian *reducción* of Guanabacoa, where he assembled a ragtag militia of around 35 Spaniards, 80 Amerindians, and 220 blacks. When the settlers refused to pay the ransom, Sores hung several captives, including some black men. Before departing, his men raided and burned the city. Virtually nothing remained standing. Havana was flattened, reduced to a smoking ghost town. Sores's fellow Huguenots desecrated churches, stabbed images of virgins and saints, burned crucifixes, and ripped the clothing off religious statues and mockingly wore it on their heads as hoods. Corsair attacks persisted regardless of whether Spain and France were at war; nine took place between 1556 and 1566.[9]

Spain responded by deploying a career military officer to govern Cuba and entrusting him with the job of reinforcing Havana's fortifications. Captain-General Diego de Mazariegos left for Cuba in 1555, armed to the teeth, clad in a coat of mail, and equipped with a broad assortment of weapons that included four harquebuses, four crossbows, and three swords. Tragedy struck him on the way to Cuba, however; his ship was wrecked and several passengers drowned, among them his wife, his children, and his lieutenant governor. When he reached Cuba, he imposed military rule and began preparations to build a new and stronger fortification that would also serve as the official residence of future captains-general.[10] Mazariegos's return to Spain in 1565 was also dramatic. His sworn enemies seized the vessel he was traveling in, took him hostage, and demanded a hefty ransom. Spanish naval forces soon freed Mazariegos and apprehended his captors, who were sentenced to forced labor in Havana's military constructions.

It was common to punish captured enemies with hard labor in ship's galleys, in quarries, and on construction sites. When captured by Spaniards in 1598, a young Dutch privateer named Piet Heyn was sentenced to row inside a Spanish galley. Others were sentenced to work in construction alongside black slaves; some of these slaves had been commandeered by Havana officials from as far away as Santiago.

Local citizens were often required to contribute to military construction by surrendering their slaves to work on such projects or by making cash donations. In fact, all free blacks and mulattos were vulnerable to conscription into such backbreaking labor; if they refused to work, they faced heavy fines and 100 lashes.[11] Guanabacoa's indigenous inhabitants were also compelled to do hard labor.

El Castillo de la Real Fuerza was completed in 1577. It was a magnificent Renaissance-style stone-and-mortar structure with a heavily fortified pointed bastion protruding out of each of its four corners. It was protected by ten-foot-wide walls and was surrounded by a moat. A massive and continuous influx of funds was needed to pay for its construction and for future military structures, armaments, ammunition, supplies, and salaries for officers and troops, which were estimated to number 450 regular soldiers by the century's end.[12] Because Cuba was unable to meet those expenses, *situado* funds came from other locations in the circum-Caribbean, particularly Mexico. The rationale was that because Havana protected the fleets, it needed financial support from the jurisdictions that most benefited from that protection.

"Papists" vs. "Heretics": Wars of Religion on Land and Sea (1559–1603)

As if territorial expansion, trade supremacy, and dominance of the seas were not good enough reasons for continuous war in Europe, the spread of Protestantism further fueled hostilities among European nations. Spain willingly took on the role of leading the Counter-Reformation against countries that had large Protestant populations or that had established various brands of Protestantism as their official faith.

One of the primary theaters of the period's religious wars was the Netherlands, which had been part of the Holy Roman Empire and had come under direct control of the Spanish Crown in 1555. Under Philip II, the region endured increased taxation and violence against Protestants, whose numbers were rapidly growing, particularly in the north. Calvinist Protestantism had become the dominant religion there by the 1560s.

In 1568, Dutch Protestants revolted against Spanish intolerance and oppression. Early in the conflict, three predominantly Catholic provinces in the south seceded from the Seventeen Provinces and accepted Spanish rule, while the remaining United Provinces continued fighting for political and religious independence. The United Provinces established a republican state in 1581. Spain, which had cemented a dynastic alliance with Catholic Portugal the previous year, responded with a heavy hand, dispatching a large army under the command of the infamous Duke of Alva. The Dutch struggle for independence and religious freedom turned into a long-lasting, multination conflagration that came to be known as the Eighty Years' War (1568–1648).

The polarization that took place in Europe along religious lines also played out in the Caribbean. Following the Franco-Spanish peace treaty of 1559, Crown-sanctioned French corsair activities subsided, but the incursions of piratical Huguenots persisted and in at least one instance led to the formation of a temporary Huguenot settlement in San Juan Evangelista (the Isle of Youth). English piracy increased during the reign of Charles I, king of England, Scotland, and

Ireland (1625–1649), and became more aggressive as Anglo-Spanish relations became more tense during the Thirty Years' War (1618–1648).

Reformism began in the fifteenth century, when Catholic priest John Huss led a reformist movement in Bohemia. Martin Luther, whom the pope excommunicated in 1521, posed a greater challenge. Lutheranism expanded in several German principalities and city-states that were part of the Holy Roman Empire. Parallel reformist movements emerged in Switzerland, France, and the Netherlands and eventually in Scotland. Reformism also took hold in England but by different means and with different motivations and results. By the mid-1560s, two discernible opposing blocs had formed: a southern European Catholic bloc led by Spain and a northern European Protestant bloc led by England. These religious realignments had significant reverberations throughout the Caribbean as aggressive Protestant zeal fueled the desire of Huguenots and Dutch and English privateers to attack Cuba and other Catholic Spanish possessions.

A valuable ideological weapon of the Reformation era and the wars against Catholic Spain was the "Black Legend." Fed by the works of an unwitting Bartolomé de las Casas, English, French, and Dutch Protestants portrayed Spaniards as backward, dishonest, fanatical, idolatrous, cruel, and lazy papists. Richly illustrated Dutch, English, and German editions of las Casas's *Brief Account of the Destruction of the Indies* circulated throughout Europe with titles such as "Spanish Cruelties and Tyrannies."[13]

Spain's relations with England soured further when Elizabeth I was crowned in 1559. She openly supported the Dutch insurrection and aided the Huguenot forces fighting in France. English incursions in the Spanish-claimed Caribbean spiked during Elizabeth's rule. These actions originally took the form of well-organized, large-scale expeditions headed by armed smugglers such as John Hawkins, John Oxenham, and Francis Drake. Their primary objective was to smuggle African slaves into Spain's Caribbean possessions in exchange for bullion and tropical products. The first instances of English mercantile piracy took place in 1562–1563, when Hawkins's men raided a Portuguese vessel off the coast of Sierra Leone, captured the 300 slaves on board, crammed them into the *Jesus of Lubeck*, and smuggled them into Santo Domingo in exchange for sugar, hides, and precious woods.

In 1567 and 1568, Hawkins commanded two smuggling expeditions that used the violent tactics of pirates. The second one ended disastrously: he lost almost all of his ships and three-fourths of his men were killed by Spanish soldiers at San Juan de Ulúa, off the coast of Veracruz, the point of departure of the fleet of New Spain. Hawkins and Drake escaped (barely), but Oxenham and others were captured, convicted of heresy by the Inquisition, and burned alive.

After decades of increasing tensions and confrontations in the northern Atlantic and the Caribbean, Anglo-Spanish hostilities broke out in 1585, when the English Crown dispatched over 7,000 troops to the Netherlands to fight against Spanish forces. That year, Queen Elizabeth began dispensing licenses to privateers to carry out acts of piracy against Spain's Caribbean possessions and vessels. She managed to build a formidable counter-armada of privateers. The largest, most dramatic, and most significant confrontation between Anglican England and Catholic Spain was Spain's massive attack against England in 1588, which culminated in the destruction of Spain's "invincible" armada. Spain rebuilt its naval forces, largely with galleons built in Havana, and continued to fight England until Elizabeth's death in 1603. However, Spain had received a near-fatal blow that ended its standing as Europe's most powerful nation and the virtually undisputed master of the Indies.

Many of the battles of the Anglo-Spanish War of 1585–1603 were fought in the Caribbean, not by regular English troops but by privateers, former pirates who now had a more venerable status because of the English Crown's formal sanction. During those years, over seventy-five documented English privateering expeditions targeted Spanish possessions and vessels.[14] Early in 1586, Drake's forces seized Santo Domingo and kept it for around a month. Before departing, they plundered and destroyed the city, taking a huge bounty. Drake's armed iconoclasts destroyed church images and ornaments and even erected a defensive palisade that featured wooden images of saints in the hope that the Spanish soldiers' Catholic fervor would keep them from firing.

Later that year, Drake and his men attacked the port city of Cartagena. They eventually landed at Cabo San Antonio (Cuba's westernmost point) to water the vessels. The sight of Drake's convoy spread terror among *habaneros*, who had called for and received reinforcements from New Spain and had installed a chain made of cedar and metal that stretched across the mouth of the bay.[15] While the attack never materialized, "El Draque" became the region's boogeyman: the mere mention of his name continued to inspire fear long after his death.

French pirates carried out numerous attacks against Santiago and at other eastern and central locations. In 1578, they obliterated the town of La Sabana on the northern coast. Trinidad was terrorized into depopulation, and the residents of other settlements had to be transplanted to safer inland locations.

The most notorious and best-documented offensive of the period by French corsairs was the 1604 attack on Santiago. That year, Huguenot corsairs led by Gilbert Girón burned and sacked the city and took twenty hostages, most famously Bishop Juan de las Cabezas Altamirano. They demanded a ransom of

100 hides, cassava bread, and other provisions. The prelate later described the abuses he suffered: "They took me in shirt sleeves and beat me repeatedly, they broke my leg with a musket." The hostages remained captive in a corsair vessel for eight days while Girón waited for the ransom to be collected. Residents managed to lure Girón inland, where they ambushed him. The lance of Salvador Golomón, a free black man, lethally pierced Girón's body. The corsair's head was later cut off and paraded on a stake all the way to the town of Bayamo, where, reportedly, adults and children alike cheered effusively.[16]

Relentless attacks by corsairs and pirates forced Spain to strengthen its defenses and expand its troop presence, actions that required a massive and continuous transfer of funds. In the aftermath of the destruction of its armada, Spain shifted its strategy and began funneling its resources toward the erection of new and stronger fortifications throughout the circum-Caribbean. In 1589, Field Marshal Juan de Tejeda began serving as Cuba's governor. He and engineer Juan Bautista Antonelli directed the construction of two new forts, one at each end of the entrance of the bay—El Morro in the east and the smaller La Punta fortress in the west. By 1594, El Morro had the largest garrison of all three forts (204 men), followed by La Real Fuerza (136 men), and La Punta (110 men). El Morro had a battery of twelve cannons that were named after the twelve apostles. Both fortifications were completed in 1630. Authorities did not begin to fortify Santiago de Cuba until 1632, when they erected El Morro de San Pedro.[17]

While there is evidence that funds for military expenses flowed from Mexico to Havana as early as the 1560s, such transfers were not institutionalized until the early 1580s, when the Crown ordered Mexico and other jurisdictions to send regular *situados* (silver coin shipments) to pay for the military expenses Havana and other port cities incurred. *Situado* transfers became the economic lifeline of Cuba, Puerto Rico, Santo Domingo, and Florida. During the late 1500s, Havana alone received a yearly influx of 700,000 silver reales. In the first three decades of the next century, allocations dropped to around 570,000 reales each year. In 1602–1603, *situado* funds constituted nearly two-thirds of all revenue received by the island's royal treasury.[18]

Although Havana came to depend on *situado* funds, those transfers were not always reliable. They were routinely delayed by shipwrecks or corsair assaults. When this happened, the region's fortified port cities became temporarily insolvent. In a 1580 letter to Philip II, Alcaide Melchor Sardo de Arana described the pernicious effects of delays in *situado* shipments: "Soldiers stationed here face many needs because they are owed much money and [because of] the small sums of *situado* money coming from the mainland. This has caused some to desert being unable to sustain themselves"; all in all, the soldiers were owed 20,000 ducados and they in turn owed money to local merchants.[19]

To cope with long delays in *situado* transfers, local authorities were forced to draw from other resources, as was the case in 1570, when they borrowed from the *caja de difuntos* (funds left by those who had died intestate). In 1582, Captain-General Gabriel de Luján requested that *situados* come exclusively from Veracruz to ensure a more regular delivery. That request was granted in 1584.[20]

Pirate Businessmen: Dutch Privateers (1604–1648)

There was not a single year of peace in Europe during the first half of the seventeenth century. This was particularly evident in Spain, which began the century at war with the Dutch and subsequently fought against almost every other European nation. The Spanish Crown and its Portuguese ally were embroiled in the continent's major conflicts, most of which were intertwined with the ongoing Eighty Years' War, which overlapped with the Thirty Years' War. These two wars ended with the Peace of Westphalia (1648), when a defeated Spain was forced to recognize the independence of the Netherlands, Bohemia, and Switzerland and the right of those nations to remain Protestant. Spain also lost its dynastic alliance with Portugal, which had declared its independence in 1640.

Although Spain and the Netherlands had been fighting each other since the 1560s, the Dutch were latecomers to the Caribbean. They did not arrive until after the mid-1590s, when the Dutch Republic was no longer on the defensive in its long conflict against Spain. Spain imposed a trade embargo on the rebellious Dutch provinces, depriving them of access to salt and goods that had been previously supplied by Portuguese merchants. This pushed them into smuggling and piracy. Dutch smugglers were particularly interested in the rich salt deposits of Punta Araya (in present-day Venezuela), the pearl fisheries of La Margarita, and the treasures Spanish fleets transported. The extent and regularity of Dutch smuggling and piracy was such that between 1599 and 1605 over 760 Dutch vessels sailed to Punta Araya, the primary source of salt, which was essential to the profitable herring business.[21]

In January 1606, Spanish vessels under Admiral Juan Álvarez de Avilés successfully fought thirty-one armed smuggler vessels off the southeastern coast of Cuba. Twenty-four of those vessels carried the tricolor ensign of the Dutch Republic.[22] After the truce of 1609 between Spain and the Dutch Republic, violent incursions came to a halt as Dutch privateers shifted their attention to South America. However, in 1621, when the twelve-year truce between Spain and the

Dutch Republic expired, war reignited. Significantly, in that year, the republic chartered the Dutch West India Company and gave it a monopoly over trade and navigation in the Americas and in the profitable transatlantic slave trade.

Dutch privateering peaked in the 1620s and 1630s, when the Dutch West India Company began operations. Dutch privateers became businessmen of sorts. In addition, during these decades, the company began serving military functions. In 1625, one of the company's fleets commanded by Boudewijn Hendricksz staged a major attack on San Juan, Puerto Rico. The fleet left five weeks later, but not before looting and destroying the city. In 1626, Hendricksz's fleet blockaded Havana with the intention of capturing the next Spanish fleet. During the next three years, Dutch ships mounted an unrelenting campaign against Spanish ships and repeatedly blockaded the Bay of Havana.

In 1628, Piet Heyn, the Dutch privateer who had been captured and forced into slavery thirty years before, carried out his long-awaited revenge. Now hold-

Figure 7.2. Celebratory engraving of the Dutch capture of the Spanish fleet, Matanzas, 1628. Source: Théodore de Bry and Matthaeus Merian, *Vierzehender Theil Amerikanischer Historien* (Hanau: Bey David Aubrj, 1630). Reprinted courtesy of the John Carter Brown Library at Brown University.

ing the title of vice admiral of the Dutch West India Company, Heyn launched the most successful and profitable attack ever against the Spanish fleet. Commanding thirty-two vessels armed with 700 cannons, he led the capture of the silver-laden convoy after it left Havana. Admiral Juan de Benavides ordered his vessels to seek refuge in the Bay of Matanzas, where soon thereafter, Heyn's men captured or destroyed all of them. The bounty was prodigious: 178,000 pounds of silver and 125 pounds of gold, in addition to pearls, indigo, cochineal, hides, sugar, and spices—all told, a bounty of 4 million pesos, a 50 percent return for the Dutch West India Company's shareholders. Because of his disastrous decision to shelter his fleet inside the Bay of Matanzas, Benavides was arrested and returned to Spain in shame. He was court-martialed and sent to jail in 1629. Heyn, meanwhile, returned a hero to his native Holland. Anxious to return to battle, he was killed by a cannonball that struck him in 1529. Five years later, Spanish authorities hung the disgraced Benavides in Seville's main square.[23]

Dutch privateer ships continued to harass vessels and ports over the next decade. They launched a failed attack on Havana in 1629, raided Santiago in 1635, and continued to sail off the coast of Havana with the intention of raiding convoyed and individual vessels. Spain's treasure fleets were routinely forced to delay their departures and change routes to avoid capture. In 1638, a peg-legged privateer, Cornelius Jol, menaced Havana for over a month with a 20-ship fleet. His men captured two Spanish vessels.[24] Two years later, another formidable Dutch squadron appeared near Havana. This time, however, bad weather saved the fleet: a storm dispersed the privateer vessels, destroying some of them.

Notably, Jol's second in command was a Cuban mulatto runaway slave named Diego Martín, who was sometimes referred to as Lucifer. This seafaring maroon led a life of piracy, rose to the rank of ship captain, and married a Dutch woman. Decades later he joined the buccaneer forces of François l'Olonnais.[25] He was not the only runaway to choose this type of life. Other blacks and mulattos joined pirate and privateer vessels as places of freedom and refuge and as sources of fortune and fame. Spanish authorities and colonial settlers actually feared enslaved and free blacks and mulattos, whom they viewed as the natural allies of pirates and privateers.

After decades of continuing war between Spain and the Dutch Republic and intense Dutch piracy in the Caribbean, not a single recorded corsair or pirate attack from any nation took place in and around Cuba between March 1641 and the end of 1651.[26]

Wars of Commerce and Buccaneering (1649–1700)

After the Peace of Westphalia, international wars of religion yielded to wars of commerce and navigation, reconfiguring the alliance patterns that had underpinned war and peace for the previous half-century. During the second half of the seventeenth century, Spain and the Netherlands were at peace and often fought together against England and other common enemies. Hostilities between Spain and England subsided, except for the final years of the English Protectorate (1657–1659), when Oliver Cromwell declared war on Spain, and in 1665, when Spain sided with the Dutch Republic against England. Relations between Spain and Portugal also changed during this period. The Portuguese, who had been at war since 1640, began fighting for liberation. Spain finally recognized their independence in 1668.

Also during this period, the Dutch Republic challenged and overtook England for mastery over the seas and commercial dominance of the Atlantic. The

Dutch Republic, which had only a few small Caribbean possessions to protect, championed the doctrine of free trade, while the English Parliament increased its mercantilist trade restrictions to keep its colonies from trading with other European nations. Particularly odious were the Navigation Acts of 1651. England was at war with the Netherlands on and off for over two decades, fighting Dutch naval and commercial ascendancy during three Anglo-Dutch Wars (1652–1654, 1665–1667, and 1672–1674).

Under Louis XIV and his chief minister, Mazarin, France was the period's most bellicose European power. It was formally at war with other European nations during thirty-three of the last fifty years of the seventeenth century. This included two major wars: the War of Devolution (1683–1684), against the Triple Alliance of England, Spain, and the Dutch Republic; and the Nine Years' War (1688–1697), against a coalition of Austria, the Holy Roman Empire, the Dutch Republic, Spain, England, and Savoy. In war after war and treaty after treaty, France peeled off parts of Spain and its empire, culminating with its formal annexation of western Hispaniola in 1697.

Ongoing international rivalries became intertwined with England's internal wars of religion. Spain sided with English royalist Catholics, and the absolutist Catholic monarchy of Louis XIV established an unlikely alliance with England's Republican Puritans. England, Scotland, and Ireland endured three civil wars in the mid-seventeenth century. The first lasted from 1642 to 1646. Shortly before the second Civil War (1648), Scotland switched sides and began supporting the restoration of Charles I, who offered the Scots the temporary establishment of Presbyterianism as official faith. Parliamentarian forces captured and beheaded the English monarch in January 1649 and established a republican commonwealth four months later. A third civil war broke out in 1650 that was mostly fought in Scotland. It ended the following year with the definite defeat of royalist forces.

An increasingly authoritarian Cromwell disbanded Parliament and assumed the title of lord protector in 1653. The next year, he declared war on Spain and launched the ambitious Western Design, the object of which was to secure possession of large Caribbean islands in order to gain control of Spain's main trade routes. France joined Cromwell's side in 1657. After a brief time of peace following the ascent of Charles II to the English Crown in 1660, tensions resurfaced, culminating with renewed hostilities with Spain from 1665 to 1667.

Following a short-lived peace between France and Spain in 1659–1660, hostilities flared up again as the French Crown fought to become the undisputed power in the continent. Both nations went to war again in 1667 (the War of Devolution), when Spain joined England and the Dutch Republic against France's expansionist offensive.

As this dizzying litany of conflagrations demonstrates, international alliances had almost nothing to do with religion or with whether a government was a monarchy or a republic. Catholics fought against Catholics, Protestants battled fellow Protestants, republican nations declared war against and battled other republican states, and kings sent troops against other monarchies. Commercial opportunism had become the guiding force behind most international conflicts.

As had been the case during the previous century and a half, European wars reverberated beyond the line, and often Caribbean settlers and buccaneers engaged in conflicts that did not correlate with European events. When Spain and the English Protectorate were at war in Europe (1654–1660), for example, they fought major battles throughout the circum-Caribbean. In fact, in this case, the Western Design was the cause of Anglo-Spanish hostilities in the European theater. Likewise, during all three of the Anglo-Dutch commercial wars, Dutch and English forces slaughtered each other at sea and on land. As was the case in Europe, Caribbean buccaneers did not have religious motives—they were not religious to begin with. What they shared with European leaders was a desire to gain and accumulate wealth.

Cromwell's Western Design began in December 1654 with the deployment of over thirty-five vessels and nearly 10,000 troops. He ordered General Robert Venables to land troops in Spanish territories "and to surprise their forts, take or beat down their castles and places of strength, and to pursue, kill, and destroy by all means whatsoever all those who shall oppose or resist you therein."[27] Lacking a specific primary target, General William Penn's fleet and Venables's land forces decided to capture Santo Domingo. They were repelled there and proceeded toward the island of Jamaica, which was poorly defended and had a population of only around 1,500 inhabitants. The Spaniards there surrendered and retreated to Cuba. Their slaves fled to freedom in remote locations in Jamaica, where they built maroon communities.

The wresting of Jamaica from Spanish hands was a significant development. Thus far, the English, French, and Dutch had occupied only smaller islands that were relatively distant from Cuba. Jamaica was much closer to Spain's premier island colony and it was also close to the relatively neglected colonies of Hispaniola and Puerto Rico. Jamaica, the third largest of the Greater Antilles, had an area twenty-five times larger than that of Barbados. It became an invaluable English possession. Unlike the Leeward and Windward Islands, Jamaica was strategically located within striking distance of Cuba and Hispaniola. Its large size and mountainous topography made it a haven for stateless peoples, including black maroons and buccaneers.

Jamaica evolved into a largely autonomous buccaneer enclave. England had a limited yet somewhat functional government presence in Jamaica and shared with the buccaneers a desire to protect the island from a possible Spanish recapture. In Jamaica, as elsewhere in the region, buccaneers lived and died beyond the line: they had their own informal institutions, their own rules about crime and punishment, and a fluid social structure based on egalitarian and democratic decision-making practices. They were also more violent and more lawless than their corsair and privateer predecessors.

The first buccaneers were mostly land-based cattle hunters who subsisted by selling or bartering smoked or salted meat with passing vessels. The word buccaneer derives from the Taino word *bucán*, the name of the stone or wood structures Amerindians used to barbecue various kinds of meat. In the 1650s, they became increasingly maritime, launching interminable and fierce attacks against vessels and villages, exhibiting a strong preference for Spanish targets. Buccaneers regularly attacked Spanish vessels and took them as prizes when they could. At least on one occasion, in 1656, they blockaded the port of Havana. Unlike earlier pirates, the buccaneers did not actually attack heavily fortified Havana. Instead, they targeted smaller population centers: Santiago, Sancti Spíritus, and Puerto Príncipe.

Because buccaneers were only loosely connected to their metropolitan authorities, they followed an autonomous "foreign policy" that shadowed the rhythms of Europe's war and peace only when it benefited them. French and English buccaneers mostly gravitated to enclaves dominated by their fellow countrymen; that is, French buccaneers went to Tortuga and English buccaneers gravitated to Port Royal, the capital of Jamaica.

In light of the peace between Spain and England in 1660, Jamaica governor Eduard D'Oyley received and conveyed orders for Port Royal's buccaneers to stop aggressions against Spanish prizes. Most buccaneers challenged those orders and forced the governor to issue commissions (licenses) that allowed buccaneers to attack Spanish targets.

A new governor, Thomas Modyford, arrived in Jamaica in 1664 with instructions to stop buccaneer aggression against Spanish ports and vessels and to instead foster peaceful trade with Spaniards. The following year, the notorious privateer Henry Morgan launched an attack against Cuba after he had promised Modyford that he would attack only Dutch vessels and islands and that he would spare the islands under Spanish control. His buccaneers briefly captured the town of Sancti Spíritus, demanding a ransom before departing. Without any regard for the English government's foreign policy, in 1666 Modyford carried out one of the most flagrant beyond-the-line actions of the century. Much to the satisfaction of the buccaneers, he declared war against Spain's Caribbean vessels and possessions.

In 1668, Morgan staged another assault on Cuba, this time against the town of Puerto Príncipe. Morgan's warning was eerily reminiscent of the sixteenth-century *requerimiento* proclamation that Spanish conquerors were supposed to read before attacking indigenous villages. "If you do not surrender voluntarily," Morgan warned, "you shall soon see your town in a flame and your wives and children torn in pieces."[28] Morgan's men carried out unspeakable atrocities in Puerto Príncipe, including torturing captives and starving women and children. Deeply concerned about a buccaneer insurrection and aware of the role they could play in defending the island against Spain, Modyford had no option but to turn a blind eye.

Although Spain was mostly on the defensive, it retaliated, declaring war on Jamaica's buccaneers and licensing its own corsairs, as its adversaries had been doing for a century and a half. It commissioned Portuguese-born Manuel Pardal Rivero as admiral of the Spanish corsairs. Rivero attacked Jamaica three times in 1670.

Responding to pressures from Spain, England agreed to put an end to buc-caneering as the Treaty of Madrid stated, which both nations signed in 1670. This concession was in exchange for Spain's promise not to reconquer England's Caribbean possessions. Fearful of the Jamaican population's reaction to this ban, Governor Modyford delayed the publication of the treaty for several months. English authorities arrested him in 1671, and the following year they arrested Morgan. English buccaneer aggression subsided after that.

French buccaneering followed similar patterns. Tortuga was a buccaneer post with tortuous and violent beginnings. It was strategically located in the Wind-ward Passage between Cuba and Santo Domingo. Spaniards first settled Tortuga, precariously so, in 1625, over 130 years after Spain first claimed it. Spanish troops forced the buccaneers out of Tortuga in 1654 but left it unprotected, making it easy for them to return. Tortuga-based buccaneers staged numerous attacks on Spanish possessions and vessels and launched a major offensive against Hispan-iola in 1659. That year, the French and English governments jointly appointed Frenchman Jérémie Deschamps de Rausset as governor. In 1662, England took over Tortuga, but it continued to be a haven for the English, French, and Dutch alike. Two years later, it came under French rule under Bertrand d'Ogeron, who

Figure 7.3. Engraving of buccaneers led by Henry Morgan staging an attack on Puerto Príncipe in 1668. Source: Alexander Olivier Exquemelin, *De Americaensche Zee-roovers* (Amsterdam: Jan ten Hoorn, 1678). Reprinted courtesy of the John Carter Brown Library at Brown University.

was appointed governor of Tortuga and St. Domingue. He found himself in a bind, as had Modyford: he had to balance the wisdom of following policy orders from the metropolis and the buccaneers' insatiable thirst for loot.

In 1666, Tortuga-based French Calvinist buccaneer Jean-David Nau (François l'Olonnais) began attacking Spanish vessels even though France and Spain were at peace. As negotiations for peace among France, England, and the Netherlands began in May 1667, France declared war on Spain and turned its attention to its colonial possessions. L'Olonnais was reputed to be the most brutal and cruelest pirate ever. In 1667, when he organized an expedition against Havana, he found it to be well defended by numerous warships. He landed elsewhere on the island, where his men unleashed their legendary brutality. They captured a Spanish ship and slaughtered its entire crew. The following year, l'Olonnais's men took San Juan de los Remedios. Although he was captured by the Spanish in Darien (presently in Honduran territory), he and a few survivors managed to escape, but not before, as Alexander Oliver Esquemeling described it, "he drew his cutlass, and with it cut open the breast of one of those poor Spanish, and pulling out his heart, . . . began to bite and gnaw it with his teeth, like a ravenous wolf."[29]

Buccaneering activities subsided in the last two decades of the seventeenth century. In 1686, the French and English governments agreed to curb buccaneering. The great Jamaican earthquake of June 7, 1692, symbolically marked the end of an era. Its epicenter was near Port Royal, which was destroyed. Thirty-three acres of land slipped below the water and a giant tsunami submerged the city. The death toll reached an estimated 5,000. Although survivors rebuilt it, Port Royal was once again destroyed in 1704, this time by a massive fire. The Treaty of Ryswick (1697), which marked the end of the Nine Years' War, dealt a near-mortal blow to buccaneering as Spain formally ceded to France the contested territories of western Hispaniola (St. Domingue) and the notorious Tortuga island.

Cultural Imprint

Havana, Manuel Moreno Fraginals once wrote, was a city that "lived facing the sea." Its economic roles as a primary port and its defensive functions manifested themselves through various aspects of material culture that included popular religiosity, the plastic arts, and literature. *Habaneros*, for example, embraced Santa Bárbara, the patron of artillerymen, as the city's unofficial patron saint. In the iconic representation of her, she is placed atop a fortified, cannon-armed tower. What is believed to have been the first canvas painting ever made on the island was a portrait of Santa Bárbara. Likewise, the patron of the port town of Regla, across the bay, was venerated as a protector of mariners.

Reportedly, in 1557, the city's only official musician was Juan de Emberas, a Flemish man tasked with playing the drums whenever a vessel entered the port. The first work of literature written on the island was Silvestre de Balboa's *Espejo de paciencia*, an epic poem about the 1604 French corsair attack and the citizenry's response to it. The first scientific book written in Cuba was entitled *Arte de navegar* (The Art of Sailing). Written by a Havana resident and physician named Lázaro Flores, it was published in Madrid in 1673.[30] Scholars of Cuban architecture have recognized that the roofs of some buildings were constructed using shipbuilding techniques and designs; the convent of Santa Clara is one example. The city's status as a harbor also influenced language. Moreno Fraginals has demonstrated that Cuban vocabulary and slang adopted numerous words related to sailing and navigation, for example *botar* (to throw away, from the word *bote* [boat]) and *singar* (to copulate), which originally meant to row with one oar. *Verga*, meaning a ship's central mast, became slang for penis, and houses of prostitution were nicknamed *atarazanas* (shipyards).[31]

8 ～

Deceivingly Sweet

Sugar, Slavery, and Resistance

*Entre la producción del azúcar y el comercio de esclavos hubo desde un principio
tan estrecho enlace, que todo lo que influía en aumentar o disminuir aquella daba
en este un resultado equivalente.*

JOSÉ ANTONIO SACO

Three concomitants of sugar production soon manifested themselves.
The first was the tendency to amalgamate factories. . . . The second was the
tendency to grow sugar for export and to import food. . . . The third . . . was
the problem of the world market. . . . Overshadowing all these questions,
however, was the crucial problem of labour.

ERIC WILLIAMS

In his classic book *Cuban Counterpoint*, Fernando Ortiz recognized sugar and
tobacco as the island's main historical characters. He associated "doña Azúcar"
(Madam Sugar) with Cuba's misfortunes: slavery, latifundia, rigid social hierarchies, dependency, colonialism, neocolonialism, and dictatorship. Sugar, Ortiz
concluded, was essentially un-Cuban. The other protagonist, "don Tabaco," while
not exclusively a frontier product, flourished at a distance from and with relative
independence from the long arm of the colonial state and the insatiable demands
of sugar production for capital, large plots of land, coerced workers, and government support. In Ortiz's view, tobacco engendered all that is good in Cuban
culture: free labor, small landholdings, democracy, liberalism, national pride.[1]

This chapter examines the first act in the Cuban counterpoint drama, intro-
ducing the villainous "doña Azúcar" and discussing her socioeconomic, cultural, and ecological impact. Doña Azúcar had an inseparable co-actor, slavery.
Together, they constitute the sugar and slavery binomial, doubtless the most

significant, transformative, and enduring factor in the history of the Caribbean. The intimate connection between sugar and slavery had deep roots in the Mediterranean and in Atlantic islands such as Madeira and Cape Verde. It was replicated in Hispaniola and continued to spread virally, infecting almost every island in its path and large extensions of the coastal areas that circumvent the Caribbean. The sweet and bitter binomial first reached the region in the second decade of the sixteenth century, when settlers in Spanish Jamaica and Hispaniola began producing small amounts of molasses and coarse sugar with primitive mills. Later in the century, similar operations spread to Puerto Rico and Cuba. Sugarcane and slavery continued to spread up and down the Lesser Antilles, eventually infecting every island in the region.

The "Sugar Revolt"

The phrase "sugar revolution," which was first used by French scholars, has become commonplace in the scholarship on the Caribbean to describe the profound economic, social, and environmental transformations brought about by the emergence of sugar production as dominant economic activity. Barbados, beginning in the 1640s, was the first Caribbean island to experience such a revolution, which historian Barry W. Higman defines as having six "central elements": "[1] a swift shift from diversified agriculture to sugar monoculture, [2] from production on small farms to large plantations, [3] from free to slave labour, [4] from sparse to dense settlement, [5] from white to black populations, and [6] from low to high value per [capita] output."[2]

Eighteenth- and nineteenth-century Cuban sugar plantations and slavery have been the subjects of unremitting scholarly examination. However, there is a noticeable dearth of scholarship on the first sugar-producing activities of the late 1500s and 1600s. Three notable exceptions are Francisco Castillo Meléndez's "Un año en la vida de un ingenio cubano (1655–1656)," Mercedes García Rodríguez's *Entre haciendas y plantaciones*, and Alejandro de la Fuente's essay "Sugar and Slavery in Early Colonial Cuba." In that pioneering work, de la Fuente contends that the earliest sugar estates did not fit the plantation model Caribbeanists commonly use because Cuba's first sugar-producing units were "self-sufficient agricultural concerns" where a limited number of slaves manufactured sugar "in an artisan-like manner." Those units were not exclusively devoted to sugarcane but also produced food crops, raised animals as sources of food and energy, and reserved much of the land for grazing and for the extraction of wood. Moreover, de la Fuente questions the assumption that sugar production generated "a given set of social and productive relations." In other words, he rejects the idea that sugar had a deterministic effect on Cuba's social structure during the seventeenth century.[3]

Cuba's earliest sugar production units fit several of Higman's "central elements" of a sugar revolution, but the social and economic transformations that occurred in Cuba between the 1590s and 1660s did not reach revolutionary proportions. While sugar's share among Cuba's exports increased during this time, sugarcane did not come even close to becoming a monocrop. In fact, during the second half of the seventeenth century, sugar was third among Cuba's exports, behind hides and tobacco; it accounted for only one-fifth of all exports. While sugarcane estates were much larger than regular farms (*estancias*), they were small when compared to early sugar plantations elsewhere in the Caribbean, and while the Cuban sugar revolt increased the proportion of blacks and slaves, white inhabitants remained a large percent of the population. Throughout the 1600s, there were more free individuals than slaves, but the number of blacks surpassed the number of whites at some point in the mid-1600s. I propose the term "sugar revolt" to describe what transpired when sugar production based on slave labor boomed in Cuba in the seventeenth century. I use this term to contrast that boom with the more profound, transformative, and overwhelming shift to sugar and slavery that first took place in Barbados in the 1640s and later echoed across the Caribbean. These profound changes did not happen in Cuba until the nineteenth century, when sugar production dominated the economy and the bulk (at times, the majority) of the population consisted of slaves.

De la Fuente's distinction between the first *ingenios* (sugar-producing units) and the later plantations is basically one of scale and degree, not fundamentals. The early incarnations were smaller, used less sophisticated technology, were worked by fewer slaves, and exhibited a lower degree of specialization.[4] I argue that while early sugar-producing estates did not revolutionize Cuba's economy, society, and demographic makeup, individual units had a profoundly transformative impact within their confines and in surrounding areas that was not dissimilar from what transpired on islands revolutionized by sugar. For these reasons, I do not discard the term "plantations" altogether but rather qualify it by using the term "early plantations."

I also subscribe to the widely held view that from the very beginning, in Cuba and elsewhere, sugar depended on, and thereafter further fostered, a particular set of material and socioeconomic circumstances, practices, beliefs, and ideologies that transcend time and space. In fact, the causative connection between sugar and a host of damaging and destructive ramifications—historian Eric Williams called them "concomitants of sugar"[5]—has been a constant in the history of the Caribbean. From the beginning, sugar production fostered the concentration of land in a few hands; a dependence on slave or otherwise coerced and brutalized labor; the institutionalization of violence; sharp, racialized social hierarchies consisting of a small white elite, a small intermediary stratum, and a large labor force made up of African slaves and their descendants; authoritarianism; vulnerability to highly fluctuating foreign markets; a reliance on government support that inevitably was conducive to corrupt practices; and ecological degradation. These bitter by-products were evident during Cuba's sugar revolt.

Long before Williams excoriated the bitter legacies of sugar, Cuban and other scholars had done so. Among the first was Ramiro Guerra, who in 1927 published *Azúcar y población en las Antillas*. Guerra viewed the plantation as the region's most pervasive and insidious institution, the source of the Caribbean's social, economic, and political ills. Likewise, Ortiz saw sugar as the root of most everything that was wrong with Cuba. Since then, many other scholars have recognized the destructive legacies of sugar. V. S. Naipaul poignantly stated that the epigraph of the Caribbean's history could well be "cane is bitter." "It is a brutal plant," he added, "tall and grass-like, with rough, razor-edged blades." W. R. Aykroyd expounded on the "sweet malefactor," and George Beckford blamed the plantation for the region's underdevelopment and persistent poverty.[6]

The very nature of sugar and its particular requirements endow its production with peculiarities that make it an extraordinarily complex socioeconomic system. Because sugarcane requires immediate milling and processing once it is cut so the canes will retain their sucrose content, sugar production has historically combined agricultural and industrial processes at one location and generally under the same owner. This contrasts with tobacco, cotton, and cocoa, which can be grown in one place and transported for processing elsewhere— even across the Atlantic and beyond. For example, when Cuban farmers began producing tobacco leaves in the sixteenth century, they exported them (legally or illegally) for processing in Seville, London, or Paris, where factory workers transformed them into snuff and pipe tobacco. This distinction is important because sugar challenged the dominant imperial scheme that reduced colonies to producers of raw materials while their metropolises reserved for themselves the more profitable manufacturing stages.

Expanding sugar markets, particularly in Europe, made large-scale sugar production possible and necessary. European demand increased sharply in the 1600s, when, as Sidney W. Mintz wrote, "sugar began to change from a luxury and a rarity into a commonplace and a necessity in many nations."[7] It became

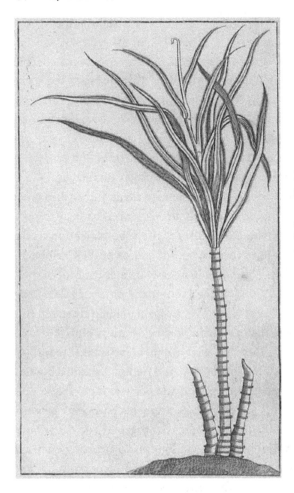

Figure 8.1. Sugarcane plant.
Source: James Grainger, *The Sugar-Cane: A Poem in Four Books with Notes* (London: R. J. Dodsley, 1764), frontispiece. Reprinted courtesy of the John Carter Brown Library at Brown University.

an increasingly important consumer product as Europeans developed a taste for bitter tropical products such as cocoa, tea, and coffee that required sweetening.

The emergence of specialized sugar-producing units in the last decade of the sixteenth century and first ten years of the seventeenth century expanded production and export capabilities. In 1602, Cuba exported 4,233 *arrobas* to Seville. According to de la Fuente's estimates, between 1603 and 1610, yearly exports from Havana averaged 6,300 *arrobas*. Export levels doubled between the early 1600s and the second third of the century, a period when Cuba was the largest exporter of sugar among the Spanish colonies; during that time, the island's yearly exports averaged 50,000 *arrobas*. By mid-century, Havana alone reportedly exported around 60,000 *arrobas* each year.[8]

Havana and its hinterland benefited from the regularization and expansion of the fleet system. Convoyed trade vessels on their way to Spain carried substantial amounts of Cuban sugar. Those exports were taxed time after time: export taxes were collected in Havana (36 reales per *arroba* in 1638); 15 percent import taxes were assessed in Seville, the city through which all American imports to Spain had to enter; and an additional 10 percent tax was levied when the sugar was transferred to other Spanish ports.[9]

Early Sugar Plantations

Because it has flourished so well in the Caribbean, one would think that sugarcane was indigenous to the region. It was not. The long-stemmed species of the Gramineae (grass) family was introduced to the New World during Columbus's second voyage.

Even in their earliest and most artisanal incarnations, sugar plantations required the coordinated alignment of numerous factors. Some were structural: a favorable climate, including adequate temperatures, sunshine, and rainfall during the planting, growing, and harvest seasons; abundant, fertile, and well-irrigated flatlands; good rivers and bays; and favorable ocean currents and winds to facilitate trans-Atlantic shipping. Those conditions had existed in Cuba for millennia.

Human agency produced the other necessary factors, such as substantial amounts of capital, a supply of reliable labor (i.e., slaves), machinery and tools, and the know-how of sugar masters and other specialized workers. Other essential factors were adequate roads and ports, reliable navigation and trade systems, and the legal and financial support of local authorities and the Spanish Crown.

Land was the first requirement for sugar production. Without it, cane could not be cultivated. Nor could an array of ancillary agricultural products: food such as plantains and *yuca* to feed slaves, fodder for oxen and mules, and the vast woodlands required to satisfy the need for wood—as a construction material, as firewood, and as fuel in sugar production. Land cultivated with cane always constituted a small proportion of the typical early sugar plantation. Most of the land remained as either *monte* (wilderness) or woodland. In the second half of the 1600s, an estimated 60 percent of all plantation land consisted of woods.[10] This was a conscious strategy on the part of elite landowners: their control of vast landholdings reduced the access of farmers and peasants of all races. Thus, from the beginning, one of the historical concomitants of the plantation, concentration of land wealth, limited sugar production to a small number of landowners. This produced a sharply hierarchical socioeconomic structure characterized by a planter elite at the top and slaves at the bottom.

While sugarcane production never reached monocrop status, it absorbed land otherwise destined for growing vegetables and fruits and raising cattle. Resources gravitated to more profitable non-edible cash crops (sugar and tobacco) at the expense of other economic activities. This resulted in the scarcity of and rising prices for cassava, meats, and other food, which made Havana vulnerable to food shortages. Tensions between the types of agricultural activities were made patent in clashes among local authorities. Opponents of sugar expansion claimed that it created dependence on imported food. For example, in 1651, the cabildo of Havana demanded that all farmers "remove and pull out all the cane fields" and devote the land to cultivating *yuca*, corn, and other food plants.[11]

Planters acquired and accumulated land in different ways. One way was through land grants. Local cabildos distributed these to well-connected individuals who belonged to or were related to Cuba's proto-aristocracy. The cabildo of Havana made land grants during the second half of the 1500s for purposes other than growing sugarcane, mostly for cattle-ranching *hatos*. Some of the grantees and their heirs eventually transformed part of that land into sugar-producing units. Scores of individuals received additional allotments throughout the sixteenth-century sugar revolt. For example, the patriarch of the Rojas clan, Alfonso de Rojas, who held several high political positions in the cabildo of Havana, benefited from numerous land grants, including one consisting of the 934-square-mile Isle of Youth, then known as San Juan Evangelista.[12]

While production of small quantities of molasses and low-grade sugar (*azúcar quebrada*) for local consumption started early in the colonial period, the first wave of sugar mill construction took place in the 1590s. Sugar plantations popped up mostly in the extended periphery of Havana, an arch that extended west to Baracoa, east to Matanzas, and south to Bejucal. Reportedly, Cuba's first sugar venture—a unit with a water-powered mill—was built in 1576 in El Cerro, on the outskirts of the capital city. Around twenty mills were built between 1595 and 1600. In 1603, fourteen of thirty-one active sugar plantations were located in the jurisdiction of Havana. Seven years later, although the number of plantations had decreased to twenty-five, 80 percent of them were situated in Havana's hinterland.[13] These included a significant number of water-run mills built on the banks of La Chorrera, three miles west of the city.

Significant numbers of sugar production units also emerged around Bayamo and Santiago. At the dawn of the seventeenth century, seventeen of the island's thirty-one early sugar plantations were located in these jurisdictions. By 1617, Bayamo had eleven and Santiago had sixteen. Sugar was the single largest legal export from those areas, which were the most heavily populated after the city of Havana. In 1617, a single owner, Captain Francisco Sánchez de Moya, had five plantations in Santiago; he also administered the copper mines of El Cobre.[14]

Seeking to boost the economy, the Spanish government played an important role in stimulating sugar production. Laws, decrees, and special licenses responded to the incessant requests of Cuba's elite. In 1595, the Crown issued an *asiento* (special monopolistic license) to Pedro Gómez Reynel to import 1,000 slaves per year. Also that year, the Crown allowed Cuban planters to import sugar-making machinery and tools duty free and it reduced the rate of tithes on planters' profits by 50 percent. The government further stimulated the founding and expansion of the first sugar plantations in 1602, when it facilitated a major loan earmarked for the financing of sugar production.[15]

Imperial authorities also responded to planters' lobbying by extending to Cuba *el privilegio de ingenios*, which protected indebted planters from having their land, slaves, and equipment seized for failure to repay loans.[16] Planters and their allies, which included cabildo members and colonial officials, recognized that the threat of property seizure was too high a risk; it kept potential investors from setting up mills and discouraged current planters from expanding their ventures. The *privilegio de ingenios* and the favorable laws outlined above are early examples of another of sugar's concomitants: sugar planters' chronic dependence on government support and subsidies, be it the Spanish Crown, the viceroyalty of New Spain, or local authorities. This gave way to a salient characteristic of the insular elites—a penchant for pleading for special considerations, tax exemptions, and honorific titles. This behavior reached its apogee in the late 1700s. Two centuries later, historian Allan J. Kuethe nicknamed those entitled elites "*los llorones cubanos*" (Cuban crybabies).[17]

Having substantial amounts of capital was another precondition for the establishment and operation of sugar-producing units. In early colonial Cuba, as elsewhere in the circum-Caribbean, sugar production was never a poor man's enterprise. It has been estimated that in the early 1600s the cost of erecting a sugar plantation ranged from 3,000 to 20,000 ducados.[18] Some planters invested capital they had accumulated from ranching, various other business activities, and ill-gotten funds. They also sought financing from merchants and other *refaccionistas* (lenders), including fellow planters and even clergymen. They used their assets, including land, slaves, tools, and machines, to guarantee such loans. Even after the *privilegio de ingenios* was implemented, lenders found ways to get around the safeguards that were intended to protect such assets.

The 1602 loans, which totaled 40,000 ducados, ranged from 200 to 4,400 ducados per planter. The funds arrived in Havana from Veracruz with the fleet

of 1601 and were finally disbursed the following year.[19] Because the loans pre-
ceded the extension of the *privilegio de ingenio* to Cuba, each borrower had to
guarantee his/her loan with land and other properties as collateral and designate
guarantors who would become responsible for the loan in case of default.

While those loans undoubtedly helped spur on the sugar boom, the funds
proved insufficient. The planters had requested a larger amount, and in 1602
a group of fourteen individuals requested additional loans in the amount of
80,000 ducados. This petition was denied. Records of outstanding debts shed
light on how the borrowers fared. Nearly a decade after the 1602 loans were disbursed, fourteen had not repaid their loans and a total of eighteen loan guarantors had been forced to pay the debts. Six of the original beneficiaries had died,
half of them leaving their mortgaged properties to surviving widows. Five of the
properties went to other hands, as was the case with the Tres Reyes plantation,
which was seized by guarantor Francisco López de Piedra, who dismantled it,
most likely to cover his guarantee. He also gained control of a plantation that
belonged to Antonio de Matos de Gama. In 1611, only eleven of the seventeen
estates remained in the hands of their original owners or surviving relatives.[20]

Of all the expenses related to establishing and running a sugar plantation,
the largest was usually acquiring and sustaining an adequate number of slaves.
Sugar production and slavery were intimately linked throughout the Caribbean,
New Spain, and Brazil. Together they formed vicious cycles: more slaves, more
sugar, more slaves, more sugar. . . . The direct connection between sugar and
slavery was attributable to the widespread belief that African slaves were exclusively endowed by nature to endure extraordinary physical abuse that whites
could not withstand. Their condition of bondage, furthermore, created a year-
round reliable labor force. It also allowed masters to keep them captive and
exploit them virtually to the point of disability or death.

Growth in the slave population almost always correlated with an increase in
sugar production. As José Antonio Saco remarked almost 140 years ago, whenever sugar production rose, the slave trade experienced a parallel increase.[21] For
example, in 1645, when the sugar revolution in Barbados was just beginning, the
island had a population of 36,000 free or indentured whites and around 6,000
black slaves (a 6:1 ratio). (Around that time, Cuba, which was 256 times larger
than Barbados, had roughly the same number of slaves and fewer whites.) By
1667, the slave population of Barbados had exploded to 50,000, the result of
massive slave imports, while the number of whites had fallen to 8,300, inverting
the race ratio to six blacks for every white person).[22] In Cuba, the sugar revolt
caused a parallel growth in the number of slaves and amounts of sugar exports

Figure 8.2. Engraving depicting slaves cutting sugarcane under the close supervision of whip-cracking overseers. Source: "Working in Sugar Cane Fields, 19th cent.," in Edmund Ollier Cassell, *History of the United States* (London, 1874–1877), 2:493, available at *The Atlantic Slave Trade and Slave Life in the Americas: A Visual Record*, compiled by Jerome Handler and Michael Tuite and sponsored by the Virginia Foundation for the Humanities, http://www.slaveryimages.org/detailsKeyword.php?keyword=Cassell&recordCount=10&theRecord=3, accessed September 7, 2017.

but not the sharp ratios of blacks to whites. It did, however, produce a small black majority and overwhelming slave majorities on plantations. The proportion of enslaved individuals in the sugar-producing district of Jesús del Monte (1691), for example, was 59 percent, twice the proportion in the city of Havana.[23]

The larger and better financed the plantation, the bigger the number of slaves and the larger the sugar output. Records pertaining to the seventeen recipients of the 1602 royal loan show that the number of slaves varied widely. The planters who received the largest loans (between 3,000 and 4,400 ducados) owned the most slaves, an average of 22.4; recipients of midsize loans (2,000–2,500 ducados) owned an average of 13.4 slaves; while recipients of loans of 1,000 ducados or less had an average of 6.25 slaves. Later in the century, when sugar production expanded, the average size of *dotaciones* (slave work forces) increased. Members of the Maldonado family, for example, owned plantations with larger slave populations; one of their plantations had thirty-one slaves and another had fifty-five.[24]

Cuba's general slave population had a substantial masculinity index of around 150, but the gender imbalance was much higher on plantations. On the seventeen plantations that received loans in 1602, enslaved men outnumbered women 5 to 1. One of those plantations, the San Diego, which was located in Matanzas, had an all-male *dotación* of twenty-three. Five decades later, the plantation Nuestra Señora del Rosario had twenty male slaves and one woman named María Motembo; she eventually escaped in the company of a creole slave named Luis.[25]

During the 1600s, the average price of a slave hovered between 300 and 400 pesos. Younger and healthy slaves and those with particular skills, such as rope making or carpentry, sold for higher prices. The cost of slaves increased around 25 percent from the 1640s to the 1680s because supplies dropped when Spain and Portugal, Cuba's traditional source of slaves, were at war.[26]

Also significant were the costs associated with maintaining slaves. Spanish law required masters to adequately feed and clothe their slaves. Providing sufficient nutrition was usually in the planters' best interest; it kept slaves healthier and increased their productivity. Masters also provided medical services, however rudimentary. Estimates for the 1670s show that each slave generated maintenance expenditures of 15–20 reales per year, half of which covered food expenses. The slaves' diet was high in animal protein from beef, pork, and turtle meat. Plantains were another diet staple. Maintenance costs also included clothing made from rustic *cañamazo*, which was made from hemp, linen, or cotton, and *jerga* (sackcloth). One set of clothing was typically distributed twice a year. Slaves were typically housed in *bohíos*, which were built almost exactly like West African huts. Antonio de Ribera, who owned sixteen slaves, had ten *bohíos* on his plantation.[27]

Even in the 1600s, growing sugarcane and producing sugar had a destructive effect on the environment. Plantations produced large amounts of waste. In 1636, local citizens complained to the Spanish government, pointing out that La Chorrera was polluted with waste from sugar mills that included bagasse, ashes, a variety of chemicals, and animal urine and excrement. Another environmental concern was deforestation. Sugar production required huge amounts of lumber, a need that led to some deforestation. Havana's cabildo issued prohibitions against cutting trees in El Vedado and on common lands. A 1662 ordinance prescribed 200 lashes or four years of hard labor for anyone caught in El Vedado with an ax or a machete. Even the Crown got involved in protecting El Vedado; in 1670, Regent Mariana de Austria ordered that no tree be cut there.[28]

From Canefield to Port

The production of sugar was a complicated endeavor. The entire process, which included clearing the land, preparing the soil, planting, harvesting the crop, manufacturing the sugar and molasses, packing the produced goods, and transporting them to port, took over a year. Once mature, sugarcanes were harvested, a final agricultural phase carried out by machete-wielding slaves. The next three stages of production were industrial: milling to extract *guarapo* (sugarcane juice) from cane stalks, boiling that juice to generate molasses saturated with sugar crystals, and purging through filtration to separate the crystals from the molasses. Molasses was a valuable by-product that was exported and used locally as raw material for *aguardiente*.

Cutting cane, one of the most grueling and dangerous production tasks, was done by slaves during *la zafra* (the harvest season), which could last from December to July because sugarcane planting was staggered to avoid having all the cane mature at the same time.

After sugarcane stalks were harvested, they were transported to the mill, where the manufacturing phases took place under simple structures called *casas*. Earlier and smaller plantations had fewer *casas* and often combined several manufacturing phases under the same structure. In 1609, Juana García Rodríguez's plantation had only one *casa*, where milling, boiling, and purging took place. In 1622, the San Pedro plantation in Cojimar had two, one of which was devoted exclusively to purging, while in 1655–1666, Juan Aréchega's Nuestra Señora del Rosario plantation had three, one for each manufacturing phase.[29]

Figure 8.3 shows a sugar mill from one of the French Indies in about 1655. Perhaps seeking to demonstrate the sugar-making process rather than present

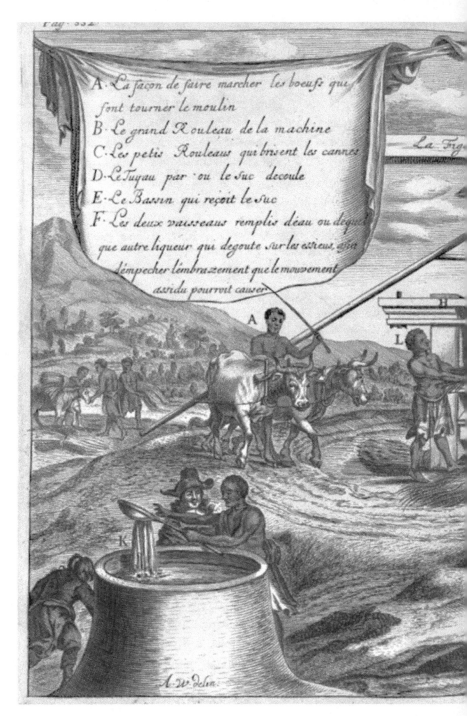

Figure 8.3. Engraving of a sugar mill worked by slaves and powered by oxen showing the different phases of sugar production: crushing the sugarcane stalks, channeling the sugarcane juice into a skimming vat, and boiling the juice to produce molasses saturated

G. L'essieu du grand Rouleau qui fait
   mouvoir toutes les roües de la machine

H. Les pieces de bois entrelassees qui lient
   et serrent la machine

I. Les planches, sur lesquelles les Negres
   posent les cannes de Sucre

K. Les grandes chaudieres dans lesquelles on
   fait bouillir le Suc iusques à ce quil soit epaissi

L. Les negres qui servent le Moulin, et qui
   poussent les Cannes entre les Rouleaux.

à Sucre

with sugar crystals. Source: Charles de Rochefort, *Histoire naturelle et morale des iles Antilles de l'Amérique par Rochefort* (Rotterdam, 1667). Reprinted courtesy of the John Carter Brown Library at Brown University.

an accurate depiction of what actual mills looked like, the illustration shows milling and boiling equipment without any shelter. The roofs of Cuban mill houses were made of palm leaves or tile, but it is possible that some parts of the manufacturing process may have occurred outdoors.

While some mills were hydraulic, most were muscle powered (generally by oxen). Regardless of what type of energy was used, most mills consisted of three vertical stone rollers, between which slaves inserted freshly cut canes. Once the juice was extracted, it ran through *canoas* (open or covered channels) into large vats, where foam and impurities were skimmed off. There are records of at least a few plantations of this period operating with two different types of mills. This was the case in Nuestra Señora del Rosario; one of the mills there was described as being of the Brazilian style.[30]

Once impurities were removed, the *guarapo* was poured into a succession of vats and cauldrons of different sizes, where it was boiled, often inside another structure called *casa de calderas*, where it was subjected to high temperatures. This process, also known as crystallization, turned the fresh juice into viscous molasses saturated with crystalized sugar.

In the final manufacturing phase, the *purga*, the crystals were separated from the molasses, first in a *resfriadera* (cooling vat), where the first stage of separation was completed manually with large spoons. The next step was to pour the crystal-saturated molasses into one-*vara*-long clay conical forms. Through the force of gravity, most of the remaining molasses dripped out of the small end of those cones into yet another set of *canoas*, leaving behind dry sugar crystals. This process, which could last several weeks, left higher-quality sugar on the top of the cone while darker, lower-quality sugar accumulated near the bottom. Contemporary inventories show that some plantations had large numbers of forms, as many as 1,000–1,500.[31] After the *purga*, workers packaged the sugar in boxes of 30–40 *arrobas* to be hauled to port.

In general, Spain sought to limit colonies such as Cuba to the role of exporters of raw materials and importers of manufactured goods by, for example, prohibiting the sale and use of tobacco mills. This was not possible with sugar because it had to be manufactured where the cane was harvested. Special royal provisions actually allowed the importation of some sugar-making machines tax free. While most cauldrons were imported from Spain and Portugal, there is evidence that some were locally manufactured using copper extracted from the mines of El Cobre. Copper was so essential that at one point authorities distributed it at cost among planters who wanted it. Documentation also proves that at least some forms were built by sugar masters and other skilled workers.[32]

Sugar production required the knowledge and skills of sugar masters at every stage of manufacturing. Half-scientists and half-artists, many sugar masters arrived in Cuba with experience from southern Spain and other sugar-producing locations such as Madeira, the Canary Islands, and coastal Brazil. One of the first sugar masters to arrive was Antonio Matos, who came from Madeira in 1593.[33] Sugar masters were the ones who erected and maintained mills. Using their sight and their refined senses of smell, taste, and touch, they determined the precise time to move the molasses through a succession of cauldrons of different sizes, calculated the optimum level of crystallization, and oversaw the purging process. They also had the skills to repair a variety of sugar-producing machines and equipment—a mill's broken roller, for example—and to construct clay forms and other implements. Some slaves learned the skills necessary to be sugar masters.

Sugar masters could decide how long they would commit their labor to planters and they had the freedom to work for more than one planter at a time. . According to *protocolos notariales* for the period 1599–1608 that Alejandro de la Fuente has analyzed, contracts ranged in length from one to three years. Some contracts stipulated payment for year-round work, while others specified wages for different *tareas* (specific jobs). The salaries for yearlong contracts averaged around 1,000 reales, while *tareas* commanded between 26 and 55 reales each. One sugar master, Antonio de Salazar, charged two reales for each form he manufactured. Another sugar master, Nicolás Hernández, signed at least three contracts between 1603 and 1604, working for two different masters, Governor Juan Maldonado and planter Luis Hernández. Maldonado payed him by *tarea* at the rate of 44–55 reales. The sugar master charged Hernández 1,100 reales for a year of labor. His colleague, Miguel Estrada, apparently worked simultaneously for two of the period's largest planters, Lucas de Rojas and Bishop Juan de las Cabezas Altamirano.[34]

The sugar industry went into a deep crisis in the last third of the seventeenth century. Prices declined in the 1670s to 24 reales per *arroba*, almost a third of earlier values. The late-seventeenth-century crisis was a response to a variety of factors, many of them caused by shifting currents in international trade, revealing the industry's vulnerability to market fluctuations—Eric Williams's third concomitant of sugar production. Much of the problem stemmed from Brazil's massive sugar exports to Iberia after Spain recognized Portugal's independence in 1668 and commercial relations were restored between the two kingdoms. Slave prices also shot up, making it harder for planters to expand their *dotaciones* or replace deceased and disabled slaves. From the onset of the crisis in the

1670s to 1687, one-third of all Cuban sugar plantations ceased operations. A final blow struck in 1692, when a hurricane destroyed forty out of the island's seventy plantations.[35]

The crisis was intertwined with a longer, broader, and deeper economic crisis that historian Woodrow Borah has referred to as New Spain's century of depression. According to Borah, that empire-wide crisis was triggered by a great epidemic that began in 1576–1579. It decimated the indigenous population of Central Mexico and lasted until around 1720. Fewer Amerindian workers translated into a reduction in food production and a steep fall in silver production starting around 1590. During the first three decades of the seventeenth century, Mexico's annual silver exports ranged between 24 and 31 million pesos, but by mid-century they had collapsed to 12 million. In 1656–1660, they decreased further to an annual average of 3 million pesos. All of this impacted Cuba as the number of fleet and individual vessels visiting Havana dropped. This translated into decreased imports to and exports from Cuba and reduced royal treasury receipts, from a yearly average of 363 million maravedís in 1658–1666 to an annual average of 221 million maravedís in 1685–1688.[36]

Seventeenth-Century Human Cargo

The slave trade was the cruelest and most brutal enterprise of the Atlantic world. It created pain, pestilence, violence, racism, and death. It degraded millions of African captives but it also degraded slave traders, masters, overseers, and government officials. Slave trading and slavery had a corrupting and degrading effect on virtually every segment of society. It bred greed and malfeasance; it made men, women, and children crueler and lazier; it worsened the labor conditions for free workers of all races; and it corrupted the institutions of family and marriage and most government, church, and civil institutions.

Estimating the number of slaves imported to Cuba is an extraordinarily challenging task, in great measure because documentation is scarce and because smuggling and other corrupt practices hid reality and falsified information. In 1653–1654, for example, slave traders landed a cargo of 500 slaves, but only 230 were declared in order to reduce the import tax and the slave tax. This fraud was perpetrated in collusion with Governor Francisco Gedler, who received a 4,000-peso bribe. An additional 3,700 pesos were distributed among other complicit officials.[37]

As discussed in chapter 5, the first phase of the Atlantic slave trade, which lasted to 1580, consisted mostly of imports from the Upper Guinea region of West Africa.[38] Slave-trading patterns started to change in the 1590s, when Portuguese merchants began to export African slaves in large numbers from the port city of Luanda. This shift changed the ethnic composition of slaves brought to Cuba and other parts of the Caribbean, and Angolan and Congolese slaves began to account for the preponderance of the new arrivals. This was the case until around 1640, when Portuguese traders had a virtual monopoly of the slave trade to Spanish colonies. This is evidenced in Havana's baptismal records, which indicate that over half of all slaves baptized during the 1590s were identified as Angolans.[39]

Data on fourteen slaving expeditions whose final destination was Havana shed much light on the evolution of the slave trade from the mid-1590s to the late 1690s. Six of those expeditions occurred during the Angolan trade period; all of them originated in Luanda and other ports in the region. In contrast, in the period 1653–1698—a third phase of the slave trade to Spain's colonies—only one of the eight slave ships that reached Havana had departed from Angola. One had come from Cape Verde and the other six had sailed from various Caribbean slave entrepôts, including Barbados, Curaçao, and Jamaica. During the post-1650 period, the amount and proportion of imported Angolans dropped. Slave origins became increasingly diversified and slaves from the Guinea Coast and Congolese ports constituted over half of all imports.

One of the notable characteristics of the period 1619–1639 was the substantial number of children on slave ships.[40] According to slave import data from those years, children constituted around 31 percent of human cargo originating in Angolan ports.[41]

In 1976, as thousands of Cuban soldiers, most of them descendants of slaves, were fighting in Angola on the side of the MPLA (Popular Movement for the Liberation of Angola), renowned Cuban historian Manuel Moreno Fraginals published a short piece entitled "Manuel de Angola" in the national newspaper *Granma*. In it, he described how Manuel, whose African name is unknown, was baptized in a collective ceremony, most likely soon after he arrived in Cuba. Baltazar Gónzalez officiated at the ceremony on October 7, 1685. In preparation for the baptism, the priest anointed Manuel with consecrated oil. An Arará couple from Dahomey, Andrés and Francisca, stood as godparents. Moreno Fraginals wrote that Manuel "was from over there and [three centuries later] is from here," meaning that he had always been both African and Cuban.[42]

Cultural Rebels, Peasants, and Members of the Republic

Earlier in the book, I discussed three forms of slave resistance: rebellions, *marronage*, and the quest for freedom via self-purchase and *coartación*. Slaves and their free descendants resisted culturally by retaining and transculturating aspects of African languages, religious beliefs, values, and practices such as ritual drumming as a means of communication and giving African names to their children. This section examines the resistance of slaves and *horros* against the sugar and slavery binomial: their aspiration to forge dignified and stable family units, autonomous peasant communities, and assert their citizenship.

Maintaining an intact family structure was high among the slaves' desires. Period records demonstrate the lengths to which slaves went to remain close to or rejoin their close relatives. Likewise, while slavery pushed all slaves to the bottom of the social ladder, occasionally they managed to recreate African hierarchies. Some *bozales* retained monarchical titles, prerogatives, and even social distinctions marked by clothing, body scarring, and tooth filing.

Slaves resisted other cultural impositions through negotiation and deceit, if necessary. Religion was one such imposition. Upon arrival, slaves such as Manuel de Angola were baptized by Catholic priests. This ritual was performed as a matter of course: the priests offered the new arrivals no spiritual preparation and paid little, if any, attention to their spiritual well-being. Laws required masters to allow religious instruction and time for daily prayers, but that was never the norm. African spirituality did not disappear but was instead repackaged syncretically. Slaves and former slaves held on to common West African beliefs and practices such as worshipping animistic deities, divination, and sacrificing animals.

In bondage and in freedom, Africans and their descendants opposed the plantation socioeconomic system. As Puerto Rican sociologist Ángel G. Quintero Rivera has asserted, they created "counter-plantation" spaces that were conducive to autonomous cultural and artistic productivity. In such spaces, they actively sought the formation of what Sidney W. Mintz has called "reconstituted peasantries," in essence establishing small units of land where free blacks and mulattos could cultivate their own food crops, as they had done for centuries in their ancestral homelands. As David Wheat has documented, black agricultural workers were the backbone of food agriculture in Santo Domingo, Puerto Rico, and Cuba.[43] Slaves persistently negotiated access to provision grounds where they could plant the crops and raise the pigs and fowl that would guarantee them food security and provide a degree of autonomy and even some income.

Historian María Elena Díaz has concluded that almost every household in the mining town of El Cobre had at least one family member working as a peasant. She argues that by the end of the seventeenth century, the royal slaves of El Cobre had successfully established a "reconstituted peasant community."[44]

Horros, meanwhile, actively pursued land ownership as they sought to become farmers. As was the case elsewhere in the Caribbean, free blacks stayed as far away as possible from sugar plantations, which they correctly associated with slavery and persistent exploitation and abuse. Havana's *protocolo* and cabildo records point to substantial levels of farmland ownership among free blacks and mulattos. The cabildo routinely granted *horros* access to land that could be turned into farms, ranches, and even hunting grounds. In 1561, for example, the free black woman Beatriz Nizarda asked for a land grant from the cabildo of Havana, which she eventually received. She and her husband Diego de Rojas, also a *horro*, raised pigs and food crops. In 1579, they hired an extra hand: Diego Toribio, an Amerindian whom they paid 25 ducados for six months of labor. Another example is that of a black freedman named Juan Gallego, who received a one *caballería* plot for cultivating *yuca*, which cabildo officials recognized was "for the good of this village." Like Beatriz, Diego, and Juan scores of *horros* owned ranches and farms, some of which had thousands of mounds of *yuca*. When *horros* from Havana's farm belt complained directly to the king about the discrimination and abuses they endured, they emphasized that they cultivated "all types of crops" with which they "sustained" Havana's population and the crews of passing fleet vessels."[45]

Free blacks and mulattos, aware of their legal rights, fought attempts to enslave or re-enslave them. They resisted laws and practices that blurred differences between them and those who remained in bondage. Despite the free status of *horros*, laws meant to regulate slave behavior were commonly applied to them also. These included prohibitions against wearing elegant clothing, jewelry, and other luxury items; gambling; selling or purchasing alcoholic beverages; being in the streets after curfew; and serving as clergymen or government officials.[46]

A series of petitions Havana's *horros* presented to the Crown in the early 1600s outlined many of their grievances. They protested against being forced to work on military constructions and in cane fields. They even complained about being compelled to serve as mail carriers, which forced them to walk great distances to the point of "losing their health." On moral grounds, they objected to denigrating impositions on their wives. Particularly odious was the practice of compelling married *horras* to dance in the streets on holidays such as Corpus Christi Day. As the *horros* put it, they endured "perpetual slavery."[47]

In these claims, *horros* outlined their long record of service to king and community. They pointed out their work in military constructions and their contributions to feeding large fleet crews and keeping city dwellers from starving by producing most of the cassava bread and vegetables they consumed. Hundreds had fought bravely against invading corsairs and had even joined a formal black and mulatto battalion to help protect Havana. In no uncertain terms, *horros* claimed their full status as citizens, as "*miembros de la república.*" King Philip IV responded to their claims by issuing decrees that banned forced labor assignments and abuses at the hands of *rancheadores*, relaxed restrictions on what they could wear, and liberated freed women from denigrating impositions. However, as anthropologist Marvin Harris once wrote, "the Crown could publish all the laws it wanted, but in the lowlands, sugar was king."[48]

While sugar and slavery were inseparable, early Cuba did not become a slave-based monocrop society at any time during the 1600s. Because ranchers, crop farmers, local and colonial authorities, and urban residents needed workers, the sugar economy did not consume all of the available labor force. In addition, slaves, both African-born and creole, male and female, and urban and rural, resisted and contested the two-headed monster that sought to deprive them of their dignity and freedom.

Conclusion

As stated in the introduction, this book's chapters stand both as individual essays and as coordinated parts. While each of the chapters offers its own topic-specific interpretations and conclusions, when the chapters are read together, they provide answers to several overarching questions. They emphasize the relationship between geographical space and human actions, they put Cuba in its broader Caribbean and Atlantic contexts, they examine complex interactions among diverse racial and ethnic groups, they trace the development of distinc tive economic systems and social structures, and they discuss the genesis of a variegated Cuban identity and culture(s) that are the result of transculturation among three primary cultural roots, themselves the product of centuries of transculturation in the Amerindian Caribbean, Iberia, and western Africa. The book thus is built on the premise that understanding Cuba's complex early history requires consideration of many interrelated aspects—a "total history" approach, to use the terminology of the Annales school—that connects the geographical, the economic, the political, the social, and the cultural.

The goal of these concluding paragraphs is to tie together those aspects as they interconnected in the three specific contexts examined throughout this book: the military and mercantile port city of Havana, the early sugar plantations that dotted Havana's hinterland, and the transgressive Cuba of the east.

Havana's privileged location and its proximity to favorable prevailing winds and currents (the geographical) resulted in human activities that were largely related to transatlantic navigation and trade and the defense of ports and navigation routes (the economic). This favorable location, however, bred the envy of Europe's naval powers, as attested by unremitting attempts to wrest Havana and Cuba from Spanish hands. Thus, very early on, the port city thrived largely on *situados* and other allocations of military funds and fleet vessels and their crews. Havana also developed ancillary economic activities such as shipbuilding and tavern keeping, products such as *aguardiente* and locally manufactured cannons, and services such as laundering soldiers' uniforms and cooking meals for sailors.

Havana's militarization required and produced particular government structures and institutions (the political). Governors became captains-general with broad powers over both civilians and the military; military officials and political officers clashed continuously, the result of overlapping jurisdictions and prerogatives; and laws protected fleet crews and military personnel from prosecution for crimes and transgressions. Havana's role as a military bastion and navigation hub also produced a distinct type of society (the social), which included a substantial proportion of soldiers of all ranks, a general population that swelled during annual fleet calls, a strong presence of black and mulatto women who contributed to a robust service sector, and a multinational and multiracial contingent of skilled laborers who raised fortifications, built ships, tailored fancy dresses and uniforms, made gold and silver jewelry, sang and played instruments to entertain the rest of society, and buried the bodies and prayed for the souls of the dead.

As discussed at the end of chapter 7, Havana's military and mercantile roles also impacted the cultural. The city and, to some extent, the island's culture (architecture, painting, music, and literature) came to reflect a singularly maritime and martial spirit.

Sugar and the sugar plantation offer another opportunity to recognize the interconnectedness of material realities and human phenomena. As seen in chapter 1, geological processes that took place millions of years ago produced extraordinarily fertile soils (the geographical) that proved ideal for sugarcane cultivation and by extension for sugar manufacturing (the economic). Sugar production generated what economists call linkages, both backward and forward. Backward linkages involved a variety of economic actors, among them slave traders, coppersmiths who fashioned cauldrons, and blacksmiths who turned iron into anything, be it nails, spoons, or shackles. Sugar cultivation generated numerous economic activities, such as producing food crops to feed the slaves, maintaining and repairing mills and other equipment, and hunting after runaways. Forward linkages included the production of *aguardiente*, warehousing, pier activities related to exporting sugar, and insurance and financial services.

Laws and government institutions (the political) promoted sugar production and helped maintain social order. The Crown issued royal orders designed to foster the construction and expansion of sugar plantations, the viceroyalty of

New Spain provided credit for the same purpose, and local cabildos made land grants and helped build the necessary infrastructure of roads, aqueducts, and wharfs. A local bureaucracy regulated and taxed sugar exports, while a law-and-order apparatus policed behavior, maintained social peace, and hunted and punished maroons and criminal transgressors.

The plantation produced a peculiar type of society (the social). First and foremost, it was a slave society, a rigidly hierarchical caste-like system. However, it was made more fluid in large measure because of the agency of individuals who purchased themselves and organized *horros* who directly addressed the king to demand respect and equal treatment under the law. Plantation society was also multiracial and multiethnic: white, Cuban- or Iberian-born planters were at the top; then came an intermediate polychromatic stratum that included overseers, sugar masters, *rancheadores*, farmers, and stevedores; and at the very bottom were enslaved blacks, including Muslims from Senegal and pantheistic men and women from Upper Guinea and the Congo.

Lastly, the cultural. While the plantation was less conducive to miscegenation than other parts of the Cuban landscape, it provided opportunities for asymmetrical cross ethnic interactions and for transculturation. Slaves responded to and challenged European ideals, norms, and practices. They learned Spanish, but in the process they created pidgin dialects that included African vocabularies, syntaxes, and cadences. Although planters and overseers forced slaves to plant and cut cane, they strove to "reconstitute" (as Mintz called it) African peasantries by giving slaves provision grounds. Although slaves were sold away from kinfolk and loved ones, they went to unimaginable lengths to reunite with them. And when priests taught them to venerate the Virgin Mary and Catholic saints, they used icons to conceal their continued worship of West African deities.

The Cuba of the east was largely shaped by its location (the geographical). It was distant from the Gulf Current and North and Central America but was next to the Windward Passage and close to Hispaniola and Jamaica. Unlike the west, the east was largely mountainous and rich in copper. The region's geography had an impact on the economy. Because of its location, its capital, Santiago, was left out of the fleet routes and consequently lost economic and strategic importance vis-à-vis Havana. At the margins of the fleet system, the island's east and center came to depend on Havana for legal trade and recurred to foreign smugglers to expand the market for their exports and to supplement their imports. Bayamo, Manzanillo, and to a lesser extent Santiago became epicenters of illicit trade. The prevalence of smuggling geared the region's economy toward the production of the crops and products foreign traders desired most: hides, tobacco, ginger, and precious woods.

All of this impacted the social. Eastern Cuba developed a more fluid and relaxed social hierarchy, conditions that favored more egalitarian interactions among individuals of different races, and miscegenation. The region's exports were mostly the products of largely independent ranchers, rustlers, and free peasants. There were, of course, slaves in the east, but they did not endure the same levels of exploitation that slaves who were forced to build forts and cut sugarcane did. Slaves involved in copper mining enjoyed relative autonomy and access to land.

The geographical and the economic helped shape the political and vice versa. Distant from Havana, the east had a reduced official and military presence that afforded the region a degree of autonomy vis-à-vis an increasingly powerful and hegemonic Havana. Local interests clashed with those of the capital city in matters of trade, navigation, taxation, and the extent of local power. The region's inhabitants asserted their independence by voicing grievances directly to the Crown, breaking laws against smuggling, evading taxes and levies, and, when necessary, combating officials and troops dispatched from Havana.

This political culture of independence, civil disobedience, rebelliousness, and social transgression was also manifested in popular religiosity, music, and diet (the cultural). For various reasons, including the survival of larger numbers of indigenous inhabitants and their descendants, the east was fertile ground for transculturation and syncretism. This was the part of Cuba that produced the unrepentant transgressor Paula de Eguiluz, the multicultural Ginés Sisters band, and a syncretic mulatto virgin named Caridad. Such was early colonial Cuba. These foundations were reflected in subsequent centuries. Their echoes are still heard today.

Notes

Acknowledgments

1. Martínez-Fernández, "Geography"; Martínez-Fernández, "1492"; Martínez-Fernández, "Forging of Creole Cuba"; Martínez-Fernández, "Far beyond the Line."

2. "Digital Book Collections," *John Carter Brown Library*, https://www.brown.edu/academics/libraries/john-carter-brown/jcb-online/digital-book-collections; "Image Collections," *John Carter Brown Library*, https://www.brown.edu/academics/libraries/john-carter-brown/jcb-online/image-collections.

Introduction

1. The English-language literature on early colonial Cuba is scant. Two notable exceptions are María Elena Díaz's *The Virgin, the King, and the Royal Slaves* (2000) and Alejandro de la Fuente's *Havana and the Atlantic* (2008). Wright's *The Early History of Cuba* was originally published in 1916. She later published two books in Spanish on early colonial Cuba, one covering the sixteenth century (*Historia documentada de San Cristóbal de La Habana en el siglo XVI*, 1927), and the other the first half of the seventeenth century (*Historia documentada de San Cristóbal de La Habana en la primera mitad del siglo XVII*, 1930). Several useful general books in Spanish cover periods of the sixteenth and seventeenth centuries, among them Sainz, *Cuba y la Casa de Austria*; Arriaga Mesa, *La Habana, 1550–1600*; Macías Domínguez, *Cuba en la primera mitad del siglo XVII*; and García del Pino, *El corso en Cuba*, which, despite its title, covers many topics beyond piracy. The first five volumes of Marrero's *Cuba: economía y sociedad* are invaluable for anyone interested in those centuries. A few extant works focus exclusively on Santiago and the east. See, for example, Wright's *Santiago and Its District (1607–1640)*; Bacardí Moreau, *Crónicas de Santiago de Cuba*; Portuondo Zúñiga, "Trayectoria histórica de Santiago de Cuba"; and Díaz, *The Virgin, the King, and the Royal Slaves*.

2. Childe, *Foundations of Social Archaeology*.

3. O'Gorman, *La invención de América*; Crosby, *Columbian Exchange*.

4. Rama, *La ciudad letrada*; Naipaul, *The Overcrowded Barracoon*.

5. Ortiz, "Los factores humanos de la cubanidad."

6. Aykroyd, *The Sweet Malefactor*; Naipaul, *The Middle Passage*, 57; Ortiz, *Cuban Counterpoint*.

7. Mintz, "Reflections on Caribbean Peasantries."

8. Irene Aloha Wright Papers, Library of Congress. Portal de Archivos Españoles is available at http://pares.mcu.es/, accessed September 12, 2017.

Chapter 1. Geography and the Shaping of Early Colonial Cuba

Epigraph sources: Massip, *Factores geográficos de la cubanidad*, 6; Diamond, "What Does 'Geographic Determinism' Really Mean?"

1. For information on Cuba's geological development, see Stanek, Cobiella-Reguera, Maresch, and Grevel, "Geological Development of Cuba"; Pardo, *Geology of Cuba*; Iturralde-Vinent, "Cuban Geology"; and Emery and Uchupi, *Geology of the Atlantic Ocean*.

2. For animation of plate tectonic movement over millions of years, see Christopher R. Scotese, "Plate Tectonics and Paleogeography, 240 Ma to +250 Future," https://www.youtube.com/watch?v=uLahVJNnoZ4, accessed September 12, 2017; and Christopher R. Scotese, "North Atlantic (0–200 Ma)," https://www.youtube.com/watch?v=l6EIC83xcQk, accessed September 12, 2017. See also Ron Blakey, "Paleographic Map of the Americas, 275 Ma," detail, http://jan.ucc.nau.edu/rcb7/namP275.jpg. For an interesting illustration of Pangea with current political borders, see https://media.wnyc.org/media/resources/2013/Sep/13/pangea_politik_archive.jpg, accessed September 12, 2017.

3. Stanek, Cobiella-Reguera, Maresch, and Grevel, "Geological Development of Cuba"; Emery and Uchupi, *Geology of the Atlantic*, 338.

4. Stanek, Cobiella-Reguera, Maresch, and Grevel, "Geological Development of Cuba."

5. Iturralde-Vinent, "A Short Note on the Cuban Late Maastrichtian Megaturbidite."

6. Handwerk, "New Underwater Finds Raise Questions about Flood Myths"; Sullivan, "In Cuban Depths."

7. Alonso and Clark, "Cuba Confronts Climate Change," 10–13. Also see Pérez, "Cubans Find Preparing for Climate Change Hard, Expensive and Essential."

8. The primary reference source for the geographical and climatological facts and statistics used in this book is Cuba, Oficina Nacional de Estadísticas, *Primer compendio de estadísticas*.

9. These maps are examples: Peter Martyr d'Anghiera, "Isla de Cuba," 1511; Giacomo Gastaldi, "Isola Cuba Nova," 1548; Paulo Forlani, "Isola Cuba," 1564; Tomaso Porcacchi, "Isola Cuba," 1572; and Gerald Mercator, "Cuba Insula," 1607.

10. Varela quoted in Rojas, *Isla sin fin*, 39.

11. Wright, *Historia documentada de San Cristóbal de La Habana en el siglo XVI*, 1:20.

12. Alchon, "The Great Killers in Precolumbian America."

13. Gebelein, *A Geographic Perspective of Cuban Landscapes*, 7.

14. Herrera, *Memoria sobre huracanes en la isla de Cuba*, 46; Schroeder, *Cuba*, 30.

15. Herrera, *Memoria sobre huracanes en la isla de Cuba*, 46; Milne, *A Catalogue of Destructive Earthquakes*, 30, 36; Taber, "The Great Fault Troughs of the Antilles," 100.

Chapter 2. Indigenous Inhabitants

Epigraph sources: Nápoles Fajardo, "El behique de Yariguá," 136–139; Childe, *Foundations*, 32.

1. Childe, *Foundations*; Childe, *Man Makes Himself*. Some Cuban anthropologists prefer

the terms Etapa Preagroalfarera, Etapa Protoagrícola, or Etapa Agroalfarera. See, for example, Tabío, "Nueva periodización," 103.

2. Throughout this book, I follow Irving Rouse's classification system as presented in his book *The Tainos*.

3. Fitzpatrick, "The Pre-Columbian Caribbean," 308.

4. Rouse, *The Tainos*, 51–57; Tabío, "Nueva periodización," 105.

5. Fitzpatrick, "The Pre-Columbian Caribbean," 310.

6. Velázquez quoted in Marrero, *Cuba*, 1:232.

7. Rouse, *The Tainos*, 60–61; Dacal Moure and Rivero de la Calle, *Art and Archaeology*, 33–34, 55.

8. Tabío, "Nueva periodización," 108.

9. Ricky, *Native Peoples A to Z*, 2:467; La Rosa Corzo, "Orientación," 150–151.

10. Dacal Moure and Rivero de la Calle, *Art and Archaeology*, 36–38, 58.

11. Keegan, "Archaic Influences in the Origins and Development of Taíno Societies."

12. Rouse, *The Tainos*, 49–70.

13. Keegan, "Archaic Influences in the Origins and Development of Taíno Societies," 2–3, 7; Wilson, "Cultural Pluralism and the Emergence of Complex Society in the Greater Caribbean," 7–12.

14. Wilson, "Cultural Pluralism and the Emergence of Complex Society in the Greater Caribbean," 7–12.

15. Marrero, *Cuba*, 1:23.

16. Columbus, *The Log of Christopher Columbus*, November 6, 1492, 104–105.

17. Figueredo, "The Indians of Cuba," 121–145.

18. Deagan, "Reconsidering Taíno Social Dynamics after Spanish Conquest," 612–616.

19. Pané, *An Account of the Antiquities of the Indians*, 3–16.

20. Some maintain that *cohoba* was made from the seed of *Anaderanthera peregrina*. Pané, *An Account of the Antiquities of the Indians*, xi, 16, 21, 26; Stevens Arroyo, *Cave of the Jagua*, 58, 122–123.

21. Hofman, Mol, Hoogland, and Valcárcel Rojas, "Stage of Encounters," 598–599, passim; Valcárcel Rojas, *Archaeology of Early Colonial Interaction at El Chorro de Maíta*, 162–198.

22. Deneven, *The Native Population of the Americas in 1492*, xxiii, passim.

23. Deneven, *The Native Population of the Americas in 1492*, xxi, xxxiii, xxix, 290.

24. Deneven, The *Native Population of the Americas in 1492*, table 1, xxviii.

25. Pérez de la Riva, "Desaparición de la población indígena cubana," 62; Guerra y Sánchez, Pérez Cabrera, Remos y Rubio, and Santovenia y Echaide, *Historia de la nación cubana*, 1:230.

26. "Padrón de vecinos, solteros, estantes, indios y negros horros de La Habana y Guanabacoa (1582)," in Marrero, *Cuba*, 2:332–334 (hereafter cited as "1582 List"). See Yaremko, "'Gente bárbara'"; Yaremko, *Indigenous Passages to Cuba*; and Barreiro, "Beyond the Myth of Extinction."

27. Pospíšil, "Physical Anthropological Research on Indian Remnants in Eastern Cuba," 229; Marchueco-Turiel et al., "Cuba."

28. Poole, "What Became of the Taíno?"; Marchueco-Turiel et al., "Cuba"; Serna Moreno, "Las supervivencias lingüisticas de origen Taíno en el oeste de Cuba," 84.

29. Barreiro, "Indians in Cuba."

30. Marx, "Cuba's Forgotten Tribe Experiencing a Rebirth."

Chapter 3. First Encounters, Inventing America, and the Columbian Exchange

Epigraph sources: Ortiz, "Por Colón se descubrieron dos mundos," 180–190; O'Gorman, *La invención de América*, 17.

1. O'Gorman, *La invención de América*; Crosby, *Columbian Exchange*; Zerubavel, *Terra Cognita*.

2. "Privileges and Prerogatives Granted to Columbus," in Commager and Cantor, *Documents of American History*, 1:1–2.

3. MacGregor, *A History of the World in 100 Objects*, 399–403.

4. "Privileges and Prerogatives Granted to Columbus," 1–2.

5. Columbus to Queen Isabella and King Ferdinand, undated (1500–1502), in Columbus, *Book of Prophecies*, 67.

6. Gould, *Nueva lista documentada de los tripulantes de Colón en 1492*.

7. Columbus, *The Log of Christopher Columbus*, September 10, 1492, 62, October 10, 1492, 67, October 11–12, 1492, 71–77, October 21, 24, 1492, 90–91.

8. Columbus, *The Log of Christopher Columbus*, November 2, 1492, 99–101; Toscanelli to Ferman Martins, June 25, 1574, in Vignaud, *Toscanelli and Columbus*, 316.

9. Oaths reproduced in Thacher, *Christopher Columbus*, 327–332.

10. Columbus, *The Log of Christopher Columbus*, October 28, 1492, 93, November 27, 1492, 119.

11. Columbus, *The Log of Christopher Columbus*, December 3, 1492, 122.

12. Columbus to Queen Isabella and King Ferdinand, February 15, 1493, in Cowans, ed., *Early Modern Spain*, 32; also see Columbus, *The Log of Christopher Columbus*, November 4, 1492, 101.

13. De Anglería, *Décadas del Nuevo Mundo*, 271.

14. Columbus, *The Log of Christopher Columbus*, November 14, 1492, 109, October 21, 1492, 89, October 8, 1492, 72.

15. Columbus, *The Log of Christopher Columbus*, November 6, 1492, 104–105.

16. O'Gorman, *La invención de América*, 16–17; Zerubavel, *Terra Cognita*.

17. Harari, *Homo Deus*, 237.

18. For further information on the Ecumene and its graphic representations, see Pinet, *The Task of the Cleric*, x–xix; Brotton, *A History of the World in 12 Maps*, 100, 170.

19. Quote in Pohl, *Amerigo Vespucci*, 81; see also Harari, *Homo Deus*, 238.

20. Peter Martyr d'Angheira to Cardinal Ascanio Sforza, November 1, 1493, quoted in Zerubavel, *Terra Cognita*, 71–72.

21. Columbus's narrative of the third voyage, in Columbus, *Four Voyages*, 129–130.

22. Some sources claim that Vespucci embarked on four expeditions to the New World. However, many scholars feel that the sources that mention four voyages are suspect. There is a consensus that he made only two voyages, one in 1499 and a second one in 1501–1502. Fernández-Armestos, *Amerigo*, 71; Vespucci quoted in Zerubavel, *Terra Cognita*, 79.

23. Narrative of Columbus's fourth voyage, in Columbus, *Four Voyages*, 187–188.

24. Crosby, *Columbian Exchange*.

25. De las Casas, *Historia de las Indias* 1:332–333.

26. Hamilton, *American Treasure*.

Chapter 4. The Manufacturing of Cuba: Conquests, Demographic Collapses, and Government Institutions

Epigraph sources: Heredia, "Les Conquerants," 407; Naipaul, *The Overcrowded Barracoon*, 254.

1. Rama, *La ciudad letrada*, 18; Naipaul, *The Overcrowded Barracoon*, 254.

2. Rama, *La ciudad letrada*, 18; Naipaul, *The Overcrowded Barracoon*, 254.

3. Machiavelli, *The Prince*, 115.

4. Menéndez Pidal, *Spaniards in Their History*; Castro, *Ibero América*; Castro, *Structure of Spanish History*.

5. Machiavelli, *The Prince*, 115.

6. "Relación de varias cantidades de maravedís, dadas de órden de los Señores Reyes á Cristóbal Colón, antes y al tiempo de su primer viage a Yndias" (1492), in *Colección de documentos inéditos relativos al descubrimiento, conquista y organización de las antiguas posesiones españolas de ultramar*, 1st series, 19:456–458; "Provisión para que los de Palos den las dos carabelas que les está mandado por los del Consejo," April 30, 1492, in Fernández de Navarrete, *Colección de documentos concernientes a la persona, viages y descubrimientos del Almirante D. Cristóbal Colón al gobierno y administración de los primeros establecimientos de Indias y a la Marina Castellana*, 1:11–13.

7. Weckmann, *The Medieval Heritage of Mexico*, 10.

8. On the subject of *juicios de residencia*, see Macías Domínguez, *Cuba en la primera mitad del siglo XVII*, 193–194, 203–232.

9. Guerra y Sánchez, Pérez Cabrera, Remos y Rubio, and Santovenia y Echaide, *Historia de la nación cubana*, 1:119–120; de la Fuente, "Sociedad, 1510–1770," 156; Ordenanzas de Cáceres (1573), in Pichardo Viñals, *Documentos para la historia de Cuba (época colonial)*, 108–129.

10. Wright, *The Early History of Cuba*, 330; García del Pino, *El corso en Cuba*, 55, 222; Marrero, *Cuba*, 4:206–207.

11. Lindsay, Captives as Commodities, 18; Chilcote, *Portuguese Africa*, 3–6; Thornton, *Africa and Africans*, 43–71; Wheat, *Atlantic Africa*, 42–44.

12. Royal order for the officials of the Audiencia of Santo Domingo, August 2, 1511, in Chacón y Calvo, *Cedulario Cubano*, 381–386.

13. Governor of Santiago to the president of the Council of the Indies, June 15, 1619, in Wright, *Santiago and Its District (1607–1640)*, 129; Macías Domínguez, *Cuba en la primera mitad del siglo XVII*, 184, 477–478.

14. "Título de gobernador de las Indias a Frey Nicolás de Ovando," September 3, 1501, in Fernández de Navarrete, *Colección de documentos concernientes a la persona, viages y descubrimientos del Almirante D. Cristóbal Colón al gobierno y administración de los primeros establecimientos de Indias y de la Marina Castellana*, 2:255–257.

15. Royal order from King Ferdinand to Viceroy Diego Columbus, June 6, 1511, in Chacón y Calvo, *Cedulario Cubano*, 327.

16. Guerra y Sánchez, Pérez Cabrera, Remos y Rubio, and Santovenia y Echaide, *Historia de la nación cubana*, 1:66.

17. Quote from de las Casas, *Historia de las Indias*, 3:114 (my translation); de las Casas, *Devastation of the Indies*, 45; "Relación o extracto de una carta que escribió Diego Velázquez, teniente de gobernador de la Isla Fernandina (Cuba) a S.A. sobre el gobierno de ella. Año de 1514," in Pichardo Viñals, *Documentos para la historia de Cuba (época colonial)*, 79.

18. De las Casas, *Devastation of the Indies*, 51.

19. Text of *requerimiento* in Hall, *Religion in America*, 17–18; de las Casas, *Historia de las Indias*, 4:162.

20. Pérez, *Cuba*, 20; Instituto de Historia de Cuba, *Historia de Cuba (la colonia)*, 90.

21. Royal order of May 8, 1513, in *Colección de documentos inéditos relativos al descubrimiento, conquista y organización de las antiguas posesiones españolas de ultramar*, 2nd series, 1:41; Marrero, *Cuba*, 1:177–178; Guitar, "Encomienda System," 250–251.

22. The average number of *encomendados* per *encomienda* was 155 in 1522. The average size of *encomiendas* generally increased from west to east: 88 in Havana, 118 in Puerto Príncipe, 147 in Trinidad, 140 in Bayamo, and 189 in Santiago. See Marrero, *Cuba*, 1:177–178; Cabildo of Santiago to Emperor Charles V, November 23, 1530, in Pichardo Viñals, *Documentos para la historia de Cuba (época colonial)*, 96–97.

23. Royal order of Charles V for Governor Guzmán, November 9, 1526, in *Colección de documentos inéditos relativos al descubrimiento, conquista y organización de las antiguas posesiones españolas de ultramar*, 2nd series, 1:351–353; Marrero, *Cuba*, 1:184–188; Cabildo of Santiago to Emperor Charles V, November 23, 1530, in Pichardo Viñals, *Documentos para la historia de Cuba (época colonial)*, 96–97; *Procuradores* of Santiago to Emperor Charles V, March 17, 1540, in de la Sagra, *Historia física, política y natural de la isla de Cuba*, appendix 88, 47–49.

24. Arciniegas, *Biografía del Caribe*, 64; Lockhart, *The Men of Cajamarca*, 90–102.

25. De la Fuente, "Sociedad, 1510–1770," 156–159.

26. "1582 List"; "Socioeconomic Survey of 1534," in Marrero, *Cuba*, 1:148–149 (hereafter cited as "1534 Survey") (also see 1:177–178, 197); Alonso de Cadenas y Lópe and Barredo de Valenzuela y Arrojo, *Nobiliario de Extremadura*, 94; Roig de Leuchsenring, *Actas capitulares del Ayuntamiento de La Habana*, tome 1, 1:257–258; Altman, "Marriage, Family, and Ethnicity in the Early Spanish Caribbean," 233–235; replies of Vasco Porcallo de Figueroa to interrogation by judges of the Audiencia of Santo Domingo, March 13, 1522, in *Colección de documentos inéditos relativos al descubrimiento, conquista y organización de las antiguas posesiones españolas de ultramar*, 2nd series, 1:119–126.

27. Pérez de la Riva, "Desaparición de la población indígena cubana," 80–83; de las Casas, *Devastation of the Indies*, 41.

28. De las Casas, *Devastation of the Indies*, 46; Wright, *The Early History of Cuba*, 156.

29. Pérez de la Riva, "Desaparición de la población indígena cubana," 62, 84.

30. Roig de Leuchsenring, *Actas capitulares del Ayuntamiento de La Habana*, tome 1, 1:79; "Lista de los que partieron para Méjico con Hernán Cortés," in de la Pezuela, *Historia de la isla de Cuba*, appendix 1, 355–371; Aparicio Laurencio, *Los días cubanos de Hernán Cortés*, 30.

31. "1534 Survey"; Gonzalo Fernández de Guzmán to Emperor Charles V, October 31, 1534, Biblioteca Nacional José Martí, Havana (hereafter BNJM), Colección Morales, vol. 81, folder 7; Arriaga Mesa, *La Habana, 1550–1600*, 132.

32. Guerra y Sánchez, Pérez Cabrera, Remos y Rubio, and Santovenia y Echaide, *Historia de la nación cubana*, 1:230.

33. Marrero, *Cuba*, 1:158–159.

34. De las Casas, *Devastation of the Indies*, 47.

35. Marreo, *Cuba*, 1:121.

36. King Ferdinand to Viceroy Diego Columbus, June 15, 1510; and royal order prohibiting residence to sons, daughters, and grandchildren of those convicted by the Inquisition, October 5, 1511, both in Chacón y Calvo, *Cedulario Cubano*, 271.

37. Instituto de Historia de Cuba, *Historia de Cuba (la colonia)*, 170–171; Enríquez Almendarez, "Dos cartas del obispo de Cuba Fray Alonso Enríquez Almendarez en contestación a una Real Cédula de Felipe III," 181–192; Macías Domínguez, *Cuba en la primera mitad del siglo XVII*, 17; Valdés, *Historia de la isla de Cuba*, 73.

38. Cabildo of Santiago to Emperor Charles V, May 2, 1532, in *Colección de documentos íneditos relativos al desculorimiento. Conquista y organización de las Antiguas posesiones españolas de Ultramar*, 2nd series, tome 4, 2:253.

39. Captain-General Luján to King Philip II, December 7, 1582, in Wright, *Historia documentada de San Cristóbal de La Habana en el siglo XVI*, 1:305–306.

40. Wright, *The Early History of Cuba*, 53–54.

41. Wright, *The Early History of Cuba*, 54–55; Fletcher, "Conflict and Conformity," 63. Also see Alonso López, "Mohínas de la Inquisición."

Chapter 5. The Emergence of Creole Society

Epigraph sources: Franqui, *Diario de la revolución cubana*, 1; Pérez, *Cuba*, 31.

1. Authorities in Santiago de Cuba repeatedly complained to the Crown about the city's neglected and decaying defense system. See, for example, Governor of Santiago to King Philip III, July 6, 1620; and Cabildo of Santiago to King Philip IV, August 15, 1636, both in Wright, *Santiago and Its District (1607–1640)*, 134–135, 173–174, respectively.

2. Pérez, *Cuba*, 20.

3. Moreno Fraginals, *Cuba/España, España/Cuba*, 71–72; Morales, *Conquista y colonización de Cuba*, 63; Governor Severino de Manzaneda to King Charles II, March 25, 1690, in Pichardo Viñals, *Documentos para la historia de Cuba (época colonial)*, 158–160.

4. Marrero, *Cuba*, 2:156; de la Fuente, *Havana and the Atlantic*, 55; García del Pino, *El corso en Cuba*, 219; Sainz, *Cuba y la Casa de Austria*, 231.

5. Havana *protocolos notariales* of January 19, January 21, and March 8, 1587, in de Rojas, *Índice y extractos del archivo de protocolos de La Habana, 1586–1587*, 248–250, 279; and October 12, 1585, in de Rojas, *Índice y extractos del archivo de protocolos de La Habana, 1578–1585*, 378–381; Marrero, *Cuba*, 2:348.

6. Royal order of December 12, 1518, in *Colección de documentos inéditos relativos al descubrimiento, conquista y organización de las antiguas posesiones españolas de ultramar*, 2nd series, 1:85; Arriaga Mesa, *La Habana, 1550–1600*, 28; Marrero, *Cuba*, 4:91; Weiss, *La arquitectura colonial cubana*, 62; Hernández Oliva, *Naufragios*, 91; García del Pino, *El corso en Cuba*, 45.

7. Arriaga Mesa, *La Habana, 1550–1600*, 260; Macías Domínguez, *Cuba en la primera mitad del siglo XVII*, 439; Cabildo minutes of August 12, 1550, in Roig de Leuchsenring, *Actas capitulares del Ayuntamiento de La Habana*, tome 1, 2:3–5.

8. Pérez, *Cuba*, 31.

9. Benítez-Rojo, *The Repeating Island*, 45.

10. Sainz, *Cuba y la Casa de Austria*, 167; García del Pino, *El corso en Cuba*, 237; *Protocolos notariales* of December 4, 1578 and August 20, 1579, in de Rojas, *Índice y extractos del archivo de protocolos de La Habana, 1578–1585*, 5, 202.

11. García del Pino, *El corso en Cuba*, 55, 58, 194.

12. Marrero, *Cuba*, 2:291, 285; Sainz, *Cuba y la Casa de Austria*, 236.

13. García del Pino, *El corso en Cuba*, 20–22, 63, 190; de la Pezuela, *Historia de la isla de Cuba*, 344–346.

14. García del Pino, *El corso en Cuba*, 19, 22, 37; Marrero, *Cuba*, 4:105; Governor Pedro de Valdés to King Philip III, January 3, 1604, in Pichardo Viñals, *Documentos para la historia de Cuba (época colonial)*, 134–154; Wright, *The Early History of Cuba*, 53. Also see Newquist, "Contraband in the Convento?" 87–103.

15. Antonio Correa to Manso de Contreras, no specific date (1607–1609), in Wright, *Santiago de Cuba and Its District (1607–1640)*, 67–71. A *grifa* is a person of partial African descent with blondish or reddish curly hair.

16. Pérez, *Cuba*, 29.

17. Marrero, *Cuba*, 1:146; Alonso de Cadenas y López and Barredo de Valenzuela y Arrojo, *Nobiliario de Extremadura*, 94.

18. Williams, *From Columbus to Castro*, 57.

19. Mintz, "Reflections on Caribbean Peasantries."

20. Hernández González, "Canary Island Immigration to the Hispanic Caribbean," 6.

21. Boyd-Bowman, *Patterns of Spanish Emigration*, 8; de la Fuente, *Havana and the Atlantic*, table 4.1, 87.

22. De la Fuente, "Población libre y estratificación social, 1510–1770," 26; Hernández González "Canary Island Immigration to the Hispanic Caribbean," 2–3.

23. Mörner, *Race Mixture in the History of Latin America*, 16; Marrero, *Cuba*, 1:147; de la Fuente, *Havana and the Atlantic*, 89; La Rosa Corzo, *Runaway Slave Settlements*, 37. For information on the case of two enslaved white women, see Fletcher, "Conflict and Conformity," 64–65.

24. Royal order for Diego Columbus, April 8, 1513 and royal order of November 17, 1526, prohibiting Cuba's residents to leave the island, both in *Colección de documentos inéditos relativos al descubrimiento, conquista y organización de las antiguas posesiones españolas de ultramar*, 2nd series, 1:36, 363–366; Sainz, *Cuba y la Casa de Austria*, 67; Pérez, *Cuba*, 35; Wright, *The Early History of Cuba*, 195.

25. "1534 Survey."

26. Wright, *The Early History of Cuba*, 88, 230, 335–336.

27. Wright, *The Early History of Cuba*, 119, 246, 177–178; Bacardí Moreau, *Crónicas de Santiago de Cuba*, 102–103; Sainz, *Cuba y la Casa de Austria*, 92–93, 115.

28. Petition of Jácome Justiniano Velázquez to the Cabildo of Havana requesting remuneration for his post of *alcalde*, 1604, in García del Pino and Melis Cappa, *Documentos para la historia colonial de Cuba*, 91–104; Memorial by Antonio Velázquez Bazán, heir to Diego Velázquez (no date), in *Colección de documentos inéditos relativos al descubrimiento, conquista y organización de las antiguas posesiones españolas de ultramar*, 1st series, 10:80–86.

29. Sainz, *Cuba y la Casa de Austria*, 92–93, 357; Marrero, *Cuba*, 2:418; Mira Caballos, *El indio antillano*, 223.

30. Marrero, *Cuba*, 2:377; de la Fuente, "Sociedad, 1510–1770," 163; de la Fuente, *Havana and the Atlantic*, 195; Arriaga Mesa, *La Habana, 1550–1600*, 126, 144; *protocolo notarial* of March 1, 1579, in de Rojas, *Índice y extractos del archivo de protocolos de La Habana, 1578–1585*, 52; *Protocolo notarial* on dowry of Úrsula de Merlo, August 12, 1609 (Havana), BNJM, Colección Pérez, folder 529.

31. Roig de Leuchsenring, *Actas capitulares del Ayuntamiento de La Habana*, tome 1, 1:53.

32. García del Pino, *El corso en Cuba*, 29; La Rosa Corzo, *Runaway Slave Settlements*, 37.

33. Cabildo minutes of February 25 and March 3, 1559, quoted in Roig de Leuchsenring, *Actas capitulares del Ayuntamiento de La Habana*, tome 1, 1:50–53; "1582 List."

34. "1534 Survey"; Altman, "Towns and the Forging of the Spanish Caribbean," 34–35; Alonso de Cadenas y López and Barredo de Valenzuela y Arrojo, *Nobiliario de Extremadura*, 94; Wright, *Historia documentada de San Cristóbal de La Habana en el siglo XVI*, 1:83; Marrero, *Cuba*, 2:379; Arriaga Mesa, *La Habana, 1550–1600*, 142.

35. Wright, *The Early History of Cuba*, 245.

36. Bishop Diego Sarmiento (1556) quoted in Pérez de la Riva, "Desaparición de la población indígena cubana," 83; Mendizabal et al., "Genetic Origin, Admixture, and Asymmetry in Maternal and Paternal Human Lineages in Cuba," 213. Parallel studies show similar proportions for Puerto Rico's contemporary population: 0 percent of males with indigenous Y-chromosomes, 85 percent with European/Mediterranean Y-chromosomes, and 15 percent with sub-Saharan Y-chromosomes. See Vilar et al., "Genetic Diversity in Puerto Rico and Its Implications for the Peopling of the Island and the West Indies," 352–368.

37. Aparicio Laurencio, *Los días cubanos de Hernán Cortés*, 22; Roig de Leuchsenring, *Actas capitulares del Ayuntamiento de La Habana*, tome 1, 1:258–259; Guerra y Sánchez, Pérez Cabrera, Remos y Rubio, and Santovenia y Echaide, *Historia de la nación cubana*, 1:348.

38. Marrero, *Cuba*, 2:379; Altman, "Towns and the Forging of the Spanish Caribbean," 34–35; Bishop Diego Sarmiento to Emperor Charles V, July 25, 1544, in Pichardo Viñals, *Documentos para la historia de Cuba (época colonial)*, 101–107; Captain-General Luján to Emperor Charles V, February 27, 1582, in Wright, *Historia documentada de San Cristóbal de La Habana en el siglo XVI*, 1:83; Arriaga Mesa, *La Habana, 1550–1600*, 142, 144.

39. Wright, *The Early History of Cuba*, 188–189.

40. See Katzew, *Casta Paintings*.

41. "1582 List."

42. See Alegría, *Juan Garrido*.

43. Roig de Leuchsenring, *Actas capitulares del Ayuntamiento de La Habana*, tome 1, 1:114; Wheat, *Atlantic Africa*, 102.

44. "1534 Survey."

45. Juan de Ynestrosa and Juan de Rojas to Emperor Charles V, April 1, 1563, in Wright, *Historia documentada de San Cristóbal de La Habana en el siglo XVI*, 1:199–200; Lucena Salmoral, *Regulación de la esclavitud negra en las colonias de América Española*, 100.

46. Instituto de Historia de Cuba, *Historia de Cuba (la colonia)*, 143; de la Fuente, "Los matrimonios de esclavos en La Habana, 1585–1645," 510; de la Fuente, "Población libre y estratificación social, 1510–1770," 24.

47. Wheat, *Atlantic Africa*, 20–23, 26–33, 47–48; de la Fuente, "Esclavitud, 1510–1886," 134–137; de la Fuente, "El mercado esclavista habanero, 1580–1699," 371–395; Marrero, *Cuba*, 2:362.

48. Wheat, *Atlantic Africa*, 99, 101–102, 213.

49. Marrero, *Cuba*, 2:360; La Rosa Corzo, *Runaway Slave Settlements in Cuba*, 39; de la Fuente, "Sugar and Slavery," 144.

50. Royal proclamation mandating that slaves be married and that women constitute one half of all cargoes in Lucena Salmoral, *Regulación de la esclavitud negra en las colonias de América Española*, 33–34; Wright, *The Early History of Cuba*, 198.

51. Guerra y Sánchez, Pérez Cabrera, Remos y Rubio, and Santovenia y Echaide, *Historia de la nación cubana*, 1:141; Arriaga Mesa, *La Habana, 1550–1600*, 221.

52. Sainz, *Cuba y la Casa de Austria*, 111; Roig de Leuchsenring, *Actas capitulares del Ayuntamiento de la Habana*, tome 2, 43; Macías Domínguez, *Cuba en la primera mitad del siglo XVII*, 282–284.

53. Report by the Audiencia of Santo Domingo (1689), in García del Pino and Melis Cappa, *Documentos para la historia colonial de Cuba*, 186–197; Marrero, *Cuba*, 2:295.

54. Ordenanzas de Cáceres (1573), in Pichardo Viñals, *Documentos para la historia de Cuba (época colonial)*, 122.

55. Roig de Leuchsenring, *Actas capitulares del Ayuntamiento de La Habana*, tome 1, 1:116; "Actas de cabildos (1597–1657)," October 22, 1610, in BNJM, Colección Pérez, folder 9; Ordenanzas de Cáceres (1573), in Pichardo Viñals, *Documentos para la historia de Cuba (época colonial)*, 119–121; Marrero, *Cuba*, 5:35.

56. Barcia, *Seeds of Insurrection*, 16.

57. Saco, *Historia de la esclavitud desde los tiempos más remotos hasta nuestros días*, 162; La Rosa Corzo, *Runaway Slave Settlements*, 40.

58. Petition by the Cabildo of Havana to the Council of the Indies (1611), in Wright Papers, folder 54-1-32.

59. Marrero, *Cuba*, 3:368–369; testimony given by Los Morenos Horros de la Ciudad de La Habana, June 19, 1609, in Wright Papers, folder 54-2-10 (June 1623); and notarized establishment of a company between Boroto and Cepero, April 6, 1587, in de Rojas, *Índices y extractos del archivo de protocolos de La Habana, 1586–1587*, 289.

60. Partida IV, Title XXI, Law VI, and Partida IV, Title V, Law I, in Burns, *Las Siete Partidas*, 901, 979.

61. *Protocolos notariales* of January 23 and September 24, 1579, in de Rojas, *Índices y extractos del archivo de protocolos de La Habana, 1578–1585*, 39, 232.

62. Wheat, *Atlantic Africa*, 143; "1582 List."

63. De la Fuente, "Esclavitud, 1510–1886," 143; Moreno Fraginals, *Cuba/España, España/Cuba*, 90; Díaz, *The Virgin, the King, and the Royal Slaves*, 256–258.

64. *Protocolos notariales* of September (no day), 1585 and October 12, 1585, in de Rojas, *Índices y extractos del archivo de protocolos de La Habana, 1578–1585*, 352–353, 378–381; Marrero, *Cuba*, 2:348; Sainz, *Cuba y la Casa de Austria*, 201.

65. Cabildo minutes of July 4, 1561, in Roig de Leuchsenring, *Actas capitulares del Ayuntamiento de La Habana*, tome 1, 2:228–229; Wheat, *Atlantic Africa*, 150; de la Fuente, *Havana and the Atlantic*, 176.

66. De la Fuente, "Los matrimonios de esclavos en la Habana, 1585–1645," 526.

67. De Árrate y Acosta, *Llave del Nuevo Mundo*, 184; Morrison, *Cuba's Racial Crucible*, 7.

68. De la Fuente, *Havana and the Atlantic*, 181; Wright, *The Early History of Cuba*, 313–314.

69. Cabildo minutes of April 23, 1557, in Roig de Leuchsenring, *Actas capitulares del Ayuntamiento de La Habana*, tome 1, 2:149–150 (also see 1:117); Marrero, *Cuba*, 2:170, 5:35; Arriaga

Mesa, *La Habana, 1550–1600*, 224; García de Palacios, *Sínodo de Santiago de Cuba de 1681*, 15–16.

70. Marrero, *Cuba*, 2:370.

71. De la Fuente, "Los matrimonios de esclavos en la Habana, 1585–1645," 524–526; Wheat, *Atlantic Africa*, 172–173.

72. Mendizabal et al., "Genetic Origin, Admixture, and Asymmetry in Maternal and Paternal Human Lineages in Cuba," 213. For similar percentages among Puerto Ricans, see Vilar, et al., "Genetic Diversity in Puerto Rico and Its Implications for the Peopling of the Island and the West Indies," 352–368.

Chapter 6. The Cuban *Ajiaco*

Epigraph source: "Bilingual Blues," in Pérez-Firmat, *Life on the Hyphen*, 180–181; Ortiz, *Cuban Counterpoint*, 98.

1. Ortiz, "Los factores humanos de la cubanidad," 24.

2. Ortiz, *Cuban Counterpoint*, 98.

3. Fuentes, *Buried Mirror*, 17.

4. Sublette, *Cuba and Its Music*, 45–46; Wheat, *Atlantic Africa*, 17 and passim.

5. De la Fuente, "Los matrimonios de esclavos en la Habana, 1585–1645," 520; last will and testament of *horro* Francisco de Rojas, June 10, 1579, in de Rojas, *Índice y extractos del archivo de protocolos de La Habana, 1578–1585*, 129–131.

6. Valcárcel Rojas, *Archaeology of Early Colonial Interaction at El Chorro de Maíta*, 165. Parallel research by Kathleen Deagan at Taino sites in Hispaniola supports this contention. See Deagan, "Reconsidering Taíno Social Dynamics after Spanish Conquest," 603 and passim.

7. Valcárcel Rojas, *Archaeology of Early Colonial Interaction at El Chorro de Maíta*, 70–71, 95–97, 138, 203–204.

8. Valcárcel Rojas, *Archaeology of Early Colonial Interaction at El Chorro de Maíta*, 247, 260, 301, 305–307.

9. García del Pino, *El corso en Cuba*, 50; Macías Domínguez, *Cuba en la primera mitad del siglo XVII*, 134.

10. Deagan, "Reconsidering Taíno Social Dynamics after Spanish Conquest," 615–616; "Actas de cabildos (1597–1657)," January 4, 1606, in BNJM, Colección Pérez, folder 9; Marrero, *Cuba*, 5:145, 3:230–232.

11. De la Fuente, "Economía, 1570–1700," 74; Arriaga Mesa, *La Habana, 1550–1600*, 319–320.

12. Marrero, *Cuba*, 5:131; Wright, *Historia documentada de San Cristóbal de La Habana en la primera mitad del siglo XVII*, 15.

13. Ortiz, "Los factores humanos de la cubanidad," 24.

14. Benítez-Rojo, *The Repeating Island*, 68; Benítez-Rojo, "La cultura caribeña en Cuba," 2; Morejón, "Cuba and Its Deep Africanity," 940.

15. Wheat, *Atlantic Africa*, 14, 214, 256, 263.

16. Wright, *The Early History of Cuba*, 333–337.

17. Wright, *The Early History of Cuba*, 336.

18. Maya Restrepo, "Paula de Eguiluz," 73–74.

19. Maya Restrepo, "Paula de Eguiluz," 78–79; Barceló, *Manual Agustiniano*, 50, 96.

20. Maya Restrepo, "Paula de Eguiluz," 77.

21. Maya Restrepo, "Paula de Eguiluz," 84.

22. Maya Restrepo, "Paula de Eguiluz," 85–87; Ortiz, *Brujas e inquisidores*, xx–xxiii; Carpentier, *La música en Cuba*, 26.

23. Bellingrad and Otto, *Magical Manuscripts in Early Modern Europe*, 7–10, 98; Maya Restrepo, "Paula de Eguiluz," 87–88.

24. Maya Restrepo, "Paula de Eguiluz," 72.

25. De la Torre, *La Habana*, 117–118; Carpentier, *La música en Cuba*, 28–32.

26. Song by Teodora Ginés (1580), in Bacardí Moreau, *Crónicas de Santiago de Cuba*, 105. My translation.

27. Carpentier, *La música en Cuba*, 33.

28. Carpentier, *La música en Cuba*, 29–30.

29. De la Torre, *La Habana*, 117–118; Carpentier, *La música en Cuba*, 28–32.

30. My translation. Scholars have not identified Aroba; most likely he/she was a Muslim person. Cervantes Saavedra himself endured five years in captivity in Algiers at the hands of Muslim pirates. A later verse says that the "Indiana amulatada" had vassals who rendered her tribute, perhaps an allusion to the Iberian Muslim practice of collecting tribute from Christians in Iberian territories they dominated. Cervantes Saavedra, *Novelas ejemplares*, 439–440.

31. Lapique Becali, *Cuba Colonial*, 34–35. The term *zarabanda* points to possible African roots: Zarabanda was the Congo deity of metal and war. Robert Stevenson, however, claimed that the genre originated in Mexico. See Chasteen, *National Rhythms, African Roots*, 192–193; Stevenson, "The First Dated Mention of the Sarabande," 29–31. Despite its reputation as indecent and even obscene, the genre made it to Seville's Corpus Christi procession of 1593.

32. Emilio Bacardí Moreau quoted in Guerra y Sánchez, Pérez Cabrera, Remos y Rubio, and Santovenia y Echaide, *Historia de la nación cubana*, 1:360–361.

33. Pané, *An Account of the Antiquities of the Indians*, 3–4; Benítez-Rojo, *The Repeating Island*, 14.

34. Murrell, *Afro-Caribbean Religions*, 111, 144–145; Andrews, *Dictionary of Nature Myths*, 173; James, *Historical Dictionary of Angola*, 178.

35. Wright, "Our Lady of Charity," 709–717.

36. Portuondo Zúñiga, *La Virgen de la Caridad del Cobre*, 74; Benítez-Rojo, *The Repeating Island*, 13–14.

37. "Declaración del Capitán Juan Moreno, negro, natural del Cobre de 85 años," in Portuondo Zúñiga, *La Virgen de la Caridad del Cobre*, 298–302.

38. Murrell, *Afro-Caribbean Religions*, 111–112.

39. Buscaglia Salgado, *Undoing Empire*, 30, 55; Lipski, *El español de América*, 39–40.

40. Buscaglia Salgado, *Undoing Empire*, 30, 57; Weiss, *La arquitectura colonial cubana*, 86–98.

Chapter 7. The Cockpit of Europe

Epigraph sources: De Balboa, *Espejo de paciencia*, 55; Williams, *From Columbus to Castro*, 71.

1. Williams, *From Columbus to Castro*, 69–94.

2. Dunn, *Sugar and Slaves*, 11–12.

3. Gosse, *The History of Piracy*, 144.

4. Hanke, *The Spanish Struggle for Justice*, 148.

5. Report of Juan Velázquez on the 1537 corsair attack in *Colección de documentos inéditos relativos al descubrimiento, conquista y organización de las antiguas posesiones españolas de*

ultramar, 2nd series, 6:22–23; Roig de Leuchsenring, *Actas capitulares del Ayuntamiento de La Habana*, tome 1, 1:184–185; Hoffman, *The Spanish Crown and the Defense of the Caribbean*, 26; Wright, *Historia documentada de San Cristóbal de La Habana en el siglo XVI*, 1:13.

6. Hoffman, *The Spanish Crown and the Defense of the Caribbean*, 26, 47.

7. Bacardí Moreau, *Crónicas de Santiago de Cuba*, 85.

8. De la Fuente, *Havana and the Atlantic*, 13.

9. Guerra y Sánchez, Pérez Cabrera, Remos y Rubio, and Santovenia y Echaide, *Historia de la nación cubana*, 1:159–161, 167; Wright, *The Early History of Cuba*, 239–241; de la Fuente, *Havana and the Atlantic*, 2.

10. Wright, *The Early History of Cuba*, 244–245; Pichardo Viñals, *Documentos para la historia de Cuba (época colonial)*, 4–6.

11. Sainz, *Cuba y la Casa de Austria*, 111.

12. Arriaga Mesa, *La Habana, 1550–1600*, 61; Wright, *Historia documentada de San Cristóbal de La Habana en la primera mitad del siglo XVII*, 47.

13. Chartier, "Materiality and Mobility."

14. Morales-Carrión, *Puerto Rico and the Non-Hispanic Caribbean*, 19n38.

15. Report by Diego Fernández de Quiñones to the Crown on the state of Havana's fortifications, 1582, in Wright, *Historia documentada de San Cristóbal de La Habana en el siglo XVI*, 1:290–291.

16. Cruz-Taura, *Espejo de paciencia*, 224; Macías Domínguez, *Cuba en la primera mitad del siglo XVII*, 334.

17. Arriaga Mesa, *La Habana, 1550–1600*, 61.

18. De la Fuente, García del Pino, and Iglesias Delgado, "Havana and the Fleet System," 102–103; Melchor Sardo de Arana to King Philip III, August 26, 1580, in Wright, *Historia documentada de San Cristóbal de La Habana en el siglo XVI*, 1:235–237; Marrero, *Cuba*, 4:195; Macías Domínguez, *Cuba en la primera mitad del siglo XVII*, 409–410.

19. Quote from Sardo de Arana to King Philip III, in Wright, *Historia documentada de San Cristóbal de La Habana en el siglo XVI*, 1:235–237, my translation; also see Arriaga Mesa, *La Habana, 1550–1600*, 181.

20. Ortiz de la Vega, *Anales de España desde sus orígenes hasta el tiempo presente*, tome 9, 3:267; Wright, *Historia documentada de San Cristóbal de La Habana en el siglo XVI*, 57–58.

21. Butel, *The Atlantic*, 90.

22. Moreno Fraginals, *Cuba/España, España/Cuba*, 73.

23. Marrero, *Cuba*, 3:111; Williams, *From Columbus to Castro*, 84; Marley, *Wars of the Americas*, 173.

24. Wright, "The Dutch and Cuba," 628.

25. Marrero, *Cuba*, 3:118–120.

26. García del Pino, *El corso en Cuba*, xi; Marley, *Wars of the Americas*, 198–209.

27. Burchett, *A Complete History of the Most Remarkable Transactions at Sea*, 387–388.

28. Quoted in Exquemelin, *The Buccaneers of America*, 135; also see Marrero, *Cuba*, 3:137–140.

29. Exquemelin, *The Buccaneers of America*, 104.

30. Moreno Fraginals, *Cuba/España, España/Cuba*, 46; Guerra y Sánchez et al., *Historia de la nación cubana*, 1:345–364; Scarpaci and Portela, *Cuban Landscapes*, 51–52; García del Pino, *El corso en Cuba*, 76–77.

31. Marrero, *Cuba*, 5:159, 162; Sainz, *Cuba y la Casa de Austria*, 182; Moreno Fraginals, *Cuba/España, España/Cuba*, 88.

Chapter 8. Deceivingly Sweet: Sugar, Slavery, and Resistance

Epigraph sources: Saco, *Historia de la esclavitud desde los tiempos más remotos hasta nuestros días*, 126; Williams, *From Columbus to Castro*, 28–29.

1. Ortiz, *Cuban Counterpoint*, 30, 47, 56–73.

2. Higman, "Sugar Revolution," 213.

3. Castillo Meléndez, "Un año en la vida de un ingenio cubano (1655–1656)"; García Rodríguez, *Entre haciendas y plantaciones*; de la Fuente, "Sugar and Slavery," 116.

4. De la Fuente, "Sugar and Slavery," 143n2, 116.

5. Williams, *From Columbus to Castro*, 28–29.

6. Guerra y Sánchez, *Azúcar y población*; Ortiz, *Cuban Counterpoint*; Aykroyd, *The Sweet Malefactor*; Naipaul, *The Middle Passage*, 57; Beckford, *Persistent Poverty*.

7. Mintz, *Sweetness and Power*, xxix.

8. García del Pino, *El corso en Cuba*, 54; de la Fuente, "Sugar and Slavery," 122–123; Marrero, *Cuba*, 4:9–10; Morales, *Conquista y colonización de Cuba*, 71.

9. García del Pino, *El corso en Cuba*, 54; De la Fuente, "Sugar and Slavery," 124.

10. De la Fuente, "Sugar and Slavery," 138.

11. Request of the cabildo of Havana quoted in Marrero, *Cuba*, 4:18; García Rodríguez, *Entre haciendas y plantaciones*, 22; García Rodríguez, "Ingenios habaneros del siglo XVIII," 42–44.

12. De la Fuente, "Sociedad, 1510–1770," 157–158.

13. Carpentier, *La música en Cuba*, 35; García Rodríguez, "Felipe II y el modelo azucarero de Cuba," 1000.

14. Marrero, *Cuba*, 4:13; García Rodríguez, "Felipe II y el modelo azucarero de Cuba," 1000–1001; Saco, *Historia de la esclavitud desde los tiempos más remotos hasta nuestros días*, 257.

15. García Rodríguez, "Felipe II y el modelo azucarero de Cuba," 1000–1001.

16. García Rodríguez, "Felipe II y el modelo azucarero de Cuba," 997–1013.

17. Kuethe, "Los llorones cubanos."

18. De la Fuente, "Sugar and Slavery," 143.

19. Marrero, *Cuba*, 4:4–5: García del Pino, *El corso en Cuba*, 51–54.

20. Marrero, *Cuba*, 4:2, 7.

21. Saco, *Historia de la esclavitud desde los tiempos más remotos hasta nuestros días*, 126.

22. Sheridan, *Sugar and Slavery*, 132–133.

23. De la Fuente, "Sugar and Slavery," 126.

24. Marrero, *Cuba*, 2:360; de la Fuente, "Sugar and Slavery," 125–126, 144.

25. La Rosa Corzo, *Runaway Slave Settlements in Cuba*, 39; Castillo Meléndez, "Un año en la vida de un ingenio cubano (1655–1656)," 453.

26. De la Fuente, "El Mercado esclavista habanero," 1580–1699," 376.

27. De la Fuente, "Sugar and Slavery," 144; de la Fuente, "Índices de morbilidad e incidencia de enfermedades entre los esclavos de La Habana, 1580–1699," 16; Castillo Meléndez, "Un año en la vida de un ingenio cubano (1655–1656)," 457.

28. Marrero, *Cuba*, 2:244–245, 4:21–22; Wheat, *Atlantic Africa*, 208.

29. Last will and testament of Juana García Rodríguez, October 31, 1609, and valuation of the San Pedro plantation, April 2, 1662, both in BNJM, Colección Pérez, transcriptions of *protocolos*, folder 529; Marrero, *Cuba*, 4:26; Castillo Meléndez, "Un año en la vida de un ingenio cubano (1655–1656)," 453.

30. Carpentier, *La música en Cuba*, 35; de la Fuente, "Sugar and Slavery," 136; Castillo Meléndez, "Un año en la vida de un ingenio cubano (1655–1656)," 454.

31. De la Fuente, "Sugar and Slavery," 143.

32. Marrero, *Cuba*, 4:12–13; De la Fuente, "Sugar and Slavery," 121, 140.

33. García del Pino, *El corso en Cuba*, 40–41.

34. De La Fuente, "Sugar and Slavery," 139–140.

35. De la Fuente, "Sugar and Slavery," 139.

36. Marrero, *Cuba*, 4:20, 30–31; De la Fuente, "Sugar and Slavery," 125; Borah, *New Spain's Century of Depression*, 20, 24–26, 34, 43; Sainz, *Cuba y la Casa de Austria*, 311; Instituto de Historia de Cuba, *Historia de Cuba (la colonia)*, 155–158.

37. Marrero, *Cuba*, 3:35.

38. Wheat, *Atlantic Africa*, 23, 32–33; de la Fuente, "Esclavitud, 1510–1886," 134–137.

39. Wheat, *Atlantic Africa*, 70.

40. De la Fuente, "El mercado esclavista habanero, 1580–1699," 383.

41. Wheat, *Atlantic Africa*, 99.

42. Moreno Fraginals, "Manuel de Angola," 172–173.

43. Quintero Rivera, *¡Salsa, sabor y control!*, 98, 239; Mintz, "Reflections on Caribbean Peasantries"; Wheat, *Atlantic Africa*, 181–215.

44. Díaz, *The Virgin, the King, and the Royal Slaves*, 168–169, 258.

45. Cabildo minutes for July 4, 1561, in Roig de Leuchsenring, *Actas capitulares del Ayuntamiento de La Habana*, tome 1, 2:228–229; Wheat, *Atlantic Africa*, 150, 153–154; de la Fuente, *Havana and the Atlantic*, 176; testimony given by "Los Morenos Horros de la Ciudad de La Habana," June 19, 1609, in Irene Aloha Wright Papers, folder 54-2-10 (June 1623); Marrero, *Cuba*, 5:28.

46. Cabildo minutes for October 22, 1610, BNJM, Colección Pérez, folder 9; García de Palacios, *Sínodo de Santiago de Cuba de 1681*, 14–16; Marrero, *Cuba*, 2:364–365.

47. Testimony given by Los Morenos Horros de la Ciudad de La Habana, June 19, 1609, in Library of Congress, Wright Papers, folder 54-2-10 (June 1623); Marrero, *Cuba*, 5:28.

48. Testimony given by Los Morenos Horros de la Ciudad de La Habana in Library of Congress, Wright Papers, folder 54-2-10 (June 1623); Guerra y Sánchez, Pérez Cabrera, Remos y Rubio, and Santovenia y Echaide, *Historia de la nación cubana*, 1:219; Harris, *Patterns of Race in the Americas*, 76.

Bibliography

Archival Sources

Biblioteca Nacional José Martí, Havana
    Colección de Manuscritos
    Colección Pérez
    Colección Morales
Library of Congress, Washington, DC
    Irene Aloha Wright Papers

Published Primary Sources and Documents

Burchett, Josiah. *A Complete History of the Most Remarkable Transactions at Sea*. London: W. B. for J. Walthoe, 1720.

Burns, Robert I., ed. *Las Siete Partidas*. Vol. 4. Philadelphia: University of Pennsylvania Press, 2001.

Chacón y Calvo, José María, ed. *Cedulario Cubano (Los orígenes de la colonización)*. Vol. 1. Madrid: Compañía Ibero-Americana de Publicaciones, 1929.

Colección de documentos inéditos relativos al descubrimiento, conquista y organización de las antiguas posesiones españolas de ultramar. 1st and 2nd series. Madrid: Real Academia de la Historia, 1885–1932.

Columbus, Christopher. *The Book of Prophecies*. Edited by Roberto Rusconi. Eugene, OR: Wipf & Stock, 2004.

———. *Four Voyages to the New World: Letters and Selected Documents*. Edited and translated by R. H. Major. Gloucester, MA: Peter Smith, 1978.

———. *The Log of Christopher Columbus*. Translated by Robert H. Fuson. Camden, ME: International Publishing, Co., 1987.

Cowans, Jon, ed. *Early Modern Spain: A Documentary History*. Philadelphia: University of Pennsylvania Press, 2003.

Cuba, Oficina Nacional de Estadísticas. *Primer compendio de estadísticas del medio ambiente de Cuba, 1990–2004*. Havana: ONE, 2006.

De Anglería, Pedro Mártir. *Décadas del Nuevo Mundo*. Buenos Aires: Editorial Bajel, 1944.

De Árrate y Acosta, José Martín Félix. *Llave del Nuevo Mundo; antemural de las Indias Oc-*

cidentales. La Habana descripta: Noticias de su fundación, aumentos y estados. Havana: Comisión Nacional Cubana de la UNESCO, 1964.

De Balboa, Silvestre. *Espejo de paciencia.* Miami: Ediciones Universal, 1970.

De las Casas, Bartolomé. *The Devastation of the Indies: A Brief Account.* Baltimore: Johns Hopkins University Press, 1992.

———. *Historia de las Indias.* Vols. 1, 4. Madrid: Imprenta de Miguel Ginesta, 1875–1876.

———. *Historia de las Indias.* Vol. 3, edited by André Saint-Lu. Caracas: Biblioteca Ayacucho, 1986.

De Rojas, María Teresa, ed. *Índice y extractos del archivo de protocolos de La Habana, 1578–1585.* Havana: La Habana, 1947.

———. *Índice y extractos del archivo de protocolos de La Habana, 1586–1587.* Havana: Burgay & Cía., 1950.

———. *Índice y extractos del archivo de protocolos de La Habana, 1588.* Havana: Burgay & Cía., 1957.

Enríquez Almendarez, Alonso. "Dos cartas del obispo de Cuba Fray Alonso Enríquez Almendarez en contestación a una Real Cédula de Felipe III" (1620). *Memorias de la Real Sociedad Económica de La Habana* 2nd series, 3 (1847): 181–192.

Exquemelin, John. [Alexander Olivier]. *The Buccaneers of America.* London: George Allen & Co., 1911.

Fernández de Navarrete, Martín. *Colección de documentos concernientes a la persona, viages y descubrimientos del Almirante D. Cristóbal Colón al gobierno y administración de los primeros establecimientos de Indias y de la Marina Castellana.* Vols. 1 and 2. Madrid: Imprenta Real, 1825.

García del Pino, César, and Alicia Melis Cappa, comps. *Documentos para la historia colonial de Cuba: Siglos XVI, XVII, XVIII y XIX.* Havana: Editorial de Ciencias Sociales, 1988.

García de Palacios, Juan. *Sínodo de Santiago de Cuba de 1681.* Madrid: Instituto Francisco Suárez, 1982.

Gould, Alice Bache. *Nueva lista documentada de los tripulantes de Colón en 1492.* Madrid: Real Academia de la Historia, 1984.

Harris, Marvin. *Patterns of Race in the Americas.* New York: Walker and Co., 1964.

Lucena Salmoral, Manuel, ed. *Regulación de la esclavitud negra en las colonias de América Española (1503–1886): Documentos para su estudio.* Alcalá de Henares/Murcia: Universidad de Alcalá/Universidad de Murcia, 2000.

Machiavelli, Niccolò. *The Prince.* Edited by Adolph Caso. Translated by Rufus Goodwin. Boston: Dante University Press, 2003.

Pané, Ramón. *An Account of the Antiquities of the Indians.* Durham, NC: Duke University Press, 1999.

Pichardo Viñals, Hortensia, comp. *Documentos para la historia de Cuba (época colonial).* Havana: Editorial Nacional de Cuba, 1965.

"Privileges and Prerogatives Granted to Columbus." In *Documents of American History*, edited by Henry Steele Commager and Milton Cantor, 1:1–2. Englewood Cliffs, NJ: Prentice Hall, 1988.

Roig de Leuchsenring, Emilio, ed. *Actas capitulares del Ayuntamiento de La Habana.* Tome 1 (1550–1565). Havana: Municipio de la Habana, 1937.

———. *Actas capitulares del Ayuntamiento de La Habana.* Tome 2 (1566–1574). Havana: Municipio de La Habana, 1939.

Secondary Sources

Alchon, Suzanne Austin. "The Great Killers in Precolumbian America: A Hemispheric Perspective." *Latin American Population History Bulletin* 27 (Fall 1997): 2–11.

Alegría, Ricardo E. *Juan Garrido: el conquistador negro en las Antillas, Florida, México y California.* San Juan: Centro de Estudios Avanzados de Puerto Rico y el Caribe, 2004.

Alonso, Gisela, and Ismael Clark. "Cuba Confronts Climate Change." *MEDICC Review* 17, no. 2 (2015): 10–13.

Alonso de Cadenas y López, Ampelio, and Adolfo Barredo de Valenzuela y Arrojo. *Nobiliario de Extremadura.* Vol. 6. Madrid: Hidalguía, 2001.

Alonso López, Eugenio A. "Mohínas de la Inquisición." Unpublished paper. http://www.kislakfoundation.org/prize/200201.html. Accessed September 12, 2017.

Altman, Ida. "Marriage, Family, and Ethnicity in the Spanish Caribbean." *William and Mary Quarterly* 3rd series, 70, no. 2 (2013): 225–250.

———. "Towns and the Forging of the Spanish Caribbean." In *The Early Modern Hispanic World: Transnational and Interdisciplinary Approaches,* edited by Kimberly Lynn and Erin Kathleen Rowe, 23–44. New York: Cambridge University Press, 2017.

Andrews, Tamra. *Dictionary of Nature Myths: Legends of the Earth, Sea, and Sky.* Oxford: Oxford University Press, 2000.

Aparicio Laurencio, Ángel. *Los días cubanos de Hernán Cortés y su lucha por un ideal.* Madrid: Editorial Betania, 1987.

Arciniegas, Germán. *Biografía del Caribe.* Mexico City: Editorial Porrua, 1993.

Arriaga Mesa, Marcos. *La Habana, 1550–1600: Tierra, hombres, mercado.* Madrid: Ediciones Sílex, 2014.

Aykroyd, W. R. *The Sweet Malefactor: Sugar, Slavery and Human Society.* London: Heinemann, 1967.

Bacardí Moreau, Emilio. *Crónicas de Santiago de Cuba.* Vol. 1. Barcelona: Tipografía de Carbonell y Esteva, 1908.

Barceló, José Agustín. *Manual Agustiniano.* Santiago de Chile: Imprenta del Correo, 1872.

Barcia, Manuel. *Seeds of Insurrection: Domination and Resistance on Western Cuban Plantations, 1808–1848.* Baton Rouge: Louisiana State University Press, 2008.

Barreiro, José. "Beyond the Myth of Extinction: The Hatuey Regiment." *KACIKE: The Journal of Caribbean Amerindian History and Anthropology* (2004). https://archive.org/stream/KacikeJournal_34/barreiro_djvu.txt. Accessed October 24, 2017.

———. "Indians in Cuba." *Cultural Survival Quarterly* 13, no. 3 (1989): 56–60.

Beckford, George L. *Persistent Poverty: Underdevelopment in Plantation Economies of the Third World.* New York: Oxford University Press, 1972.

Bellingrad, Daniel and Bernd-Christian Otto. *Magical Manuscripts in Early Modern Europe: The Clandestin,e Trade in Illegal Book Collections.* Gewerbestrasse, Switzerland: Springer Nature, 2017.

Benítez-Rojo, Antonio. "La cultura caribeña en Cuba: continuidad versus ruptura." *Cuban Studies/Estudios Cubanos* 14, no. 1 (1984): 1–16.

————. *The Repeating Island: The Caribbean and the Postmodern Perspective*. Durham, NC: Duke University Press, 1992.

Borah, Woodrow Wilson. *New Spain's Century of Depression*. Berkeley: University of California Press, 1951.

Boyd-Bowman, Peter. *Patterns of Spanish Emigration to the New World (1493–1580)*. Buffalo: Council on International Studies, State University of New York at Buffalo, 1973.

Brotton, Jerry. *A History of the World in 12 Maps*. New York: Viking Books, 2012.

Buscaglia Salgado, José F. *Undoing Empire: Race and Nation in the Mulatto Caribbean*. Minneapolis: University of Minnesota Press, 2003.

Butel, Paul, *The Atlantic*. London: Routledge, 1999.

Carpentier, Alejo. *La música en Cuba*. Havana: Editorial Letras Cubanas, 2004.

Castillo Meléndez, Francisco. "Un año en la vida de un ingenio cubano (1655–1656)." *Anuario de Estudios Americanos* 39 (1982): 411–467.

Castro, Américo. *Ibero América: Su historia y su cultura*. New York: Henry Holt and Co., 1960.

————. *The Structure of Spanish History*. Princeton: Princeton University Press, 1954.

Cervantes Saavedra. Miguel de. *Novelas ejemplares*. Madrid: Libro de Oro, 1854.

Chartier, Roger. "Materiality and Mobility of a Text: Bartolomé de Las Casas' 'Brevíssima Relación de la Destruycion de las Indias' between Sevilla, Antwerp and London." Paper presented at a Workshop in the History of Material Texts, Columbia University, New York, New York, February 25, 2013.

Chasteen, John Charles. *National Rhythms, African Roots: The Deep History of Latin American Popular Dance*. Albuquerque: University of New Mexico Press, 2004.

Chilcote, Ronald H. *Portuguese Africa*. Englewood Cliffs, NJ: Prentice Hall, 1967.

Childe, V. Gordon. *Foundations of Social Archaeology: Selected Writings of V. Gordon Childe*. Edited by Thomas C. Patterson and Charles E. Orser Jr. Walnut Creek, CA: AltaMira Press, 2004.

————. *Man Makes Himself*. London: Watts and Co., 1936.

Crosby, Alfred W. *The Columbian Exchange: Biological and Cultural Consequences of 1492*. Westport, CT: Greenwood Press, 1972.

Cruz-Taura, Graciella. *Espejo de Paciencia y Silvestre de Balboa en la historia de Cuba*. Madrid: Iberoamericana, 2009.

De la Fuente, Alejandro. "Economía, 1570–1700." In *Historia de Cuba*, cord. Consuelo Naranjo Orovio, 29–68. Madrid: CSIC and Editorial Doce Calles, 2009.

————. "Esclavitud, 1510–1886." In *Historia de Cuba*, cord. Consuelo Naranjo Orovio, 129–151. Madrid: CSIC and Editorial Doce Calles, 2009.

————. *Havana and the Atlantic in the Sixteenth Century*. Chapel Hill: University of North Carolina Press, 2008.

————. "Índices de morbilidad e incidencia de enfermedades entre los esclavos de La Habana, 1580–1699." *Asclepio* 43, no. 2 (1991): 7–22.

————. "Los matrimonios de esclavos en La Habana, 1585–1645." *Ibero-amerikanisches Archiv* 16, no. 4 (1990): 507–528.

————. "El mercado esclavista habanero, 1580–1699: las armazones de esclavos." *Revista de Indias* 50, no. 189 (1990): 371–395.

————. "Población libre y estratificación social, 1510–1770." In *Historia de Cuba*, coord. Consuelo Naranjo Orovio, 17–27. Madrid: CSIC and Editorial Doce Calles, 2009.

———. "Sociedad, 1510–1770." In *Historia de Cuba*, coord. Consuelo Naranjo Orovio, 153–171. Madrid: CSIC and Editorial Doce Calles, 2009.

———. "Sugar and Slavery in Early Cuba." In *Tropical Babylons: Sugar and the Making of the Atlantic World, 1450–1680*, edited by Stewart B. Schwartz, 115–157. Chapel Hill: University of North Carolina Press, 2004.

De la Fuente, Alejandro, César García del Pino, and Bernardo Iglesias Delgado. "Havana and the Fleet System: Trade and Growth in the Periphery of the Spanish Empire, 1550–1610." *Colonial Latin American Review* 5, no. 1 (1996): 95–115.

De la Pezuela, Jacobo. *Historia de la isla de Cuba*. Vol. 1. Paris: J. B. Baillere & Hijos, 1868.

De la Sagra, Ramón. *Historia física, política y natural de la isla de Cuba*. Vol 2. Paris: Arthus Bertrand, 1842.

Deagan, Kathleen. "Reconsidering Taíno Social Dynamics after Spanish Conquest: Gender and Class in Culture Contact Studies." *American Antiquity* 69, no. 4 (2004): 597–626.

Deneven, William M. *The Native Population of the Americas in 1492*. 2nd ed. Madison: University of Wisconsin Press, 1992.

Diamond, Jared. "What Does 'Geographic Determinism' Really Mean?" http://www.jared-diamond.org/Jared_Diamond/Geographic_determinism.html. Accessed May 25, 2017.

Díaz, María Elena. *The Virgin, the King, and the Royal Slaves of El Cobre*. Palo Alto, CA: Stanford University Press, 2000.

Dunn, Richard S. *Sugar and Slaves: The Rise of the Planter Class in the English West Indies, 1624–1713*. Chapel Hill: University of North Carolina Press, 1972.

Emery, K. O., and Elazar Uchupi. *The Geology of the Atlantic Ocean*. New York: Springer-Verlag, 1984.

Fernández-Armestos, Felipe. *Amerigo: The Man Who Gave His Name to America*. New York: Random House, 2007.

Figueredo, Alfredo E. "The Indians of Cuba: A Study of Cultural Adaptation and Ethnic Survival." *Círculo: Revista de Humanidades* 3, no. 3 (1971): 121–145.

Fitzpatrick, Scott M. "The Pre-Columbian Caribbean." *PaleoAmerica* 1, no. 4 (2015): 315–331.

Fletcher, Brendan. "Conflict and Conformity: The Holy Office of the Inquisition in Colonial Cuba, 1511–1821." MA thesis, Missouri State University, 2006.

Franqui, Carlos. *Diario de la revolución cubana*. Barcelona: R. Torres, 1976.

Fuentes, Carlos. *The Buried Mirror*. New York: Houghton Mifflin, 1992.

García del Pino, César. *El corso en Cuba. Siglo XVII*. Havana: Editorial de Ciencias Sociales, 2001.

García Rodríguez, Mercedes. *Entre haciendas y plantaciones: Orígenes de la manufactura azucarera en La Habana*. Havana: Editorial de Ciencias Sociales, 2007.

———. "Felipe II y el modelo azucarero de Cuba: la Ley de privilegio de ingenios." In *III Coloquio de Historia Canario-Americana: VIII Congreso Internacional de Historia de América*, coord. Francisco Morales Padrón, 997–1013. Gran Canaria: Cabildo de Gran Canaria, 1998.

———. "Ingenios habaneros del siglo XVIII: mundo agrario interior." *América Latina en la historia económica* 13, no. 2 (2006): 41–75.

Gebelein, Jennifer. *A Geographic Perspective of Cuban Landscapes*. London: Springer, 2012.

Gosse, Philip. *The History of Piracy*. Mineola, NY: Dover Publications, 2007.

Guerra y Sánchez, Ramiro. *Azúcar y población en las Antillas*. Havana: Cultural, S.A., 1927.

Guerra y Sánchez, Ramiro, José M. Pérez Cabrera, Juan J. Remos y Rubio, and Emeterio Santovenia y Echaide. *Historia de la nación cubana.* 10 vols. Havana: Editorial Historia de la Nación Cubana, 1952.

Guitar, Lynne. "Encomienda System." In *The Historical Encyclopedia of World Slavery.* Vol. 1, *A–K,* edited by Junius P. Rodríguez, 250–251. Santa Barbara, CA: ABC-CLIO.

Hall, Timothy L. *Religion in America.* New York: Facts on File, 2007.

Hamilton, Earl J. *American Treasure and the Price Revolution in Spain, 1501–1650.* New York: Octagon Books, 1965.

Handwerk, Brian. "New Underwater Finds Raise Questions about Flood Myths." *National Geographic News,* May 28, 2002. http://news.nationalgeographic.com/news/2002/05/0528 _020528_sunkencities.html. Accessed September 4, 2017.

Hanke, Lewis. *The Spanish Struggle for Justice in the Conquest of America.* Philadelphia: University of Pennsylvania Press, 1949.

Heredia, José María. "Les Conquerants." *The Month: A Catholic Magazine* 62 (1908): 407.

Hernández González, Manuel. "Canary Island Immigration to the Hispanic Caribbean." *Oxford Research Encyclopedia of Latin American History Online* (2017).

Hernández Oliva, Carlos Alberto. *Naufragios: barcos españoles en aguas de Cuba.* Seville: Editorial Renacimiento, 2009.

Herrera, Desidero. *Memoria sobre huracanes en la isla de Cuba.* Havana: Imprenta de Barcina, 1847.

Higman, Barry W. "The Sugar Revolution." *Economic History Review* 53, no. 2 (2000): 213–236.

Hofman, Corinne L., Angus Mol, Menno L. P. Hoogland, and Roberto Valcárcel Rojas. "Stage of Encounters: Migration, Mobility and Interaction in the Pre-Colonial and Early Colonial Caribbean." *World Archaeology* 46, no. 4 (2014): 590–609.

Hoffman, Paul. *The Spanish Crown and the Defense of the Caribbean, 1535–1585.* Baton Rouge: Louisiana State University Press, 1980.

Instituto de Historia de Cuba. *Historia de Cuba (la colonia): evolución sociéeconomica y formación nacional.* Havana: Editora Política, 1994.

Iturralde-Vinent, Manuel A. "Cuban Geology: A New Plate-Tectonic Synthesis." *Journal of Petroleum Geology* 17, no. 1 (1994): 39–70.

———. "A Short Note on the Cuban Late Maastrichtian Megaturbidite (An Impact-Derived Deposit?)." *Earth and Planetary Science Letters* 109 (1992): 225–228.

James, W. Martin. *Historical Dictionary of Angola.* Lanham, MD: Rowman & Littlefield Publishing Group, 2011.

Katzew, Ilona. *Casta Paintings: Images of Race in Eighteenth-Century Mexico.* New Haven, CT: Yale University Press, 2004.

Keegan, William F. "Archaic Influences in the Origins and Development of Taíno Societies." *Caribbean Journal of Science* 42, no. 1 (2006): 1–10.

Kuethe, Alan J. "Los llorones cubanos: The Socio-Military Basis of Commercial Privilege in the American Trade under Charles IV." In *The North American Role in the Spanish Imperial Economy 1760–1819,* edited by Jacques A. Barbier and Allan J. Kuethe, 142–156. Manchester: Manchester University Press, 1984.

Lapique Becali, Zoila. *Cuba Colonial: Música, compositores e intérpretes.* Havana: Ediciones Boloña/Editorial Letras Cubanas, 2008.

La Rosa Corzo, Gabino. "La orientación este de los entierros en cuevas de Cuba: Remate de una fábula." *Latin American Antiquity* 14, no. 2 (2003): 143–157.

———. *Runaway Slave Settlements in Cuba: Resistance and Repression*. Chapel Hill: University of North Carolina Press, 2003.

Lindsay, Lisa A. *Captives as Commodities: The Transatlantic Slave Trade*. Upper Saddle River, NJ: Pearson, 2008.

Lipski, John M. *El español de América*. Madrid: Cátedra, 1994.

Lockhart, James. *The Men of Cajamarca: A Social and Biographical Study of the First Conquerors of Peru*. Austin: University of Texas Press, 1972.

MacGregor, Neil. *A History of the World in 100 Objects*. New York: Penguin Books, 2010.

Macías Domínguez, Isabelo. *Cuba en la primera mitad del siglo XVII*. Seville: Escuela de Estudios Hispano-Americanos, 1978.

Marchueco-Turiel, Beatriz, E. J. Parra, E. Fuentes-Smith, A. Salas, H. N. Buttenschøn, D. Demontis, María Torres-Español, Lilia C. Marín-Padrón, Enrique J. Gómez-Cabezas, Vanesa Álvarez-Iglesias, Ana Mosquera-Miguel, Antonio Martínez-Fuentes, Ángel Carracedo, Anders D. Børglum, and Ole Mors. "Cuba: Exploring the History of Admixture and the Genetic Basis of Pigmentation Using Autosomal and Uniparental Markers." *PLoS Genetics* 10, no. 7 (2014), http://journals.plos.org/plosgenetics/article?id=10.1371/journal.pgen.1004488. Accessed September 4, 2017.

Marley, David. *Wars of the Americas*. Vol. 1. Santa Barbara, CA: ABC-CLIO, 2008.

Marrero, Leví. *Cuba: economía y sociedad*. 15 vols. Madrid: Playor, 1971–1988.

Martínez-Fernández, Luis. "Far beyond the Line: Corsairs, Privateers, Buccaneers, and Invading Settlers in Cuba and the Caribbean (1520–1670)." *Revista de Indias* 75, no. 263 (2015): 7–38.

———. "The Forging of Creole Cuba: Race, Gender and Society in the Sixteenth-Century." In *Caribe/Caribes: Criollización y procesos de cambio*, edited by Josef Opatrný, 49–63. Prague: Editorial Karolinum, 2006.

———. "1492: First Encounters, the Invention of America and the Columbian Exchange." *Revista Brasileira do Caribe* 6, no. 11 (2005): 13–31.

———. "Geography, Will It Absolve Cuba?" *History Compass* 2, no. 1 (2004): 1–20.

Marx, Gary. "Cuba's Forgotten Tribe Experiencing a Rebirth." *Chicago Tribune*, August 10, 2004. http://articles.chicagotribune.com/2004-08-10/news/0408100264_1_taino-indians-indigenous-descendants. Accessed September 4, 2017.

Massip, Salvador. *Factores geográficos de la cubanidad*. Havana: Cultural, 1941.

Maya Restrepo, Luz Adriana. "Paula de Eguiluz y el arte del bien querer: apuntes para el estudio del cimarronaje femenino en el Caribe, siglo XVII." *Historia Crítica* 24 (December 2003): 101–124.

Mendizabal, Isabel, Karla Sandoval, Emma Berniell-Lee, Francesc Calafell, Antonio Salas, Antonio Martínez-Fuentes, and David Comas. "Genetic Origin, Admixture, and Asymmetry in Maternal and Paternal Human Lineages in Cuba." *BMC Evolutionary Biology* 8, no. 1 (2008): 213.

Menéndez Pidal, Ramón. *The Spaniards in Their History: An Analysis of Spain's National Characteristics*. Translated by Walter Starkie. New York: Norton, 1967.

Milne, John. *A Catalogue of Destructive Earthquakes, A.D. 7 to A.D. 1899*. London: British Association for Advancement of Science, 1912.

Mintz, Sidney W. "Reflections on Caribbean Peasantries." *New West Indian Guide* 57, no. 1–2 (1983): 1–17.

———. *Sweetness and Power: The Place of Sugar in Modern History*. New York: Viking, 1985.

Mira Caballos, Esteban. *El indio antillano: repartimiento, encomienda y esclavitud (1492–1542)*. Seville: Muñoz Moya, 1997.

Morales, Salvador. *Conquista y colonización de Cuba, siglo XVI*. Havana: Editorial de Ciencias Sociales, 1984.

Morales-Carrión, Arturo, *Puerto Rico and the Non-Hispanic Caribbean*. Río Piedras: Editorial de la Universidad de Puerto Rico, 1974.

Morejón, Nancy. "Cuba and Its Deep Africanity." *Callaloo* 28, no. 4 (2005): 933–950.

Moreno Fraginals, Manuel. *Cuba/España, España/Cuba: historia común*. Barcelona: Editorial Crítica, 1995.

———. "Manuel de Angola." In *La historia como arma y otros ensayos sobre esclavos, ingenios y plantaciones*, edited by Manuel Moreno Fraginals, 172–178. Barcelona: Editorial Crítica, 1983.

Mörner, Magnus. *Race Mixture in the History of Latin America*. Boston: Little, Brown, and Company, 1967.

Morrison, Karen Y. *Cuba's Racial Crucible: The Sexual Economy of Social Identities, 1750–2000*. Bloomington: Indiana University Press, 2015.

Murrell, Nathaniel Samuel. *Afro-Caribbean Religions: An Introduction to Their Historical, Cultural, and Sacred Traditions*. Philadelphia: Temple University Press, 2010.

Naipaul, V. S. *The Middle Passage*. New York: Vintage Books, 1990.

———. *The Overcrowded Barracoon*. New York: Alfred P. Knopf, 1973.

Nápoles Fajardo, Juan Cristóbal. "El behique de Yariguá." In *Poesías Completas*, edited by Juan Cristóbal Nápoles Fajardo, 136–139. Havana: Editorial Letras Cubanas, 1983.

Newquist, Ingrid Marion. "Contraband in the Convento? Material Indications of Trade Relations in the Spanish Colonies." In *Islands at the Crossroads: Migrations, Seafaring, and Interaction in the Caribbean*, edited by L. Antonio Curet, and Mark W. Hauser, 87–103. Tuscaloosa: University of Alabama Press, 2011.

O'Gorman, Edmundo. *La invención de América: Investigación acerca de la estructura histórica del Nuevo Mundo y del sentido de su devenirla*. Mexico City: Fondo de Cultura Económica, 1958.

Ortiz, Fernando. *Brujas e inquisidores: Defensa póstuma de un inquisidor cubano*. Compiled by José Antonio Matos Arévalo. Havana: Fundación Fernando Ortiz, 2003.

———. *Cuban Counterpoint: Tobacco and Sugar*. Durham, NC: Duke University Press, 1995.

———. "Los factores humanos de la cubanidad." *Revista Bimestre Cubana* 45, no. 2 (1940): 161–186.

———. "Por Colón se descubrieron dos mundos." *Revista Bimestre Cubana* 50, no. 2 (1942): 180–190.

Ortiz de la Vega, Manuel. *Anales de España desde sus orígenes hasta el tiempo presente*. Tome 9, Vol. 3. Tomás Gorchs: Barcelona, 1859.

Pardo, Georges. *The Geology of Cuba*. AAPG Studies in Geology Series no. 58. Tulsa: American Association of Petroleum Geologists, 2009.

Pérez, Inés. "Cubans Find Preparing for Climate Change Hard, Expensive and Essential." *E&E*, June 16, 2014. http://www.eenews.net/stories/1060001239.

Pérez, Louis A., Jr. *Cuba: Between Reform and Revolution.* 5th ed. New York: Oxford University Press, 2015.

Pérez de la Riva, Juan. "Desaparición de la población indígena cubana." *Universidad de La Habana* 196–197 (1972): 61–84.

Pérez-Firmat, Gustavo. "Bilingual Blues." In Gustavo Pérez-Firmat, *Life on the Hyphen: The Cuban-American Way.* Rev. ed. Austin: University of Texas Press, 2012.

Pinet, Simone. *The Task of the Cleric: Cartography, Translations, and Economics in Thirteenth-Century Iberia.* Toronto: University of Toronto Press, 2016.

Pohl, Frederick J. *Amerigo Vespucci: Major Pilot.* London: Frank Cass, 1966.

Poole, Robert M. "What Became of the Taíno?" *Smithsonian Magazine,* October 2011. http://www.smithsonianmag.com/people-places/what-became-of-the-taino-73824867/.

Portuondo Zúñiga, Olga. "Trayectoria histórica de Santiago de Cuba: 1515–1707." *Santiago* 26/27 (1977): 9–32.

———. *La Virgen de la Caridad del Cobre: Símbolo de cubanía.* Santiago: Editorial Oriente, 2001.

Pospíšil, M. F. "Physical Anthropological Research on Indian Remnants in Eastern Cuba." *Current Anthropology* 12, no. 2 (1971): 229.

Quintero Rivera, Ángel G. *¡Salsa, sabor y control!: Sociología de la música "tropical."* Mexico City: Siglo Veintiuno Editores, 2005.

Rama, Ángel. *La ciudad letrada.* Montevideo: Arca, 1998.

Ricky, Donald. *Native Peoples A to Z.* Vol. 2. Hamburg, MI: Native American Books, 2009.

Roig de Leuchsenring, Emilio. *Actas capitulares del Ayuntamiento de la Habana.* Havana: Municipio de la Habana, 1937.

Rojas, Rafael. *Isla sin fin.* Miami: Ediciones Universal, 1998.

Rouse, Irving. *The Tainos: Rise and Decline of the People Who Greeted Columbus.* New Haven, CT: Yale University Press, 1992.

Saco, José Antonio. *Historia de la esclavitud desde los tiempos más remotos hasta nuestros días.* Vol. 1. Barcelona: Jaime Jepús, 1879.

Sainz, Nicasio Silverio. *Cuba y la Casa de Austria.* Miami: Ediciones Universal, 1972.

Sánchez Baena, Juan José. "Sobre libros en Indias: de su existencia y comercio en Cuba entre los siglos XVI y XVII." In *Alma America: In honorem Victorino Polo,* vol. 2, edited by Vicente Cervera Salinas and María Dolores Adsuar Fernández, 340–362. Murcia: Universidad de Murcia, 2008.

Scarpaci, Joseph L., and Armando H. Portela. *Cuban Landscapes: Heritage, Memory, and Place.* New York: Gilford Press, 2009.

Schroeder, Susan. *Cuba: A Handbook of Historical Statistics.* Boston: G. K. Hall, 1982.

Serna Moreno, J. Jesús María. "Las supervivencias lingüísticas de origen Taíno en el oeste de Cuba." *Latinoamérica* 45, no. 2 (2007): 79–104.

Sheridan, Richard B. *Sugar and Slavery: An Economic History of the British West Indies, 1623–1775.* Kingston: Canoe Press, 1974.

Stanek, Klaus Peter, Jorge Luis Cobiella-Reguera, Walter V. Maresch, and C. Grevel. "Geological Development of Cuba." *Zeitschrift für Angewandte Geologie* 1 (2000): 259–265.

Stevens Arroyo, Antonio M. *Cave of the Jagua: The Mythological World of the Tainos.* Albuquerque: University of New Mexico Press, 1988.

Stevenson, Robert. "The First Dated Mention of the Sarabande." *Journal of the American Musicological Society* 5, no. 1 (1952): 29–31.

Sublette, Ned. *Cuba and Its Music: From the First Drums to the Mambo*. Chicago: Chicago Review Press, 2004.

Sullivan, Kevin. "In Cuban Depths, Atlantis or Anomaly? Images of Massive Stones 2,000 Feet below Surface Fuel Scientific Speculation." *Washington Post*, October 10, 2002.

Taber, Stephen. "The Great Fault Troughs of the Antilles." *Journal of Geology* 30, no. 2 (1922): 89–114.

Tabío, Ernesto E. "Nueva periodización para el estudio de las comunidades aborígenes de Cuba." *Cuba Arqueológica* 8, no. 2 (2015): 103–111.

Thacher, John Boyd. *Christopher Columbus: His Life, His Works, His Remains*. Vol. 2. New York: G. P. Putnam's Sons, 1903.

Thornton, John. *Africa and Africans in the Making of the Atlantic World, 1400–1800*. 2nd ed. Cambridge: Cambridge University Press, 1998.

Valcárcel Rojas, Roberto. *Archaeology of Early Colonial Interaction at El Chorro de Maíta, Cuba*. Gainesville: University Press of Florida, 2016.

Valdés, Antonio J. *Historia de la isla de Cuba y en especial de La Habana*. Vol. 1. Havana: Oficina de la Cena, 1813.

Vignaud, Henry. *Toscanelli and Columbus: The Letter and Chart of Toscanelli*. London: Sands and Co., 1902.

Vilar, Miguel G., Carlalynne Meléndez, Akiva B. Sanders, Akshay Walia, Jill B. Gaieski, Amanda C. Owings, Theodore G. Schurr, and The Genographic Consortium. "Genetic Diversity in Puerto Rico and Its Implications for the Peopling of the Island and the West Indies." *American Journal of Physical Anthropology* 155 (2014): 352–368.

Weckmann, Luis. *The Medieval Heritage of Mexico*. New York: Fordham University Press, 1992.

Weiss, Joaquín E. *La arquitectura colonial cubana*. Seville: Instituto Cubano del Libro/Agencia Española de Cooperación Internacional/Consejo de Obras Públicas y Transportes de Andalucía, 1996.

Wheat, David. *Atlantic Africa and the Caribbean, 1570–1640*. Chapel Hill: University of North Carolina Press, 2016.

Williams, Eric. *From Columbus to Castro: The History of the Caribbean*. New York: Vintage Books, 1970.

Wilson, Samuel M. "Cultural Pluralism and the Emergence of Complex Society in the Greater Caribbean." In *Proceedings of the XVIII International Conference of Caribbean Archaeology*, vol. 2, edited by G. Richard, 7–12. Guadeloupe: International Association for Caribbean Archaeology, 1999.

Wright, Irene A. "The Dutch and Cuba, 1609–1643." *Hispanic American Historical Review* 4, no. 4 (1921): 597–634.

———. *The Early History of Cuba*. New York: Macmillan, 1916.

———. *Historia documentada de San Cristóbal de La Habana en el siglo XVI*. 2 vols. Havana: Impresora El Siglo XX, 1927.

———. *Historia documentada de San Cristóbal de La Habana en la primera mitad del siglo XVII*. Havana: Imprenta El Siglo XX, 1930.

———. "Our Lady of Charity." *Hispanic American Historical Review* 5, no. 4 (1922): 709–717.

———. *Santiago de Cuba and Its District (1607–1640)*. Madrid: Establecimiento Tipográfico Felipe Peña Cruz, 1918.

Yaremko, Jason M. "'Gente bárbara': Indigenous Rebellion, Resistance and Persistence in Colonial Cuba, c. 1500–1800." *KACIKE: The Journal of Caribbean Amerindian History and Anthropology* 7, no. 3 (2006): 157–184.

———. *Indigenous Passages to Cuba, 1515–1900*. Gainesville: University Press of Florida, 2016.

Zerubavel, Eviatar. *Terra Cognita: The Mental Discovery of America*. New Brunswick, NJ: Rutgers University Press, 1992.

Index

LUIS MARTÍNEZ-FERNÁNDEZ is professor of history at the University of Central Florida. Over the past three decades, he has researched and published extensively on a broad range of topics and periods, including nineteenth-century slavery and abolitionism (*Fighting Slavery in the Caribbean*) and Cuba's recent history (*Revolutionary Cuba: A History*). He served as chief editor of the multiple-award-winning *Encyclopedia of Cuba: People, History, Culture.*

CPSIA information can be obtained
at www.ICGtesting.com
Printed in the USA
LVHW090105210319
611309LV00004B/25/P